This is our Story
This is our Song

Missionaries!

By Harry & Phyllis Little

Copyright © 2017 Melton Little

All rights reserved including the right to reproduce this book or any portion thereof in any form whatsoever without written permission of the publisher, except in the case of brief quotations embodied in critical articles and reviews.

ISBN-13: 978-1542529365
ISBN-10: 1542529360

Bwana Press
3707 Avenida Madera
Bradenton, FL 34210

Forward

I write this forward out of love and respect for my parents and their accomplishments in the service of God and their faith.

There are many more qualified and able to write the forward to this book and in some way I feel my words and talent in this endeavor is far from adequate and does a disservice to the story.

However, as my parents have touched so many, they have touched me. Both in life and in my father's death. My father was the most faithful man I have ever known. He never doubted the Lord, His love and His plan for him.

I have at times doubted what came after this life—until the death of my father. I've seen him twice since his passing. Those of you who have had similar experiences will need no explanation. For those who have not, I pray at some point the Lord God will touch you in a way that leaves no doubt in your mind and heart as to his existence and love for you.

Both times he visited me were shortly after his death. The first time, he made a simple request. The second warrants this forward. He set upon the edge of my bed. He was there, present, no doubt in my mind and heart. He had a simple message. He looked at me with love and simply said, "Don't worry. And don't be afraid."

I believe this is his message. No matter what peril we may encounter, there is no need to worry or fear. God is with us always, with his infinite, unconditional love.

I hope you hear this message in their story.

Melton Harry Little

Prologue

Where does the desire to become a missionary begin?

For us it was a lifelong belief in God. There was never any doubt.

This book encapsulates our time as Methodist Missionaries including our younger religious undertakings that brought us both to this wondrous decision.

We have written our full Life Legacy including Harry's many brushes with death, his years in the Navy during World War 2, his time in Bogata, Columbia working and surviving their revolution, his educational endeavors, his engineering path around the world, and how it merges with his unflagging belief in God, and his love for his wife and his family.

Phyllis describes her early years and involvement with her church throughout her life, her education, love of art, and her devastating personal setback due to a medical problem.

All this, and all we have done is in the full version of *Life Legacy, This is Our Story, This is Our Song*.

For everything about our life as Missionaries we provide you the condensed version in *This is Our Story This is Our Song, Missionaries!* We hope you enjoy it. We did!

Table of Contents

I. Harry's Early Life and Religion 1

II. Phyllis' Early Life and Religion 14

III. This is Our Story 23

IV. METHODIST MISSIONARY CANDIDATES 29

V. BRUSSELS, BELGIUM (1951-1952) 42

VI. BELGIAN CONGO, KAPANGA (1952-1956) 73

VII. BELGIAN CONGO/ 186

VIII. FURLOUGH RESIGNATION EMPLOYMENT
(1960-1961) 269

IX. MISSIONARY REUNIONS 279

X. EPILOGUE 294

XI. ODDS & ENDS 296

I. Harry's Early Life and Religion

I, Harry Little attended church all my life. My parents regularly attended services. In regards to church attendance, the whole family attended the Santa Rosa Methodist Church in Texas.

As teenagers I enjoyed Sunday School and the youth group, called Epworth League in those days. Church meals, Dinners on the Grounds, and singing were fun. However, our singing wasn't always very reverent. A favorite hymn was "Power in the Blood", which the young sang as "POWer, POWer, POWer in the Blood" with strong emphasis on the "POW."

After high school I joined the Navy days before Pearl Harbor was attacked. At times there were no Methodist Churches available and I would, when able, attend the services of the base or a nearby Unity Church.

I had a love of learning and while in basic training was offered an opportunity to attend Fleet Radio School. When I completed with good scores, I was offered further training at Aircraft Radio School which provided five months of training far more complex and advanced than Fleet Radio School. Aircraft radio training included Morse code skills, but added courses in basic electricity, vacuum tube electronics, battery chargers, radio repairs and maintenance.

While attending Aircraft Radio School, one Sunday Eugene Brewer and I went to the Park Place Methodist Church. We were the only sailors at the service. At the end of his sermon, the minister paused and said "I cannot feed all these hungry sailors."

The Potts family, all females, took us home for dinner. Amongst three pretty daughters, we were delighted with our good luck. The father and the husband of the eldest daughter were away in the service. The second daughter was single, but several years older than I was. The youngest, prettiest daughter was Eugene's age. The family spoiled us that day and on subsequent visits for several months. Eugene was smitten and bitten by the love bug. He and the youngest daughter were married before the end of the year.

Eventually my choice of Radio operator led to an opportunity to become an engineering officer and the Navy would pay for the entire course at Georgia Tech. I had many adventures and my early life history, as well as Phyllis' are available in our Life Legacy *This is Our Story, This is our Song.*

Once I was stationed in Atlanta for my education, six days each week, I worked for the Navy. The seventh day was mine. My intentions were to honor the Sabbath and attend church whenever possible.

This six-day work week paid off, my final grade point average at graduation was above average, placing me in the upper third of my class.

On the first Sunday after arrival in Atlanta, I chose the First Methodist Church on Peachtree Street, which was within walking distance of Georgia Tech. On three consecutive Sundays, not one person did any more than greet me casually then go on their way. On the third Sunday, a notice in the paper informed me of another Methodist Church just a bit further north on Peachtree Street.

Later that afternoon, while sauntering along the western sidewalk of Peachtree near Fifth Street I noticed two large churches. On my side, the First Baptist Church was closed for the afternoon. On the other side, Saint Mark Methodist Church was open for business, a noisy youth group in evidence. Three men came across the street to meet me: Huber R Parsons, Albert Armstrong, and J Tom Smith. All became lifelong friends.

Saint Mark had a wonderful youth group along with many counselors and ministers who cared.

Dr. Lester, and Mrs. Mary Rumble were an inspiration to hundreds of high school kids, college students and military personnel. The Navy programs in Atlanta (V-5, V-12, and NROTC) and the Army (ROTC and ASTP) supplied many boys for Saint Mark. As the number of boys in attendance soon exceeded the girls, the "word" got around rather quickly. More girls quickly appeared because the wartime draft had taken most men their age away.

Saint Mark Methodist Church utilized its great facilities at an excellent location. That made it possible for the friendly ministers, staff and members to meet wartime needs of a multitude of civilian and military people. This was done in spite of the fact that many Saint Mark members were somewhere else—on military duty or essential civilian assignments. Their goal was to minister to all young women and men who needed a church home.

"Gather-In" was a loose designation for Sunday afternoon food and games, Sunday morning and evening services, Sunday School, Wednesday evening fellowship, bowling, movies at the fabulous Fox Theater, plus week-end retreats at Camp Glisson, Camp Coweta, and state parks.

Their weekly bulletin, *The Remarker*, was written and published for inspiration, spiritual guidance, news and occasional gossip about dating "games" within the group. An adequate inventory of the available talent occupied several pages: singers, musicians, artists, writers, speakers, cooks, decorators, organizers, candy makers, scholars and comedians.

Mary Rumble, remarkable wife of Saint Mark's senior minister, Lester Rumble, died within a few months of my joining. One of her talents was talking "with" young people. She didn't talk "to" you, she talked with you in a way that was unforgettable. Her exceptional recipe for a happy married life included the following ingredients: love, kindness, time, patience, understanding, listening, Christian beliefs and humor.

The Saint Mark sanctuary is large, but at her funeral there were so many flowers there wasn't much room for mourners.

One of the associate ministers, Leon Smith, and his wife Anne, were a vital part of the Gather-In. They listened to people while challenging them to be real Christians.

The twins, Ben and Carlton Carruth, both former assistant ministers, but now Navy Chaplains, came for visits.

As sailors, we envied their gold stripes.

Jimmy Moore, former assistant minister, now Army Chaplain, returned from Europe where he had served in the invasion of Normandy (D-Day, 1944). Chaplains go into battle armed only with their Christian faith. They never carry weapons. This brand of courage impressed sailors who were being trained to fight with all types of firepower.

Incidentally, Jimmy took out of circulation one of the prettiest mathematicians in Atlanta. Betty Jane could do better mathematics than most engineering students. She was also a talented musician.

Back to the chaplains for a final word. Four chaplains on the torpedoed USS Dorchester gave their life jackets (Mae Wests) to other men on the ship. The four chaplains went down with the stricken ship into the frigid waters of the north Atlantic.

Another assistant minister at Saint Mark, B.C. Speers, was appointed by the Bishop to Georgia Tech in order to start a Wesley Foundation on campus. Being single and blessed with a great personality he succeeded. Six of us were the founding members. In a few years the Wesley Foundation had its own building.

TECH RELIGIOUS COUNCIL
    AND WESLEY FOUNDATION

The Tech Religious Council was established in 1944 to promote religious activity and the general welfare of the student body. The Baptists and Catholics organized clubs. Many students belonged to the Tech Y.M.C.A. (Young Men's Christian Association) on North Avenue. On a plaque above the entrance these words from the prophet MICAH, 6:8, were inscribed for all to see:
  "and what does the LORD require of you?
   to act justly, and, to love mercy,
  and, to walk humbly with your God."

During my senior year, a group of six Methodist students got together with the Rev BC Speers and started the first Wesley Foundation at Georgia Tech. The bishop of the North Georgia Conference (Methodist) assigned B.C. to Tech as his pastoral appointment. This meant he devoted himself full-time to Methodist students at Tech. Within a few years the foundation had its own building and far more than six members.

I managed to continue my church attendance through most of the war. Saint Mark helped build my commitment to my beliefs.

After the war, I was able to finish my engineering degree with my V.A. benefits. I looked for a job for a while but with so many soldiers returning, it was a difficult task.

Since I was raised in Texas near the Mexican border, I was fluent in Spanish. A Columbian company. Indega, was seeking a production manager who was bilingual. I accepted the job.

PRODUCTION MANAGER
FOR INDUSTRIAS De GASEOSAS

After an initial training period in the USA, I flew to Bogata Columbia. Industrias de Gaseosas is a Coca Cola bottling company. I worked for them as the production manager from January 1947 to after the initial revolution in April 1948, staying until August of 1948.

I seem to have a knack for finding myself in extremely interesting situations. On April 9, 1948, I arrived back at the plant a bit late from a delivery and was shocked to see ALL of our delivery vehicles inside the walled compound, employees hurrying to go home, an agitated plant superintendent anxious to get home, and the main gate being locked.

During lunch hour, Jorge Gaitan, Liberal Party presidential candidate, had been shot and mortally wounded as he left a downtown restaurant. A wild mob caught the assassin, tortured him to death, dragged his battered body through the streets. Jorge Gaitan was popular among the people who were economically depressed and desperately poor. Bogota had very few city policemen. The local army garrison was on maneuvers out of town.

Rioting, looting, shooting, bombing and burning continued for days. If I'd taken a different route back to the plant, I would have been in the middle of the chaos.

US citizens were offered evacuation but I chose to stay and continue protecting the plant. Gunfire rang out day and night and often, if anyone moved, they were shot at. The revolution caused extensive destruction of buildings. Thousands were killed. It was so widespread that clean up and new construction moved very slowly.

I stayed behind the walls of the plant in a small apartment through most of the revolution. Some of the employees brought food when they could.

One of the reasons for the rioting was to disrupt the Pan American Conference of Secretaries of State and Foreign Ministers who were meeting in Bogota. The assassination of Jorge Gaitan was used to trigger the disruption. All 21 Latin American countries sent their foreign ministers or secretaries of state to the conference. The US sent the Secretary of State, General George C Marshall. They met on the campus of an exclusive girl's school in suburban Bogota.

The water was unsafe to drink and the dignitaries sent word requesting bottled Coca-Cola. I loaded about fifty cases into a Coca-Cola truck, with large Coca-Cola logos on the doors and headed for the Conference.

Driving onto the campus, I looked down several machine gun barrels but thankfully they were silent.

I was by myself and was hauling two cases at a time upstairs when my left hand banged the shin of a man coming down the stairs.

I'd just hit the shin of Five-Star General of the Army George C Marshall. His body guard chewed me out, but he remained silent. I gave some of the Coca-Cola to the soldiers on guard. Gunfire resounded through the streets as I left the Pan Am Conference, but I arrived safely back at the plant.

"Drink Coca-Cola. Do not shoot Coca-Cola employees."

Two days later the Secretary General of the Pan American Conference appeared at the plant and asked if we had Coca-Cola in the warehouse. I assured him we had some, as sales had been slow recently! He asked if I would take a hundred cases to the National Capitol complex where government officials and guards had nothing to drink. He agreed to put two armed soldiers on the truck with me.

In a small convoy, we drove slowly to the center of the city, heading for the National Capitol complex. Some distant gunfire was heard, but none occurred on our route. Debris and wrecked vehicles littered the streets. No pedestrians were in sight. It appeared to be a ghost town.

After several miles of slow and cautious driving, we pulled into the parking garage at the rear of the capitol building. NEVER BEFORE OR SINCE HAVE I RECEIVED SUCH A WELCOME! No one had anything to drink for days. They popped the caps and drank warm Coca-Cola in one gulp. Our excitement was not yet over. My co-worker and I were fired upon by a sniper as we exited the building, but he missed due to the angle. An Army cannon blew the top off the bell tower where the shot came from before he got off a second shot. We raced back to the safety of the plant.

If you are interested in this episode of my life as well as my close brushes with death, please read our Life Legacy.

CHURCH IN COLOMBIA

The Roman Catholic hierarchy had an extremely strong influence over all of life in Colombia. The Archbisop's cathedral was just across the plaza from the National Capitol. All laws conformed to Catholic dogma and dictates. Contraceptives and all other family planning aids were forbidden by law.
With sufficient influence, a marriage could be annulled, but divorce was unacceptable. There were no churches visible except the Roman Catholic structures.
In Bogota, there was a Union Church, but it was hidden away on a side street. The only visible clue was a small bronze plaque that said "Union Church" in English. About thirty denominations were represented and served members from embassies, consulates and foreign businesses. No Colombians were present at any service. My Colombian

friends told me the priests had forbidden them to enter any church or chapel other than Roman Catholic.

LEAVING COLOMBIA

During July, I was shot at one more time; thankfully, it missed again. The plant was operating well again. I trained a Colombian foreman to satisfactorily do the majority of my work as a production manager. He was far less expensive to the company.

As an honorably discharged veteran, I had several years of GI Bill educational assistance available. During a friendly talk and discussion with Nick Thomas, it was stressed my working conditions in Bogota were good, but being a target outside the plant wasn't much fun.

When Indega hired me the agreement was confirmed by a handshake with Mr. Staton and no contract was needed. Indega offered to pay my final salary, severance pay, and travel expenses in US dollars if I traveled home by way of Panama, where they had an office.

On August 4th I flew to Tocumen Airport, Republic of Panama, traveled across the isthmus on the railroad (incidentally, the canal runs north/south and not east/west as expected), collected my money and reserved a flight from Panama City to Miami on a DC-6 airplane.

On the flight we flew through parts of a small hurricane. My seatmate was scared to death as the plane bounced through the sky on a dark and stormy night. Being tired and relaxed, I slept soundly most of the trip.

In 1948, Miami was an American tourist town and had very few Spanish speaking inhabitants. After clearing customs, I sat down in a restaurant, looked at the English language menu, automatically translated it, and gave my order in Spanish. The waiter was dumbfounded until I ordered again, this time in English. The habit of using Spanish was hard to break. Now (1995) they probably wouldn't understand an order in English. Times change.

Upon my return to Atlanta in August 1948, good fortune smiled upon me. The GI Bill granted one full month of educational benefits for each month of active military service during the Second World War, up to a maximum of four years.

Earning my bachelor's degree in 1946, only used seven months of my eligibility.

The 1948 Georgia Tech catalog listed degrees in the School of Industrial Engineering with a good friend, Colonel Groseclose, as Director.

Several courses in the undergraduate degree were more in line with my desire for more education. In those years, many engineers obtained dual degrees.

Industrial engineering would complement my electrical engineering.

In early September I enrolled in upper class industrial engineering courses. It wasn't necessary to repeat the freshman and sophomore years meaning a second degree could be obtained in less than two years.

Having met and been impressed by the Professor of Safety Engineering, Bill Cox, I enrolled in several of his courses. Safety Engineering granted only the Master of Science degree with an undergraduate degree in some field of engineering as an entrance requirement.

ST. MARK METHODIST AND NORTH AVENUE PRESBYTERIAN CHURCHES

While in the Navy at Georgia Tech I'd joined Saint Mark Methodist Church as an affiliate member, which meant my full membership remained with the Santa Rosa Methodist Church. Upon returning in 1948, I transferred my membership to Saint Mark, attending regularly, and renewing old friendships.

The Gather-In was still active with numerous attendees from high schools, colleges and businesses.

Wartime military officer training units were abolished in 1946, soon after the war ended. The new civilian student young men provided an expanding source of potential members.

Simultaneously business and commercial expansions attracted hundreds of young job seekers, both women and men. Every high school graduate in Georgia wanted to go to Atlanta, get a good job and obtain a Rich's Department Store charge card.

Many wanted to establish church relationships for fellowship, fun and a chance to meet the opposite sex. At Saint Mark, the Gather-In continued to attract mainly undergraduate students and others in that age group (16-22).

Being a bit older, I sought a slightly older group of young people while maintaining regular attendance at Saint Mark.

My wartime experience at First Methodist Church prevented me from going there again.

In early 1949 someone suggested that the North Avenue Presbyterian Church, a few blocks away from Saint Mark on Peachtree Street, had an active group of graduate students and business employees. Methodists were welcome.

For the remainder of the school year, I attended Saint Mark and Gather-In on Sunday and met with the Presbyterian young adult group during the week. The Presbyterian group had at least thirty young people at their meetings.

The family of one of the members had a large country estate near Atlanta which was ideal for picnics and bordered on a large wooded area.

On one of those picnics, I started exploring when one of the pretty young ladies said, "Harry, wait for me!"

And often I have been waiting for her ever since.

II. Phyllis' Early Life and Religion

ORMEWOOD PARK, Georgia
        PRESBYTERIAN CHURCH

Our home at 695 Woodland Avenue was next door to the Ormewood Park Presbyterian Church parsonage. Our minister, Rev. William Crane, his wife Catherine and three children, Effie, Paul and Kitty (Catherine) were a great influence in our young lives. Rev. Crane preached simple, profound sermons. He lived God's words—visiting, sharing, consoling and praying with us. We thought he was just like Jesus.

We faithfully attended Sunday School and church services, and most of the congregational meetings held quarterly after church on Sundays. At these meetings we heard about any plans for additions to the church building, new programs, changes in the purposes and goals of our church and other matters. The grownups agreed and disagreed. They chided and praised each other, and worked together for God. We children watched it all.

My best friend, Kitty Crane and I were in the Church Youth groups and classes together. We went to Smyrna Camp in the summer, heard Rev. Peter Marshall speak at a youth rally at Central Presbyterian Church (near the Georgia state capitol building in downtown Atlanta) and did lots of other activities together. Many times we just visited one another's home, poring over clothes and fashion magazines while discussing manners and make-up.

I was invited to go along on many Crane family outings, which included travels to Beechhaven near Athens, Georgia where the Crane family had started building a retirement home on family property. This spot was next to a wide, shallow river. It was a cool, lovely Georgia landscape away from highways. The family is living there today.

Kitty's older sister, Effie, was in college at Agnes Scott (the Presbyterian Women's College near Atlanta) and majoring in education & music. After graduation she went to the Belgian Congo in order to teach missionary children. Kitty's brother, Paul, was in college and while we lived there he graduated. Then he entered Columbia Presbyterian Seminary near Atlanta in order to become a minister. Kitty was finishing middle school and going on to Girl's High School.

CRANE FAMILY INFLUENCES

Often Effie and Paul had college friends (frequently children of Presbyterian missionaries) staying with them during the summer months. These young people were active and enthusiastic. They planned recreation for the youth of our church. Friday and Saturday evenings we played volleyball, badminton and horseshoes. We had races and played games in the lighted church yard. We had serious devotionals and sang camp songs. A couple of times we had cookouts—hot dogs and pot luck picnics. For the Christmas holidays, we gathered pine branches and holly to help decorate the sanctuary.

We attended small classes at church and have certificates for "Leadership Training Classes." We attended Vacation Bible School.

As we grew up, we helped with class teaching and lesson preparation. We learned to cut stencils and "run" them off on a big inked cylinder within the duplicating machine in the church office. Twice we attended sessions at the Presbyterian Camp Smyrna, south of Atlanta near Conyers, Georgia.

Kitty and all the Crane family moved to Charleston, West Virginia. Kitty went to Queen's College, a Presbyterian college in North Carolina.

AFTER HIGH SCHOOL

I attended Girl's School in high school. After graduation I obtained a job as a draftsman for Southern Bell Telephone Company in downtown Atlanta. It was fun.

During the summer, while working, I attended church at the Ormewood Park Presbyterian Church. I taught a Sunday School class of almost twelve middle-school boys—we had a great time! I read my Gideon New Testament and Sunday School literature while riding the bus to and from work.

My friend Sue brought a North Georgia College Brochure to our house. She talked with me and Mother about the two of us being college roommates. I didn't think seriously about it or beg to go to college.

But Mother and Dad talked. They came to the conclusion that it would be a good thing if I did go away for a year.

I gave the required two-weeks' notice at work and happily prepared to go off to the North Georgia hills.

I roomed in an all-girl's dorm with Sue as my roommate. We were members of the Young Women's Christian Association (YWCA).

Every Sunday the girls dressed for Sunday Church and walked to their churches. There were only two Big Churches in 1944—Methodist and Baptist.

Sue was a Methodist, so we attended that church first. The people seemed a bit "prissy" to us. The next Sunday we attended the Baptist Church. Their minister was also the Post Master of the city. He read the scripture beautifully and told wonderful stories—of conversions and changes in the lives of those who accepted Christ as their Savior.

We felt very happy and comfortable in his church, so we attended the Baptist Church that year. Dr. Harry B Forester, our Biology professor at the college, was our Sunday School teacher.

The Presbyterians in Dahlonega were a very small group. Their church building was tiny—preaching was every 6th Sunday when a visiting minister came up from Atlanta. I never attended church there.

When our first year of college was over, my dad came to take us home. Sue entered Agnes Scott College, near Decatur, to finish her education.

I took a civil service test and was hired at the Conley Quartermaster Depot southeast of Atlanta in Conyers, Georgia. My job was working for the War Department Services of Supply. I was a clerk-draftsman designing charts, etc.

We worked seven days a week and I managed to attend church services on Sunday evenings. We were quite well paid and I banked most of the money I made (for a second year of college). Though I loved NGC, I decided I couldn't return because they didn't offer a single "art" class.

I applied and was accepted as a sophomore at Auburn in Auburn, Alabama.

Most of my classes were in art—usually two hour labs. After class we spent hours "designing" stuff to complete all the homework we were given.

There was an old, red-brick Presbyterian Church just a block from the dorm where we lived. The minister appeared to me to be very old! Sunday evenings there was a meeting for college students. I attended once and found the students and leaders "up-beat" and attractive, but I decided I didn't have time to attend the group. After several weeks of Sunday morning church services—spent mostly in my own thoughts— I said, "God, I didn't hear one word that minister said. I am not coming to church anymore. I cannot see you working in this world!" Off I went to classes and the library.

The year was over too quickly. I couldn't make enough money to stay on campus for another year. Dad drove over to take me and all my "things" home to Atlanta. I confess I cried a good part of the way home. Po' Dad!

I found a summer job at Rich's Department Store in the advertising department.

That summer I took classes at the Evening College of the University of Georgia in downtown Atlanta. I took two courses: Art 208 and Advertising Design, from Mr. Jimmy Routh. He was a commercial artist and business man, and also a very good teacher. His father, Dr. James E Routh taught there for years and was Chairman of the English Department. Toward the end of the class, Jimmy Routh told me he would be changing jobs soon, to work for the *Atlanta Constitution* newspaper. If I was interested, there was an opening position for a beginning apprentice in their Advertising Department. That was welcome news!

In the fall of 1946, I interviewed for the job with the *Atlanta Constitution.* Mr. Bill McFall conducted my interview. He looked over samples of my art work and hired me, with the good recommendation from Jimmy Routh.

I loved the job.

Lu Croft became a very dear friend. She also worked at the *Atlanta Constitution* in the Public Relations Department.

Lu invited me to spend a weekend with her at her apartment on Ponce de Leon Avenue. Sunday morning we attended the North Avenue Presbyterian Church.

Dr. Vernon Broyles, Jr, was the minister. The beautiful church was packed with lively, happy people. God was working in this world!

During 1948 I became very ill and had to have an operation. I had something wrong with my ovary and they removed it. Recuperation was slow and difficult. A few months later I was back in the hospital and they were forced to remove my remaining ovary. I was devastated. It took much longer to recuperate.

Later Lu asked me to come with her to a monthly meeting of a group of young working women. It was an evening Circle Meeting of the Women of the Church. Ruth Davis, a red-headed lawyer, was the chairman of the Circle. Those dear kind ladies were so pleasant to be with that I continued to attend the meetings with Lu. I soon learned Ruth Davis lived near my Aunt Elvie Warren. They knew each other as neighbors. Several times I met Ruth for lunch—not far from the newspaper building downtown. We became fast friends.

NORTH AVENUE PRESBYTERIAN CHURCH

On March 28, 1948, I joined North Avenue Presbyterian Church. I rode the bus into Atlanta early Sunday mornings to attend a Sunday School class made up of undergraduate and graduate college students and young adults working in downtown Atlanta. The teacher was a retired Presbyterian Minister from Canada. His hair was snow white—a very fine looking man. He grew up Jewish and then converted to Christianity when he was a college student. His degree was from a seminary in Canada. The class became quite large and soon met in the Fellowship Hall. We all learned a great deal of Bible history, traditions and doctrine.

Sometime during the early part of 1948, I went with Lu and several young women to talk with Robert (Bob)White, the Director of Religious Education at North Avenue. We wanted to ask if the young adults could reserve a meeting room for a week night dinner, meeting and fellowship. Church hostess would plan and prepare the meals. Bob really tried to discourage the group—believing it would be made up of single women. The young women persisted so he decided to let them try it.

The meetings were on Friday evenings in a pleasant second story room with adjacent kitchen. Surprisingly, there were always more young men present than women! The food was delicious, especially the home made rolls. The group attracted many graduate students. Some were attending the nearby dental college. Lu and I attended—we soon made many new friends. Mrs. Allen Clapp's two oldest daughters were home from college and came bringing some of their friends.

Just before the New Year, 1949, my health was recovered enough to return to work. I returned to the Advertising Department at the *Atlanta Constitution.* It was good to be back in busy downtown Atlanta—among friends and business colleagues.

Two major operations in 1948 sapped much of my physical strength. I found I didn't have enough stamina to return to the evening classes at the University of Georgia, downtown Atlanta Division, so I withdrew from the two classes I'd registered to take. Classes, for me, were postponed for a later time.

Most Sunday mornings I managed to attend Sunday School and church at the North Avenue Presbyterian Church. I dropped out of the Women's Guild for several months.

Friday evenings, after a long busy day of work, I missed the Young Adult dinners and programs. By now thirty to forty-five young adults attended those meetings.

Finally, in the early spring (April), I attended a Young Adult dinner. The tables had been arranged in a "U" shape. I was seated to the right of center with Lu Croft and some friends. The ends of the "U" were toward the windows of the room. People sitting along the ends were partially silhouetted in the late afternoon sunlight. I looked up and saw Harry—he looked so pleasant and calm, and somehow very dear. Later that evening the song from South Pacific "Some enchanted evening you may see a stranger....across a crowded room...and strange as it seems," came into my mind.

In June, George Carmichael hosted a picnic-hamburger cookout for the Young Adult group at the home of his parents in North Atlanta. Their back yard was huge and strung with lanterns. There was a large outdoor grill, tables and chairs everywhere. I was standing and chatting with a group of young people in the pathway. Harry walked by on his way to the tables. I thought "I don't want to stay here," so I quickly said "Hey, wait for me". Now he says those were my first words to him and he is still waiting for me.

Over the next few months we spent more time together, spoke for hours on the phone, and on Thanksgiving Day 1949 he asked me to marry him. I was in love and gladly said YES!

We planned to be married when Harry's classes were finished and he graduated with a master's degree in Industrial Engineering. That would be some time in the fall, September 1950. We weren't in a rush to plan all the details, we thought we had plenty of time.

III. This is Our Story

Now we are writing *Our Story* together.

Harry became the Editor of the *Wesleyan Tech* paper. His monthly column was called: "Little Stuff." I have included a quotation from one of his columns that I kept in my scrapbook:

"There seldom passes a day that doesn't require a full share of decisions and choices. Often the choices are small and the decisions are relatively minor. But if you total all of the decisions made in a year then there is a definite pattern which will usually fit the outlines of those decisions. This pattern is a result of your conscious or unconscious decisions and may have been arrived at by default. By this, I mean that you may not have had any definite plan at the beginning of the year but at the end the actions you had taken were definite and had been done. Therefore, if you would be pleased at the pattern at the end of the year then you must of necessity plan wisely at the beginning of the year. And the one who is most able and willing to help you in your plans is the Lord. If you would claim to be a Christian then why not work at it and be the best one possible. You want to succeed as engineers in this world, which only lasts a short while. Why not consider being a real CHRISTIAN and enjoy fellowship with the saints. For the Lord will help you fulfill his plans even as he guides you in making them; AND if the Lord is with you, who can stand against you. As engineers we are taught and can see that the best, finest of materials are usually those that endure the longest, and are long remembered by men. Twenty centuries have only magnified the remembrance and merit of the best and finest of men, Jesus. The best and finest of materials is seldom remembered scarcely a century, much less twenty centuries. WALK CONSTANTLY WITH THE LORD AND HE WILL BE WITH YOU THROUGH ALL ETERNITY."—

           hwl

Sunday mornings we began to alternate attendance at church services—one Sunday at North Avenue Presbyterian Church, the next at St. Mark Methodist Church.
Both churches were designed by the same Atlanta architect—beautiful grey stone Gothic style buildings! At both churches we made wonderful life-long friendships. From Saint Mark: Huber & Margie Parsons, Colonel & Miss Agnes Groseclose, Jimmy & B J Moore and Torn & Martha Smith. From North Avenue: Mrs Allen Clapp (we met later in Africa), Lu Croft, Ruth Davis, and many others.

GOD CALLS—

During that fall quarter I frequently attended the North Avenue Presbyterian Church for the young adult meetings. That group never did have a catchy name like the group "Gather-In" at St. Mark.

On one occasion I scanned the church bulletin board which held a variety of notices. One of them was from the Methodist Board of Foreign Missions who was seeking engineers and architects to build many mission projects (hospitals, churches, schools and residences) around the world.

Before I finished reading that notice, God called me to become a missionary and fulfill part of my vision about doing something for Him.

I had no previous inclination either to become a missionary or any other full-time Christian church vocation. The lengthy process of becoming a missionary was unknown or my certainty about the call might have been less certain.

When I shared this call with Phyllis, she replied she would go wherever I went. She had no idea how many miles and locations that "going" would eventually include. As an engaged couple, we wrote for application forms and received a bundle of paper. Most of them involved questions about our work or other experience: training, education and church membership activities. Three personal references were required, including one from our pastors. We discovered later that each of our references was asked to provide three more references. Theological questions were asked, but not too many because we were going out as engineering/technical missionaries, not as preachers or evangelists.

We finally appeared before the missionary personnel committee on the campus of Scarritt College in Nashville, Tennessee. That large committee would recommend approval or disapproval of our application to be missionary candidates.

It was an important meeting for us. We encountered unusual questions from the group. The presiding official was Dr. W.A. Smart, dean of the theology school at Emory University. He avoided theology almost entirely by asking one tough practical question. As an engineer "How would we fix the leaky roof on the chapel at Emory University?" He explained several remedies had been tried and none had been completely successful. He really wasn't serious, because he knew I was an electrical engineer, who didn't fix roofs as part of my basic assignments. Although as an engineer missionary team, we would fix several leaky roofs in the Belgian Congo. Anyway, the personnel selection committee recommended the Board of Foreign Missions approve our candidacy.

Reverend Bill Davis and Doris, were applicants before the same personnel selection board on the same day. Together we went with them to Kennedy School of Missions at Hartford, Connecticut; the Ecole Coloniale in Brussels, Belgium; and the Belgian Congo. Our path would cross the Davis' path many more times over the intervening years. When we retired in 1991, their youngest son, Mark, was a veterinarian in the town of Arcadia, only a few miles east of our home in Bradenton.

A few weeks after the personnel meeting we were tentatively scheduled for attendance at the Kennedy School of Missions, Hartford Seminary, Hartford, Connecticut in September 1950. If we successfully completed that year of study, we would be commissioned as lay missionaries for the Methodist Church and sent to our overseas assignment. The Board of Foreign Missions discussed with us a possible assignment to Sarawak (formerly Borneo) for the construction of a hospital.

Our formal acceptance as missionary candidates with an assignment to Kennedy School of Missions occurred in the spring of 1950. At the same time we were informed our overseas location would be Sarawak and our task would be to build a 100-bed hospital there.

We never made it to Sarawak.

At least seven months elapsed since we'd sent for the application forms and started on that long paper trail that led to our selection as missionary candidates. Now all we had to do was complete the requirements for the master's degree, get married and get to the Kennedy School of Missions at the Hartford Seminary in Hartford, Connecticut.

WEDDING

On a lovely, warm Saturday, September 9, 1950, in the mid afternoon, we were married in the Chapel of North Avenue Presbyterian Church in Atlanta, Georgia. The church still remains on Peachtree Street in North Atlanta. Dr. Vernan Broyles Jr officiated the ceremony with the assistance of

Reverend B.C. Speers Jr, the Chaplain at Georgia Tech University. Elaine Lewis, sister of the bride, was maid of honor, and Rev. Lewis Davis served as best man. Charles Crawley and Glen Schooley were ushers.

A reception was held on the second floor church parlor in the Education Building. The reception was planned by Phyllis' mother Thelma Lewis and her dear church circle friends, Mrs. Jessica Fletcher, Mrs. Glenna Wilson, and Mrs. Moulton.

The wedding also served as a de facto Lewis/Thorne family reunion. The oldest brother of Phyllis' father, Roy, a Baptist Minister attended, as did a number of other members of the Lewis family. The Thorne family was represented by John, Mertie, Maude, and Robert Thorn, while Otho, Bee, Claude and Melva represented the Lewis family.

There was little time to celebrate as we headed out shortly after the reception ended.

*Footnote: Harry and Phyllis remained married for 65 years celebrating their 65th wedding anniversary on September 9, 2015. Harry went to the Lord two days later, September 11, 2015.

IV. METHODIST MISSIONARY CANDIDATES
(1950-1951)

ATLANTA TO HARTFORD, CONNECTICUT

After the wedding reception, we loaded all our worldly possessions into TeePee, the Oldsmobile, and left Atlanta late in the afternoon. Prior to the wedding, we'd advised our friends we were foreign missionary candidates. As a result, we received no crystal or china or beautiful but decorative items that are customary wedding gifts. Lots of stainless steel Revereware and utensils arrived, almost all of which are in use in 1995. Nearly a complete service for eight of Towle's "Candlelight" sterling silver remains in use. The service included one mysterious item we couldn't identify. Later, it was determined to be a rather ornate candle snuffer. We used it on our candles in Africa where we had no electricity. A generous supply of linens came.

We spent the first night in a small motel near Cornelia, Georgia. Next morning we decided to drive slowly along the spectacular Blue Ridge Parkway in the Great Smoky Mountains and enjoy the scenery. We didn't know how slowly we would be forced to drive! The views were beautiful, but a heavy, dense fog settled on the parkway. Visibility decreased until we couldn't see past the hood ornament. Soon our forward progress slowed to a crawl. There was no place to stop safely. Holding one door open and looking down to see the right edge of the pavement, we kept moving along. Not a single vehicle was met or passed. Apparently we were alone on the parkway.

Many hours later, almost midnight, we crept down the mountain, past the barricades that now closed the parkway to incoming traffic and into Front Royal, Virginia. For a long while every motel we approached had a "NO VACANCY" sign prominently displayed. We finally located a tiny room in a small motel and took it. It hadn't been approved by AAA. Surrounded by a rather dreary neighborhood, one of us stayed awake for the remainder of the night and watched the vehicle containing all our worldly possessions. Fortunately, the rest of the trip was uneventful.

KENNEDY SCHOOL OF MISSIONS, HARTFORD SEMINARY

While it no longer exists in 1995, the Kennedy School of Mission, Hartford Seminary provided a full year of excellent training for candidates from many boards of foreign missions in 1950.

As a childless couple, we were placed in one room of Hosmer Hall dormitory which was filled with many other missionary candidates. The rooms had no cooking facilities. All students were expected to eat in the dining hall. Some of us had hot plates for boiling water in order to make hot tea during the cold winter months. With severe restraints on finances, we managed to get ten cups of hot tea from one (1) tea bag.

On our first shopping trip to a supermarket we were behind a woman at the checkout counter. Her entire purchase was a jar of peanut butter and a six-pack of cold beer. The jar of peanut butter was okay, but the pack of beer surprised us. In 1950 no alcoholic beverages were sold in southern grocery stores.

On Monday, September 18th, we enrolled in the school, received our class assignments and obtained the required textbooks. The Board of Foreign Missions assigned us to Sarawak (formerly Borneo) for the construction of a hospital.

However, Jim Pottenger, who'd designed and started construction of the hospital at Kapanga in the Belgian Congo, died suddenly at age 32.

Some missionary candidates insisted on going to their choice of mission field. When the Board asked us if we would change our destination and go to the Belgian Congo, we replied immediately that we'd go wherever they wanted us to go. We felt our call by God wasn't restricted to a particular location or mission field.

Several other missionary candidates had parents, relatives, or friends on certain fields. That's where they wanted to go. They didn't want to be reassigned. Our own reassignment required us to enroll in French classes and African studies during the year at Kennedy School of Missions. We needed a second class of French language and some specialized studies at the Ecole Coloniale in Brussels, Belgium before going on to Africa. Our classes at Kennedy included French, Linguistics, Anthropology, Bible, African history and cultures, and a course in what could be called "How to be a Missionary."

CRICKET

Dr. Daniel J. Fleming taught an excellent course for future missionaries because he'd served as a missionary for many years in India. He authored a delightful book titled "*Each with His Own Brush,*" which explains how cultural groups can honor Christ in their individual, unique ways through art.

One day, in the midst of one of his lectures, he stopped completely and addressed a young female missionary candidate. "Cricket, what are you doing?"

Cricket, an energetic, bright lady known by her nickname had been making circular motions above her head with both hands.

Her reply broke up the class.

"I am polishing my halo!"

LINGUISTICS AND DR. GLEASON

The Hartford Seminary had a great library with a unique librarian, who was also a skilled linguist. When asked how many languages he knew, Dr. Gleason cited whole groups of languages: Teutonic, Romance, Slavic, et cetera. He could write, read and knew grammar in twenty-two languages. In a linguistics class, he told us, "if the village idiots can learn the local languages, we missionaries can learn them."

At the time we believed him.

Years later in the Congo, we'd doubt his statement. Lunda was a very tough language to master.

Unfortunately, the Kennedy School of Missions didn't attract enough students to stay alive. Hartford Seminary remains in service, with a reduced student population and fewer teachers. In the late 1970's or early 1980's the Kennedy School of Missions went out of business. They sold their library books and manuscripts to Emory University in Atlanta. Most mission boards quit giving missionary candidates one year of training and shortened their preparation to a few weeks at denominational facilities.

MARRIED LIFE IN A DORMITORY

At the Kennedy School of Missions only married couples with children lived in the apartments. Single persons and childless couples were housed in a dormitory with one room per person or per couple. As mentioned earlier there were no cooking facilities in the dorm.
Each room was small and equipped with one or two beds plus one or two study desks and a small closet space. Bathrooms and showers were down the hall. There were no telephones in any room. Instead we had one pay phone in the hallway on each floor. Our meals were eaten in the dining hall, which had a typical college menu.
We were the only Methodist couple scheduled for southern Congo conference. A single female nurse was scheduled for central Congo conference. The other Methodists were scheduled for Angola, Mozambique and India. Candidates from other mission boards were scheduled for Congo and various countries around the world. A delightful couple from Canada was in the dorm and made us an international

group. Unfortunately, we and the other students have scattered around the world on our missions. We've lost contact with most of them. A few are known to us until this day.

GERARD AND MARGIE MORRISSEY

After a few months of communal living we explored other possibilities. With our limited salaries, many candidates looked for ways to supplement their incomes. The ordained pastors obtained preaching engagements that paid them for Sunday services. Others found a variety of part-time jobs to earn additional cash. In mid-November, we read a notice that a family in nearby West Hartford needed a couple to live in their home and care for their children part-time. We went for an interview and met Gerard (Rod) and Margie Morrissey. They had two small children with a third one due in a few months. In addition, they cared for three other children who belonged to relatives who were having difficulties. We believed the arrangement would be a challenge, but one we were willing to take.

We were needed to care for six children in the afternoon and early evening as our primary duty. Our meals would be provided as we ate with the family. No salary was involved, which was good as it would have greatly complicated our pay from the Board of Foreign Missions. The house was huge, with three floors and a full basement. Our living area was the third floor with a bedroom, bathroom, study area and storage space. The Morrisseys approved us and we moved in December 9th, three months after our marriage.

That terrific arrangement lasted until we finished the school term in May.

The Morrisseys were genuine Roman Catholics. His sister was a Mother Superior, who believed in saying grace and making the sign of the cross before every meal.

Lucy, their three-year-old, added her unique touch to that custom one day when she startled her parents and us. She added a second sign of the cross when her ice cream arrived. Lucy loved ice cream and wanted God, and us, to know it.

The third Morrissey child, another girl, arrived on time and was baptized as Margie. She was a healthy, happy baby with a mass of curly hair. All the older children attended school on a very interesting schedule. They went to school most of the year in six week segments with free time between each segment and a short time for summer vacation. All the parents liked the schedule.

One weekend in the spring Rod and Margie asked us if we would care for the children while they went to New York City to see a stage play. We agreed. The children had been taught to obey us and were no problem to watch. Before our first wedding anniversary, we found ourselves in a big house with six children. We, and the children, had a great time.

We found out Margie's parents, the Davidsons, were major stockholders of the Wiremold Company. If you ever see metal or plastic molding in an office or factory it is probably a Wireway made by Wiremold. These Wireways contain electrical, telephone and computer wires. Uncounted millions of feet of Wireway have been installed.

Rod and Margie became very interested in our goal to go to the Congo and build a hospital. One day they handed us a catalog from LL Bean and asked us to choose whatever we could use. They would order and pay for it. We were happy to do so and used the items in our home overseas. At least one item, a hunting knife, is still in our possession today.

Rod had a beautiful over-and-under 16 gauge shotgun that the Marlin Firearms Factory had custom-made for him. He rarely used it and loaned the shotgun to us with the stipulation that we return it after our first term of service. Phyllis used it on many dove hunts in Congo and added doves to our food supply. We returned the shotgun in 1956. We have fond memories of the months we spent at the Morrissey home.

CHRISTMAS 1950

For our first Christmas as a married couple, we wanted to be at home. Santa Rosa was 2500 miles away. Atlanta was far closer, so we drove to Phyllis' home for our first Christmas.

Many missionary candidates didn't have autos. Margaret Boss and her brother Charles asked if they could ride with us to Chattanooga. We said yes, but it wasn't quite that easy.

Charles was married to Kathie and they had a small girl, Becky. Six people in a two door coupe for a thousand miles is rather cozy, but we survived somehow.

On the way, we got lost in Philadelphia late at night. We stopped to ask a policeman for directions. He was very kind and pointed to the restaurant behind him.

"I'm going into that restaurant for coffee. When I am out of sight, make a real quick U-turn and drive over that low median divider. Drive a few blocks and you'll see your highway."

There were no legal U-turns for miles in the direction we were headed.

We left the Boss's in Chattanooga.

We had a most pleasant holiday time. All three of Phyllis' sisters were single and at home. On the way back to Hartford, we encountered an ice storm in the Potomac River Valley at Hagerstown, Maryland. The highway had been clear. As we came over the hilltop and started down towards the river, we were on a sheet of ice that covered the highway. We made it.

HARTFORD TO ATLANTA

When our year at the Kennedy School of Missions came to an end early in May, we headed for a short visit to the Board of Foreign Missions office at 150 Broadway in New York. They informed us we would tentatively sail for Belgium sometime in July and gave us shipping instructions for our household goods.

Only a few items would go with us to Europe. Most items would be stored in New York for shipment directly to the Congo after we arrived there.

In the field, the Board provided housing, beds, furniture, and some major kitchen appliances, usually a wood stove. Missionaries were responsible for dishes, lamps, cooking utensils, silverware, linens and anything else.

We went on to spend five great days in the city of Washington, D.C.

Our accommodations were much better than when I slept on a bench around the Washington Monument during my wartime visit. In these intervening years we have visited the city many times and still have not seen everything. We will never do so. They added marvelous sights, such as the Air and Space Museum in 1976 for the Bicentennial, Viet Nam Wall, and other great memorials.

ATLANTA JUNE 8-19
—COMMISSIONED MISSIONARIES

We hadn't been formally commissioned as lay missionaries, so we called Bishop Arthur J Moore. He said his schedule was full, but he'd commission us in his office on a Saturday morning. A private ceremony didn't appeal to us. When we asked if any ordained minister could commission us, he said "Of course !"

We called John Horton, senior minister at Saint Mark, who was happy and delighted at the opportunity to commission us in the sanctuary at Saint Mark. On June 13th, we were commissioned at a special service in the presence of hundreds of family, friends and acquaintances. (Sometimes bishops do strange things.)

On June 19th, the Georgia Institute of Technology awarded me my Masters of Science in Industrial Engineering degree.

It had been a busy week. We bought, cleaned, and packed many fifty-five gallon steel barrels. With good lockable clamp lids, they were cheap, sturdy, roomy and ideal for shipping our household goods. Originally these steel barrels contained shortening, chocolate frosting and other ingredients used by large bakeries. After cleaning, we packed the barrels with dishes, glassware, silverware, linens, clothes, shoes, boots, soap, books, Kleenex, toilet paper, stationery, sanitary napkins and items given to us by our Roman Catholic friends, Rod and Margie Morrissey, in Connecticut.

ATLANTA—GREENCASTLE—NEW YORK

Each summer a conference was scheduled at Greencastle, Indiana, for all missionaries on furlough and new missionaries going out.
On the beautiful campus of De Pauw University, we spent a wonderful week listening to lectures, great sermons, lengthy stories about real missionary life and helpful hints on how to be a worthy missionary.
A veteran woman missionary, going out for her sixth term told us a memorable story. She was finally being appointed to a teaching position, which she'd been recruited to do so many years ago. Her point was, you could expect to be appointed by the resident bishop to tasks you weren't trained to do.
Sure enough, Phyllis was later appointed to do double-entry bookkeeping for the business affairs of the two-hundred bed hospital we built at Kapanga. Being trained in fine arts, commercial art, and drafting, she'd certainly never been exposed to business courses of any kind, much less double-entry bookkeeping. When the Bishop announced Phyllis'

appointment as hospital bookkeeper, she immediately recalled the words of the missionary at Greencastle.

HAZARDS OF GOSSIP

On the train from Atlanta to Greencastle we weren't dressed as "traditional" missionaries. I wore boots and a hat. Two ladies in the seat ahead of us spent several hours "gossiping" about their lives as Methodist missionaries in the Congo. When all of us got off at Greencastle station and went to the university, they looked at us with some surprise.

For a day or two, they were obviously apprehensive we might repeat some of the gossipy conversations. Of course, we did no such thing.

In any case, we couldn't remember the names, places and mission stations we'd heard about on the train. As a reward, they both became good friends and were helpful to us, then and for years afterwards. As engineer missionaries, we never really fit the stereotype of what a foreign missionary should look or act like.

SAILING FOR BELGIUM

Upon arrival in New York on June 29th, the Board told us our sailing date was delayed until late July. We were free to do whatever we wished until then. Phyllis had several relatives living in Massachusetts, so we went to visit them.

On July 17th, we returned to New York in order to obtain visas, travel tickets, some travel money advances, physical exams and check on our shipment of goods which had arrived from Atlanta.

On July 25th, we went across the Hudson River to New Jersey and boarded the SS Edam for our voyage to the port of Antwerp, Belgium.

The SS Edam sailed up the Scheldt River and into the Port of Antwerp. The Port is located in the Northwest part of Belguim. On the map below Belguim is just below the word "Belguim".

V. BRUSSELS, BELGIUM (1951-1952)

SS EDAM

On July 25th we sailed for Antwerp on the SS EDAM, an ancient "rust bucket" relic from World War One. It was so old more than one-hundred of the passengers were in steerage and only a very few in cabins. Neither the steerage area nor the cabins were air conditioned. We felt fortunate to occupy a cabin on the upper deck.

The passengers in steerage occupied a large open area below decks that had sleeping accommodations in rows of bunks with communal rest rooms plus showers. On this voyage most of the steerage passengers were students going to Europe as cheaply as possible.

In 1951, airline tickets were expensive. All transatlantic flights were on noisy piston-engined aircraft that were relatively slow. The flight lasted 11 hours. Large, fast jet aircraft were ten years away.

These travel arrangements in steerage had been created in the late 1800's in order to transport millions of immigrants to America quickly and at the lowest cost. In earlier years, many passengers brought their own food. One story explains the earliest ships of this type hauled cattle (steers) to Europe and brought people from Europe. However, I cannot confirm steerage really originated that way. Refrigerated ships weren't available yet for bulk transport of meat, so the story may be true.

Being old and equipped with an inefficient steam engine, the Edam moved slowly. As a result, the voyage required almost twelve days when many passenger liners were crossing routinely in as few as four or five days. Upon arrival in Antwerp we were told the good ship Edam had just made its last voyage! Hooray!

However, a full-year later, we met the Elwood Bartletts when they arrived by ship at Antwerp. To our surprise they were on the Edam. Evidently the owners of the ship wanted to gain all possible profit from the old rust bucket before breaking it up for scrap and over doesn't always mean over.

FESTIVAL OF BRITAIN (August 1951)

Our classes in the French language and study of the laws, geography, history and customs of Belgium and Belgian Congo wouldn't start until September. Most of the Protestant Boards of Foreign Missions sending missionaries to the Congo had cooperated in the establishment of an office in Brussels. That office assisted missionaries in locating housing, schools for children, tutors, visas and other duties. The skilled director, H. Wakelin Coxill, was a remarkable man who had a thorough knowledge of French and Belgian bureaucracy as well as local customs. None of us spoke fluent French or had any knowledge of the local bureaucracy and customs.

All medical missionaries attended the Tropical Medicine School in Antwerp. The rest of us studied French and attended the Ecole Coloniale in the city of Brussels. With Rev. Coxill's assistance, we soon located some lodging in a boarding house [pension in French] on the Avenue des Lucioles in Watermael, a suburb of Brussels. This pension was owned by Monsieur et Madame Durand. More about life there later.

With weeks to spare, we went to England late in August to visit the Festival of Britain. Our trip involved an electric train to the channel port of Ostende, a ferry boat across the English Channel to Dover and a train from Dover to London. Numerous sea and air battles were fought in this area from 1939 to 1945, so the Channel contained much wreckage from many ships and planes. Several masts and smoke stacks of sunken ships could still be seen in 1951 because the Channel is quite shallow. In addition to the ship wrecks, there are thousands of tons of bombs and millions of ammunition rounds in the Channel. I don't know if any effort has ever been made to clean out the wartime debris.

The White Cliffs of Dover are a beautiful introduction to England. Most of our week was spent in London. The Festival gathered exhibits and shows from throughout the commonwealth. One memorable evening, Tattoo was performed by The Black Watch, a regiment fully equipped with skillful drummers, bagpipe players and marvelous uniforms. Because they wore kilts on some occasions, the German Army in 1914-1918, after a disastrous battle with the Black Watch regiment, called them the "Ladies from Hell." They could fight as well as they could parade.

We went to visit Windsor Castle and one of King Henry VIII's castles. He'd built several. At Windsor Castle the guide informed us King George III had never been properly buried. His casket is stored in a hallway beneath St. George's Chapel. On our visit to the Tower of London we were allowed to see the crown jewels and the location in the yard where numerous people "lost their heads" to executioners with large axes. While viewing the crown jewels, it was difficult to comprehend the sight of diamonds and rubies the size of a hen egg and pearls almost as large as a ping pong ball. On another outing we stayed inside Westminster Abbey until closing time. As missionaries to Africa, we wanted to find the grave marker for David Livingstone. This beautiful slab is found on the floor in a walkway because after a 1000 years the Abbey is rather crowded. It gives one an odd, somewhat irreverent, feeling to walk across his grave marker. A book by Jeannette Eaton published in 1947 titled *David Livingstone, Foe of Darkness* is a great insight into his life. Livingstone died at the village of his friend, Chitambo, near Lake Bengeulu early in the morning of May 1, 1873.

When Chuma found Livingstone, he was kneeling against his bed as if in prayer. Chuma, and the loyal Africans who'd been with him for years, decided his body should be returned to his home land. "But with instinctive poetry, they buried there the heart that for 30 years had beaten for Africa." They wrapped the body in a tree bark that was placed inside sailcloth. Chuma and company carried the burden on their shoulders as they walked for a thousand miles across the wilderness. Superstitious fear of any dead body made it difficult to enter villages. Often they were refused entry and had to camp away from a village. Halfway to Zanzibar, they met a rescue party looking for Livingstone. The English Army captain wanted to bury the body there. Chuma refused and kept going towards the coast. In Zanzibar harbor they found a British navy cruiser. After nine months on the path with their precious burden, Chuma and his men entrusted the body to the captain of the cruiser for transport to London. Chuma and Susi followed in another ship. They helped to complete Livingstone's last notes and journals for publication.

On that slab in Westminster Abbey are inscribed words from one of David Livingstone's letters to the editor of the *New York Herald*. Livingstone was begging America's help to stamp out slavery:

"All I can add in my loneliness is, may heaven's rich blessing come down on everyone—American, English, or Turk—who will help heal the open sore of the world."

Outside of Westminster Abbey in the City of London there remained many signs of the destructive Nazi air raids. We visited the Methodist Central Hall and heard Dr. Norman Vincent Peale. He'd been absent when we visited his Marble Collegiate Church in New York. In London we stayed at a pleasant small hotel but didn't get accustomed to their breakfast. Americans are not likely to order kippered herring and heated tomatoes early in the morning.

BRUSSELS

We heard someone say spring comes on July 3rd and summer on July 4th with the remainder of the year being fall and winter. After fourteen months in Brussels, we agreed. Much of the weather involves fog, rain and cold winds. We bought woolen underwear although we were quite certain such clothing would never be needed in Africa. Some wartime rationing was still in effect throughout Belgium and Europe. Heating fuel was scarce and most buildings didn't have central heating. In the pension, we were allowed one hot bath per week unless we paid extra; the Durands discouraged a second bath because gas was expensive. For us a cold water bath wasn't a viable option. Therefore, we had one bath per week. Antiperspirants weren't needed. Normal activities didn't cause perspiration, they caused shivering.

Belgium derives its name from the Belgica tribe who lived in the area when Julius Caesar's legion arrived 2000 years ago. Caesar wrote that the tribesmen were fierce fighters and cannibalistic. Many other tribes have conquered and settled in the area. Therefore, modern Belgians are only distant relatives of the Belgica tribe.

Brussels started in the seventh century as a peasant village, Brocella, surrounding a little chapel dedicated to the Archangel Michael. Three centuries later Charles of France built a fort on the island of Saint Gery. A chapel was built in order to contain and honor the remains of Saint Gudule. That village, Bruocsella, was on the caravan route between the cities of Cologne and Tongres on the east and the wealthy seaports of Bruges and Ghent on the west. Bruocsella prospered and outgrew its walled enclosure. During the 14th century a second line of fortifications was built in order to include this larger territory. One of the gates, Porte d'Hal, remains.

The jewel of Brussels, the Grand Place, began to take shape in 1454 when the Town Hall (Hotel de Ville) was completed. This magnificent hall has been damaged in succeeding wars, but today (1995) is a beautiful sight. Next to it is the House of the King (Maison du Roi) and various ornate Guild Halls that were built by powerful guilds.

The ports of Bruges and Ghent were silted shut. The Port of Antwerp on the Scheldt River became the primary port for the area. Between 1550 and 1561 Brussels built the Canal

Willebroek from Brussels to Antwerp. In 1695 the Marshal of Villeroy besieged Brussels with 3,000 aerial bombs and 1,200 cannonballs. The Grand Place and Town Hall were damaged but rebuilt later.

In 1803 Napoleon Bonaparte entered Brussels and he modernized the city. A decree of 1810 dismantled the fortified walls, except the Porte d'Hal. They were replaced with a ring of splendid boulevards. After the fall of Napoleon at Waterloo, Belgium, in 1815, the country was annexed by Holland. On August 15, 1830 a revolt brought independence to Belgium with Brussels as the capital. The Low Countries, Belgium and the Netherlands, are often referred to as the Crossroads of Europe. For centuries they've been the target for invading armies. They have been the site of many decisive battles: Waterloo in 1815, Ypres in 1914 and the Battle of the Bulge in 1944. Most of the time, the invading armies were on their way somewhere else. As a result the Belgians and Dutch became skilled at frustrating their occupiers. They never had sufficient power to defeat them, but they certainly made the invaders unhappy, as we learned from Joe, our landlord's son.

Within Napoleon's Boulevards, the Old Town of Brussels is a pentagon in shape and contains the most fascinating parts of the City of Brussels.

This Old Town was originally divided into two parts by the Senne River, carrying polluted waters and industrial wastes. This river was diverted and the riverbed filled.

Within the Old Town are located: Palace of Justice, King's Palace, Fine Arts Museum, National Library, Place Albert, Koekelberg Church, Cathedral of Saint Michael and Saint Gudule, Museum of Modern Art, the Grand Place, also known as the Grote Market—their central plaza, as well as many other historic locations.

Belgians love to eat and drink beer, and the city is well supplied with many restaurants, cafes and brasseries (for the beer drinkers). On the sidewalks you can purchase one of Belgium's food specialties: frites. This is a generous sized paper cone filled with hot fried potatoes. They are delicious, but not low calorie.

Outside the Old Town is the Cinquantenaire, a huge ornate monument dedicated in 1880 for the 50th anniversary of Belgium's independence. One wing is a general interest museum and the other wing is a military museum that was badly bombed during the Second World War.

Near Brussels are two very historic sites. The first is the battlefield at Waterloo where Napoleon was defeated in 1815 by the Duke of Wellington and Von Blucher. The second location contains the Congo Museum at Terveuren.

For many of the colonial years (1908-1960), the Belgians were busy acquiring a tremendous collection of original artifacts from the Congo. A talented museum staff has been making exact duplicates of these artifacts in order to return the originals to a Congo museum. This was a unique action by a colonial power.

Unfortunately the continual unrest and the extreme political instability in Zaire has indefinitely delayed the achievement of that noble goal. In 1995, the Congo (now Zaire) remains in the grip of a very brutal dictator— Mobutu. He is not the least bit interested in museums or anything else in art, history, or culture. His only interest is staying in power as long as he can.

Brussels, and its suburbs, had an extensive street car system that was cheap to ride. This made it very easy to visit all of these locations.

{Note: In 2016, Mobutu is gone but there is still political unrest in the Democratic Republic of Congo. Elections are scheduled for 2018}.

Belgium has a monarchy. But the king is King of the Belgians and not the King of Belgium. They have had six kings: King Leopold I,(1830-1865); King Leopold II (1865-1909), who was also King of the Belgian Congo; King Albert I (1909-1932, a hero of the First World War); King Leopold III,(1932-1952, who was forced to abdicate in 1952 for his collaboration with the Nazis during World War II); King Baudoin, (1952-1992); and King Albert II (1992-present).

A beloved member of the monarchy was the beautiful Queen Astrid, who graced so many Belgian stamps. She was killed in an auto accident while King Leopold III was driving and had been drinking. Many Belgians never forgave him, and this memory probably contributed to the demand for his abdication after the Second World War.

IDENTITY CARDS AND MAIL WOES

Belgium and the Belgian Congo required every resident, citizen and alien, to carry an identity card at all times. Upon moving into an apartment or house, each resident had to register their initial arrival and their final relocation with local communal police. When registering at a hotel, each person had to have an identity card or a passport (for aliens). Remembering to carry your identity card wasn't easy for Americans who relocate without any sort of real official notification to anyone, except to the US Postal Service for mail.

We discovered the hard way that sending cash in the mail was forbidden in Belgium. The penalty was 10% of the value sent by mail.

One day, a uniformed gendarme appeared at our door looking for Madame Little. With some trepidation, Phyllis admitted she'd mailed 40 francs (80 cents) through the mail to Monsieur Florent Mortier for an item he had sold her. Together with the gendarme, we went to the police station where Phyllis paid her fine of four (4) francs. We never sent any more coins or cash through the mail in Europe.

Incidentally, the Belgians had an interesting nickname for gendarmes. FLICs--Federation Libre des Imbeciles casques; in English, Free Federation of Helmeted Imbeciles. We learned this bit of Belgian slang from our teenage friend, Joe Durand.

BOARDING HOUSE (pension)
        ON GLOWWORM AVENUE

When we arrived in Brussels the Rev. H. Wakelin Coxil helped us find living space.

We chose to live with Monsieur and Madame Durand and their son, Joe, at 11 Avenue des Lucioles in Watermael, a suburb of Brussels. We stayed there from August 1951 through February 1952. Our living space was one small room with a bath down the hall. Our meals were eaten with the family.

They spoke no English, although the teenager, Joe, had acquired a lot of American slang from US soldiers during the war years.

The boarding house was near a street car stop. The street car system was heavily subsidized by the Belgian government in order to keep the fares as low as possible. We could economically travel to anywhere in Brussels.

As we lived with the family for six months, we learned a great deal of French, with a Belgian accent, and became familiar with many customs.

December 6th is St. Nicolas day when gifts of candy and massepain are exchanged. Massepain is a delicious confection made with finely ground almonds and formed into a multitude of fascinating shapes. For Christmas, they brought in a real live Christmas tree from the forest. Then they trimmed it with many lighted candles in addition to other ornaments. Unfortunately, some of those ornaments were flammable and could burn easily. We weren't comfortable sitting next to that tree.

As the tree became progressively drier, it tended to catch fire occasionally. Monsieur Durand kept a cloth napkin in a small basin of water in order to quickly extinguish these fires. We were nervous until the tree was removed.

The Methodist Board of Foreign Missions strongly suggested single missionaries and childless couples live in boarding houses. This was a good idea when the host family had no knowledge of English and didn't want to try to learn English. It forced the missionaries to learn the language.

Joe entertained us with some of his escapades as a child during the Nazi occupation (1940-1944).

On the street cars, a group of Belgian children would distract a lone German soldier while one child crept up behind him. The culprit would slip the soldier's bayonet out of its holder and drop it noisily on the metal floor of the streetcar. The soldier would be furious but could seldom catch the perpetrator.

Elsewhere the German Army had small spotter aircraft stationed in large open parks around Brussels. Their aviation gasoline, in short supply, was stored in fifty-five gallon barrels near the landing strip.

Joe and his buddies would sneak up to the barrels, silently unscrew the bung, and tip the barrel over in order to pour out the gasoline. At that time, the boys weren't quite as tall as the barrels. It took a lot of nerve. This loss of scarce gasoline infuriated the Nazi airmen, who would shoot the culprits if they ever caught them.

In 1952, the existentialism of Jean Paul Sartre was a very popular type of philosophy in Europe. One evening, Joe and his girlfriend offered to escort us to an existentialist hangout.

The Poubelle (Trash Can) lived up to its namesake. The place was located in a cellar and was crowded with young intellectuals. I made the mistake of wearing my hat through the doorway and was greeted immediately with some raucous cries of "chapeau," and very quickly removed the offending hat.

Fortunately modern electronic music instruments and huge amplifiers had not been invented yet. As a result the music was agreeable and did no damage to our eardrums.

Two more incidental facts about life in Belgium in 1952. First, the purchaser of an automobile was presumed to know how to drive. No requirement existed for licensing drivers. If you had the money to buy a vehicle, you had the right to drive it. Vehicles were licensed and heavily taxed, but not drivers. The Durand family said they saw absolutely no need for drivers to obtain any sort of license to drive their vehicle. Second, the legal age for voting was 18 and if you didn't vote you were fined. Obviously, voter participation is much greater in Belgium than in the US.

A somewhat minor story concerned toilet paper. European toilet paper had a slick wax coating on one side and what seemed to be fine sandpaper on the other. It wasn't easy to use.

There were various other details in Belgian customs and laws that were/are quite different from anything we have in the US, but we aren't writing a historical account of Belgium and Europe.

ACUTE APPENDICITIS

On October 31st I went to class, but soon felt severe stomach pains. We went to Dr. Sommerhausen's office, where the good doctor soon diagnosed it as acute appendicitis. In a few hours, on Halloween, I was on an operating table in the Edith Cavell Hospital. Although there were no complications, they kept me in the hospital until November 6th, six days. Long stays were standard routine in those years. Nurses offered me a beer and wine list, but wouldn't allow Coca-Cola in the hospital because it had "caffeine" in it. Phyllis smuggled Coca-Cola in because I had no desire for beer or wine.

It is to be noted that Belgium and France had no age limit for drinking alcoholic beverages. Primary school children in France routinely carried table wine to school with their lunches. School cafeterias were non-existent or very rare.

STUDYING FRENCH

Our hosts, the Durands, knew no English. This gave us an excellent opportunity to learn French with a Belgian accent. We arranged formal tutoring with Madame Huge, who wisely had us work hard to really master the French language, spoken and written.

Speaking French is considerably easier than writing it correctly. For example, the spoken sound "onh" can be spelled at least a dozen ways: en, ent, ens, on, ons, ont, em, etcetera. Therefore, writing a passage correctly while your tutor is dictating is one of the questionable pleasures when learning the French language. But it is absolutely essential.

Using the proper gender is difficult because all inanimate objects, such as "the chair," have been assigned an arbitrary gender. Chair is feminine.

My knowledge of Spanish was both a help and a hindrance. The inanimate objects designated as feminine in Spanish may or may not be feminine in French. Therefore, genders must be memorized because no inanimate object has any masculine or feminine characteristics. This makes it difficult to determine the gender of nonliving objects.

Other studies were more fun with a delightful Congo veteran, Monsieur Florent Mortier. He tutored us in Belgian and Belgian Congo laws, customs and cultures. He was truly a great tutor and scholar with practical knowledge and an excellent personal library.

The laws of Belgium and the Belgian Congo were based on the Napoleonic Code, which is quite different from the English based laws we have in America. We soon determined we weren't "European" at all, but American, although the Belgian Congo laws had only two legal distinctions: natives (indigenes) and European. In Congo the indigenes were denied access to many locations and services.

We studied Belgian history back to the Belgica tribe which fought Caesar's army for so many years. They were rumored to be cannibals, as well as fierce fighters. While reading more recent Belgian history, Monsieur Mortier grinned when we read, in French, that "Belgium and its Allies Won the Second World War."—a true, but not very complete, statement.

ECOLE NORMALE CHARLES BUHL

Before going to the Congo, all foreign missionaries were required to attend classes at one of the Normal Schools that train Belgian primary and secondary school teachers. On December 5th We began classes at the Ecole Normale Charles Buhl. These classes, all in French, covered the basic courses in pedagogy as practiced in the public schools of Belgium. The school system in Belgium was quite different from any system in the US. Course materials, curricula and exams followed national standards. There were no local school boards. After primary school, the students were tested and assigned to tracks. One track led to the classic courses that prepared the best students for application to a university. As recently as 1988, only 7% of the population go on to university. The only other track led to preparation for vocational schools and terminated at the end of secondary school.

Belgium had only two major universities. The University of Louvain was an old Roman Catholic institution and the Universite Libre de Bruxelles, a "free" university, which really meant independent from Catholic hierarchy. Both universities were small because any university education was considered to be a rare opportunity you had to earn. The fact that I was a farm boy who had two university degrees was almost incomprehensible to the Durands, our hosts. Early in 1952, I successfully completed all the normal school courses and was awarded a certificate entitling me to teach French in a secondary school.

MISSIONARY EXCURSIONS

H Wakelin Coxill and the Protestant missionary office often scheduled trips to cities in Belgium and Holland during the year.

A trip to Dinant, Belgium was most interesting to us, but even more so to Louis Johnson. On his previous visit to Dinant he'd found German Army tanks in the area and they weren't too friendly. The scenery around Dinant is spectacular and quieter without tanks.

As mentioned, Belgium has been in the path of many armies. Nearly every town has been the location of at least one major battle. Statues and war memorials are scattered throughout the land. Therefore any comprehensive history of Belgium includes a bewildering array of rulers, kings, battles and invasions. This makes Belgian history a complicated subject and difficult to master. To further make the history difficult, the towns and locations often changed names to suit the current invader. For example, Charlemagne's capital, Aix la Chapelle, is now known as Aachen.

Before the fourteenth century, the city of Bruges, Belgium was a thriving seaport for Belgian commerce and business, particularly trade in cloth, tapestries, lace, rugs and spices as imports. Over the centuries, the passageway to the sea filled with silt and they had no dredges to remove it.

Today Bruges is miles from the seacoast and remains almost in the same condition it was in when ships could no longer arrive at the port docks. There are many ancient buildings, guild halls, churches and a magnificent bell tower with circular staircase. The basement crypt of one of the churches contains a life-size statue of Christ crucified that is startling in its realism. We visited the Congo Museum at Terveuren but we could not appreciate the treasures until we had lived in the Congo.

Holland is a short distance from Brussels. Bill and Doris Davis, Steve, Mark and Susan, had received their Chevrolet Carry-All and invited us to go with them to visit Rotterdam, Holland. For its strong stubbornness, this city had been subjected to saturation bombing by Nazi Stuka dive-bombers. One square mile of the downtown area was bombed into a pile of rubble.

Louis Johnson, mentioned earlier, made many friends in Belgium during the war as an army officer. He invited me to go to Liege, famous for steel products and the Browning shotguns and rifles, for a visit to a steel mill. This medium-size steel mill had four parking spaces for cars, but hundreds of spaces for bicycles. This was my second visit to a steel mill and confirmed my desire to work elsewhere.

In Belgium, we went on a trip to Breendonk, a somber, forbidding concentration camp and prison. During the First World War, a Belgian nurse, Edith Cavell, was caught, accused of spying, brought here, and shot to death by the Germans. During the Second World War it housed unwilling guests of the Nazi Army as a concentration camp. Walking through the cell blocks and looking at execution walls didn't inspire pleasant memories.

APARTMENT LIVING IN BRUSSELS

After six months in a boarding house (pension), we felt we'd learned enough about the style of living in Brussels. We located a small apartment in the same building with our friends, Max and Anita Ritter, and son, Mark.

When we moved on March 1st we made certain we notified the Watermael police of our departure and registered our arrival with the new police office, as required. We didn't want to be charged with illegal relocation of residence.

Harry & Phyllis on the balcony of our Brussels apartment

On the previous Halloween, Anita and I were patients in the Edith Cavell Hospital. Anita was in the maternity wing giving birth to their first son, Mark, and I was in the emergency operating room for an appendectomy.

About two months after we moved into the apartment below them, Max and Anita went on spring break {to Nice, France} and left their infant, Mark, with us. He was a healthy, happy baby, but we had little experience in infant care. All three of us survived and were happy to see the parents return.

On June 3rd we went to the Royal Opera House with the Ritters to see the great opera "*Aida*." It contains the processional march used at graduations in America for years.

In our own apartment, we were free to take as many baths as we wished and eat the foods we liked. An important note: as usual, the apartment had a gas stove. There were no other appliances: no refrigerator, no freezer, no washing machine or dryer, and no microwave. In those days, you bought fresh food, meat and household items every day in separate stores. No supermarkets existed. For refrigeration, you simply placed the food, vegetables and fruit on the balcony where the temperature was ordinarily freezing or frosting. Fortunately for us there was a laundry nearby.

Belgium uses the metric system for weights and measures, with kilograms for weights and liters for measuring volume. In cooking, Belgians use weights and volumes for their recipes. Teaspoons, tablespoons and cups are never used for measuring anything.

At the Durands we'd been introduced to many Belgian dishes. Some tasty and some only "interesting." An interesting dish was "filet Americain" which is raw hamburger meat mixed with a raw egg and various seasonings. We never tried it.

While living in the apartment, we bought raw hamburger meat frequently. We made it into delicious American Hamburgers, with mustard and ketchup on buns. We probably perpetuated the myth that Americans eat lots of "filet Americain."

PARIS AND CHARTRES

We had Holy Week free from classes. Even poor missionaries could afford the fare of nine dollars for a round trip to Paris. We found a room at the small Hotel d'Angleterre near the Arc des Triomphes and Champs d'Elysees. From the hotel we walked to most of the places we wanted to visit. We enjoyed the Louvre Museum which holds a world class collection of art, paintings and statues. Phyllis was thrilled to see many of the items she studied in art classes. We rode the elevator up the Eiffel Tower to get one spectacular view of Paris. Another great view was from the church up the hill in Montmartre. Our fluency in French helped us get around in Paris and France.

One evening we went to see the *Barber of Seville* at the Opera Comique. It was a delightful comedy with a young American company of performers.

A movie house in Paris introduced us to Africa in a way we hadn't studied at the Kennedy School of Missions. "The African Queen" was shown in English with French subtitles. Being the only American missionaries present, we laughed before the rest of the audience. At the opening scene, a Methodist Mission in Congo, we didn't know whether to laugh or cry. Fellow Methodist missionaries disapproved of the movie, which has a female missionary drink and sleep with a stranger. All missionaries are not saints, but we know of none who strayed quite as far as Katherine Hepburn did with Humphrey Bogart.

From Paris we made a one day bus tour to see the marvelous Notre Dame de Chartres (The Cathedral of our Lady of Chartres) with its great mismatched spires. The south spire is octagonal and was built in the 12th century. The north, taller, spire is more ornate and was built in the 16th century. An abundance of carved stone sculptures are inside and outside this ancient structure. The huge stained glass windows are alive with truly magnificent colors, particularly the "Chartres blue." It has nearly 200 windows containing the finest stained glass of the 12th and 13th centuries.

Back in Paris, we lived on hard French rolls and delicious cheeses, plus an assortment of other inexpensive meals. We couldn't afford to patronize the famous restaurants of Paris where the price of dinner required a whole month of missionary pay. During the week, we never did get to see anything outside of Paris, except Chartres. Mostly we walked around the central parts of the city in order to thoroughly enjoy the many places of interest to us within Paris.

On the Left Bank of the Seine River, we went to the outdoor used book stalls. While there, and at several other cities in Europe, we bought a number of unique books. One pair of books we bought for a few dollars is now worth $150.

In Paris we spent hours exploring the cathedral of Notre Dame and tried to imagine we sensed the presence of the Hunchback, Quasimodo. This cathedral is an awesome structure with many fierce-looking gargoyles as rainspouts.

Another excursion took us to see the grandiose tomb of Napoleon, Les Invalides. It's a magnificent memorial. Although much of Europe considered the man, Napoleon, to be an invader, bully and tyrant, the French didn't do so.

As we checked out of the hotel, I asked the doorman to call a taxi for our trip to the railroad station. He asked "Un taxi ou deux?" Fortunately Phyllis didn't hear him. He'd asked if I wanted one taxi, or two? The implication of two taxis wouldn't have pleased my American wife.

MEMORIAL DAY 1952

On Memorial Day, we went to the US Military Cemetery at Henri La Chapelle near Liege, Belgium. More than 17,000 American soldiers had been buried there. Many were casualties in the Battle of the Bulge, fought in late 1944 and early 1945 in the Ardennes Forest not too far away. More than 600,000 American men were involved in that desperate effort to stop the German Army, which had more than 500,000 men. Other casualties were brought from the important battle for the city of Aachen.

Many of the Belgians told us they were happy when the Americans won all the battles and pushed the Nazi Panzer tanks back into their own country. Local residents had hidden in caves and wooded areas until liberated by the US Army. Belgians appreciated the sacrifices so many young Americans made. They showed their appreciation when they came to the cemetery on our Memorial Day. Hundreds of Belgian school children placed flowers on every grave. Later they sang the Star Spangled Banner before Taps was played at the end of the ceremony. The cemetery is on the slope of a beautiful hill facing the east. The rising sun shines on the soldiers first.

PREPARATION FOR THE ECOLE COLONIALE EXAMS

Successful completion of an exam given by the Ecole Coloniale was required before any non-Belgian missionary can serve in the Congo. At least one of a married couple must pass.

Prior to the Ecole Coloniale courses and subsequent exams, all of us attended preparatory classes given by a university teacher, Professor La Rochette. He assembled a huge collection of French idiomatic expressions and slang, with their rough translations into English. Bill Davis promptly dubbed these legal-sized sheets, "Lippy La Rochettes Lousy Leaflets." That collection was a help to us. Idiomatic expressions and colloquialisms are difficult to learn. Quotations from famous French and Belgian writers are helpful. La Fontaine wrote numerous fables similar to Aesop's fables. Quotes from French Kings, Presidents and Generals are important. You should know who said, "They shall not pass." Professor La Rochette provided us with an introduction to French literature, but not to poetry or humor.

When you can read poetry intelligently, sing songs and tell jokes, you have mastered a foreign language. These classes with La Rochette began on January 3rd and continued for several months. No tests were given at the end. They were tutoring classes and only needed as preparation for Ecole Coloniale courses.

ECOLE COLONIALE

The Belgian government established the Ecole Coloniale for two purposes: (1) to improve the preparation of non-Belgians who wanted to teach and serve in the Belgian Congo. In nearly all cases the missionaries were Roman Catholic and Protestant. This school taught us many things that would have been impossible to learn on the job in the Congo. (2) to screen the qualifications of non-Belgian missionaries requesting entry into the Belgian Congo.

For example, a number of religious groups, including Jehovah's Witness, were not allowed to operate anywhere in the Congo. Their Watchtower periodical was always confiscated when found.

However, one unintended result of the Ecole Coloniale, was making numerous Protestant missionaries into temporary believers in Purgatory, a place of punishment. The courses and exams required intensive study of many complex subjects plus an excellent knowledge of French.

All Dutch speaking applicants could take the course and exams in Flemish, one of the two languages officially recognized in Belgium and Congo. Medical personnel were required to successfully complete the Tropical Medicine School in Antwerp. They were not required to take the Ecole Coloniale Exam. Rumor has it the Tropical Medicine route wasn't the least bit easier.

The lengthy final exams were given over a five-day period from August 4th to 8th, 1952. All questions and answers were in French. You were graded on the correctness of your French as well as the correctness of your answers. A week later the grades were posted. The optimists started at the top of that list.

Being a realist, I started at the bottom, among the worst failing grades, and finally found my name above the minimum grade for passing. Failure meant the missionary couldn't enter the Congo. Some students failed and returned to their home countries.

(Footnote: The Ecole Coloniale was located in stables built for Napoleon's cavalry. The Napoleonic "N" was seen everywhere, on columns, archways and walls because photography had not yet been invented. Like all dictators, and many other rulers, Napoleon wanted all people to know who was in charge.)

CHATEAU BOSSEY, SWITZERLAND

In September 1952, a nine-day conference was held at the Chateau Bossey near Geneva, Switzerland for young Christian laymen in Europe. We received permission to attend as the only non-Europeans. The other attendees were from Switzerland, France, Germany and the United Kingdom (England, Scotland and Wales).

A number of world-class theologians were meeting when we arrived. As a result, we were very privileged to hear a sermon "Be of good cheer, I have overcome the World" preached by Karl Barth. It made sense.

During the conference, we were seated at a table with two other attendees, one a slightly older German man. He conversed with us in excellent American dialect, not the King's English used by other Europeans. With hesitation, we asked him where he learned English. His rather surprising answer was that he'd learned his American English during the two years he was a prisoner of war in the State of Virginia. He said he much preferred being a prisoner of war to being a combat soldier in the German Army, especially as it was losing the war and suffering terrible casualties.

The multi-lingual capability of most Europeans was in evidence at the conference. In general, the sessions were held in English, which was understood by everyone in attendance. But at the meals and on excursions, the other languages were used frequently. Switzerland has four "official" languages: English, French, German and a rare language, Romansch. Switzerland really lived up to its reputation for beautiful scenery, neatness and punctuality.

In many countries, we found the local citizens had a strong preference for a specific language. In Antwerp, you spoke Flemish or English. French wasn't tolerated. In Liege, you spoke French (Walloon) or English. Flemish wasn't accepted. In France, you spoke their French or you were considered uneducated. In Switzerland you could choose from any one of a half-dozen languages with no linguistic problems. In the United Kingdom, we quickly learned we spoke American English, not the Queen's English, as used by most of the inhabitants. However, the United Kingdom does have a bewildering variety of dialects that are quite difficult to understand. The East End of London has a dialect only vaguely similar to any English. A London Bobby was kind and gave us directions. We didn't understand a word.

SWITZERLAND TO BRUSSELS

On our travels, we tried to take different routes to and from our destination. Therefore, we purchased train tickets (3rd class) for the trip down the Rhine River Valley to Cologne, Germany. From Basel to Cologne, the Allies had pounded the railroads mercilessly. The partially rebuilt roadbed was rough. In our 3rd class coach, some German tourists brought out an alcohol-fueled Sterno heater late at night. By motions, they offered us hot tea. We accepted, but kept an eye on the flame of the heater. After all, the entire coach was made of wood.

Just after dawn, we arrived at the Cologne railroad station. Cologne was almost completely leveled into piles of rubble. The Cathedral was the only structure still standing, but pockmarked from bomb blasts. A veteran of the 8th Air Force told me the Flying Fortress bomber crews used the tall spire as a guidepost for their bombing runs. It was also used as a navigation check point when they returned from raids deeper into Germany.

As far as you could see, heaps of brick, stone, twisted & blackened steel, and broken glass littered the landscape. The people, any who had survived, were living in dark basements or the open. All public utilities and transportation were gone. It was truly an awesome sight. Later we caught a train from Cologne to Brussels and passed the city of Aachen where my friend, CA Evans, had been killed. Brussels suffered some bombing, but not the long, relentless pounding that hit Cologne. The Cologne area was important to the German war effort. Brussels wasn't.

SUMMATION OF LIFE IN BRUSSELS

Our life in Brussels had been exhilarating and exhausting. Visits to London, Paris, Chartres, Amsterdam, Switzerland and Cologne, Germany exceeded our greatest expectations. Our travels in Belgium were fascinating. It surprised us when we found that the Battle of Waterloo was fought just a few miles from Brussels.

Monsieur and Madame Durand made us welcome in their boarding house (pension). We learned a lot about Belgian family life, as well as more of the French language. We felt liberated when we got our apartment. That apartment allowed us to entertain friends for meals and even have them stay overnight if necessary.

From our Guest Book we noted the following persons were our guests:

Bernie and Dudie Davis—teachers, Disciples of Christ mission

Rev John Wesley Shungu—delegate to Genera Conference, spent two nights with us, later became Bishop of the Congo

Monsieur Florent Mortier—tutor extraordinaire-Belgium & Congo

Simone Van Ooteghem—Belgian Methodist, nurse, Wembo Nyama

Jean Luckey—American Baptist, lower Congo

Georges (JOE) Durand and Claude Culot—young Belgian friends

Marie Jensen—pioneer missionary at Kapanga, 1916
Al and Mary Anne Burlbaugh—missionaries, central Congo

Although the Roman Catholic Church claimed the majority of Belgians as members, there was a significant minority who were non-Catholic. The Universite Libre (FREE) de Bruxelles was free from the hierarchy.
There are small, active Methodist Churches and other protestant denominations. Officially the constitution granted religious freedom to all Belgian citizens. However, the Royal Family and many government officials were Roman Catholics. Government schools were secular.
The Rev. Coxill preached to the missionary group. He was truly a saintly person. He was a practical person who made his sermons apply to daily life. None of us believed that we could match his example, but we could try.

MV BAUDOINVILLE

Our formal training was at end. As missionary candidates, we'd been students at the Kennedy School of Missions for one year. After commissioning as missionaries, we studied in Belgium for one year. Two full years had passed. We passed the necessary requirements to become missionaries. Now we were booked to sail for the Belgian Congo on the MV Baudoinville, a beautiful cruise liner.

AT LAST WE COULD BEGIN OUR CAREERS IN AFRICA.

VI. BELGIAN CONGO, KAPANGA (1952-1956)

MV BAUDOINVILLE--ANTWERP TO LOBITO, ANGOLA

On September 22, 1952, we traveled by train from Brussels to the Port of Antwerp. At 12:30 on the 23rd, we sailed from Antwerp on a beautiful luxury liner, the MV Baudoinville.

After two years of training, we were on our way to the mission field at Kapanga in the Belgian Congo. We would return to the USA in March of 1956 on the good ship MV Del Oro, which was neither beautiful nor luxurious, but a real workhorse freighter. In contrast to our voyage across the Atlantic Ocean on the SS Edam, the weather was great for the voyage on the Atlantic Ocean from Antwerp to Lobito, Angola.

On September 28, 1952, we stopped at Tenerife, Canary Islands. These islands were used by Columbus on his way to America in 1492. From here he sailed with the westerly winds across the wide, mid-Atlantic.

In Tenerife we toured much of the island in an antique, but well-maintained, four-door convertible. Up in the hills, magnificent views filled with beautiful tropical flowers, shrubs and trees enchanted us. We visited a large Roman Catholic Church filled with a marvelous array of jewelry and gold relics.

Later the same day we weighed anchor and sailed south along the west coast of Africa. During the late afternoon of the second day we sailed within sight of the coastline as we passed the old city of Dakar, French West Africa.

BAPTISM AT THE EQUATOR

On the 3rd of October, we were apprehensive as we approached the Equator at 0 degrees latitude and near 0 degrees longitude. King Neptune's court was prepared for us and began to initiate neophytes into the "Baptism of the Equator."

We have 16mm movies of the fierce looking characters of that court, some were from the crew and others had been baptized on previous crossings. The rite of passage across the equator included: drinks of salt water with quinine, some simulated severe haircuts with huge shears, abusive language, threats of violence and crawling on hands and knees through a canvas tube against the stream of water from a fire hose.

We missionaries were treated gently, but a poor Belgian income tax collector was subjected to much more severe treatment. After initiation, we were given beautiful certificates.

Fortunately, I never crossed the equator while in the US Navy. Their unique initiation into the Order of Shellbacks is more rigorous. All of my brothers had become Shellbacks in peace time and suffered the consequences.

As you read the above paragraph you realized that a Baptism at the Equator is not at all like a Christian Baptism. The income tax collector would certainly heartily agree to that last statement.

BANQUET AT SEA

During the evening of the ninth day at sea, the staff of the MV Baudoinville prepared and served a sumptuous formal banquet. Every imaginable type of appetizer, main courses, side dishes, desserts and drinks appeared in the course of about four hours.

At least thirty different cheeses and fruit were on a long table at one end of the dining room. We'd learned to love real cheese. On the 10th day we entered the port of Lobito, Angola near the railroad terminal of Benguela. We watched our luggage being unloaded.

At Lobito, we endured Portuguese customs and surrendered our passports. We had no Angola visas—neither tourist nor resident. The Portuguese would return our passports when we left Angola to enter the Belgian Congo at Dilolo.

On the beach at Lobito we filmed dozens of Africans scooping baskets of sardines out of the surf. These small fish thrive in the cold waters of the South Atlantic coming from the Antarctic regions.

KDL—KATANGA—DILOLO—LOBITO RAILWAY

A three day, two night trip across Angola on the KDL is very picturesque and memorable. But it is NOT pleasant. All passenger coaches were wooden, with wood seats and no air conditioning. Fuel for the locomotives was eucalyptus trees cultivated at intervals from the coast to the Congo.

During that long, uphill journey, the train stopped a dozen times in order to load more fuel and water for the boilers.

Phyllis was placed in a compartment with three women. I was placed in a compartment with four men.

Enroute we had a difficult choice. Open the windows to let in some air or close the windows to keep out some of the soot, sparks and ashes. We soon discovered why many veteran Belgians brought fruit, food and much bottled water from the ship or stores in Lobito. The food was just terrible. For breakfast the eggs were smothered in olive oil and the Portuguese coffee made Navy coffee appear weak. Gray spots on all the food were not pepper, but ashes from the locomotive's stack

DARK CONTINENT

During those next two nights we discovered the real reason why Africa became known as the Dark Continent. Not because of the skin color of the people, but because not a light could be seen! Only a few tiny cook fires in far distant villages. There are no cities and only two small towns on the route. Our new Belgian friends soon exclaimed the train ride must be familiar to us Texans. They'd seen many old Western movies, so we didn't challenge their statements. Total mileage from Benguela to Dilolo is 700 miles.

DILOLO and THE BELGIAN CONGO

About 10AM, October 9, 1952, two years after entering the Kennedy School of Missions, we finally entered our destination: Le Congo Belge. We were lucky, the Portuguese returned our own passports containing resident visas for the Congo. Customs people had misplaced one

Belgian woman's passport and she was almost in a hysterical state when we saw her. They eventually found her passport.

After the three-day trip, we were covered with soot and ashes, hungry and thirsty. That frontier town of Dilolo looked beautiful.

Panagis' tiny motel had good food and many cool drinks. A veteran Danish missionary, John Brastrup, met us. He was formally dressed in black as a genuine missionary should be dressed. He didn't recognize us, as we were two very casually-dressed, young American missionaries. We kept silent and finally, he read the names on our luggage and boxes. Uncle John was a dear friend until his retirement a few years later.

After clearing customs, we loaded our luggage into his vehicle and left for the Sandoa Mission, our nearest Methodist mission station. The road was unpaved, unmarked and sandy. On the way we stopped once for a short rest and were immediately surrounded by a huge swarm of gnats.

CLEAN REST ROOMS?

No service stations with or without rest rooms existed. For service, gasoline was stocked in fifty-five gallon barrels. It was hand pumped into your vehicle. Often we'd use an old felt hat as a filter in the funnel to keep out rust, sand and water, etc. None of those elements would burn very well in the engine. "Rest rooms" were found in the drain paths cleared from the roadway a short distance into the bush. Lions had been seen recently. Congo has an ample supply of snakes, plus flying and crawling insects. Therefore, relief trips were usually brief and taken only when urgent.

SANDOA—KANENE—KAPANGA

Sandoa Mission station was established in the early 1920's by Thomas Brinton and family. When we arrived on October 9, 1952 we noticed the tall grass (up to six feet) hadn't been cut and the mango trees had never been trimmed. No spring or stream was near the station. As a consequence, we were given two small pitchers of water for bathing. Our heads were so matted with soot, ashes and dust that we couldn't comb our hair. Irving and Stella Everett, truly saints, welcomed us. They'd been in the Congo during the Great Depression and World War II years when support was meager.

We deeply appreciated the sincere greetings. But a warm shower bath would have been welcome. We felt we'd never be clean again until we finished our four-year term.

After supper, Uncle Irving took a tattered, unbleached muslin cloth (called Americani in Congo) from a table. He uncovered a large pile of non-descript paper currency and coins. If you have ever heard either of these two expressions: "dirty money" or "filthy lucre," you'd quickly recognize that pile.

The Congolese had no billfolds or handbags. Money was carried in small squares of dirty cloth and tied to their skimpy clothing. We were asked to help Uncle Irving count the money and prepare pay packages for the local preachers and employees of the mission. Checks were never used because no one had a bank account except missionaries.

Early next morning Uncle Irving asked us to go with him to the Kanene station, about 75-miles to the east. Being near his retirement, he wanted me to drive the rather undependable car. Again the road was unmarked and unpaved with the usual rest stop "facilities" along the way.

Crossing the Lulua River on an old unpowered ferry made from dugout logs was a unique experience. After seven-years' service in the Congo and many ferry crossings, we still don't feel comfortable until we complete the ferry crossing.

Kanene is one of the oldest Methodist stations in the Congo. In 1952 there were no missionary residents there. But Jason Sendwe, a remarkable African Assistant-Doctor, was there managing a dispensary. Jason was a talented linguist who could speak and read more than twenty languages, including fluent French and English. He was a subscriber to *Time* magazine and understood it well. Our living accommodations were primitive, but we had good water and food.

On the 13th we returned to Sandoa and prepared to go to our real destination—Kapanga Mission. Everett Woodcock, on furlough, had left his vehicle at Sandoa. We drove it seventy-five miles to Kapanga.

As we entered the Kapanga Mission Station, we were truly amazed with our good fortune. Lawns were neatly cut. Flowering shrubs were all over the station. Mango trees had been trimmed about ten feet above ground level. A spring with a steady flow of good water was located near the dispensary and hospital. Howard Hardee, MD, Ruth Piper, RN, Tove Jensen, RN, and Albert Whelchel, A-3, welcomed us.

Howard was overjoyed with our arrival. Now relieved of the hospital construction project, he could devote his attention full-time to medicine.

Leon Holt, an Englishman from Liverpool with citizenship from the Union of South Africa, had supervised the construction work since Jim Pottenger had died in 1950. Mr. Holt was a rather rough character and not too kindly disposed towards Congolese, whom he referred to as Kaffirs. The mission hired him on contract in order to keep the hospital on schedule. He and his wife owned a small store in Kapanga.

The four single missionaries assigned us to the huge Grass Palace residence. This grass roofed structure was built over twenty years earlier by Ruth Piper's parents. Dr. Arthur and Mrs. Maude Piper arrived in 1914 and retired in April 1952, just six months before our arrival. {Arthur Piper was a brother to William Piper of the Piper Aircraft Company}.

The Grass Palace was 120-feet long from front door to the attached pit privy (toilet to the uninitiated). With a thick grass roof, the house was comfortably cool but the roof harbored various insects and small critters. Our own stay was pleasant but short.

KAPANGA—ELISABETHVILLE—KAPANGA

Four days later, October 19, 1952, we were asked to drive the Women's Division automobile to Elisabethville in order to deliver some personal possessions to a female missionary. The trip was an opportunity to buy some much needed food and supplies at the big city stores. Our own household goods and supplies wouldn't arrive from America until early 1953.

We drove south to the town of Sandoa, then went southeast to Kasaji, Mutshatsha, Kolwezi, Mulungwishi, Jadotville and into the city of Elisabethville. This very long trip of more than 500 miles required overnight stops.

At Kasaji, we spent the night at the old Garaganze Mission. We slept (?) on a corn shuck mattress and struggled with corn meal mush for breakfast. The missionaries were faith missionaries from England. They were poor but friendly.

The next night we spent a most enjoyable time at the Kolwezi "Bonne Auberge Inn," with good beds and great food. We enjoyed the company of a talkative Englishman, who represented the Unilever Compnay, a giant English corporation.

He told us the American Colonies, with their Revolution, should have taught the British Empire a lesson. But it didn't. The Empire was still trying to hold onto their colonies. He said the British, French, Spanish, Portuguese and South Africans should free all colonies.

And...within fifteen years there were no more colonies on the entire African Continent. Independence came, but real freedom still has not arrived in some former colonies. Black dictators have replaced white rulers.

The large City of Elisabethville was capital of the province of Katanga and headquarters of the mining company, Union Miniere.

We found hotels, shops, hardware stores, a movie house, streetlights, telephones, electricity, paved streets, restaurants, small zoo, a large copper smelter and a modern international airport. We enjoyed most of them, with the exception of the large copper smelter and the international airport which we visited on a later trip. This city was our postal address: Boite Postal 522, Elisabethville.

A few days later we drove back towards Kapanga. Between Kolwezi and Kasaji, we drove through terrible weather conditions. Traffic was no problem. "Heavy" traffic was meeting one vehicle every two or three hours.

When the rains stopped, we saw dozens of red and blue frogs alongside the roadway. Those frogs had red legs and blue bodies. In a small grove of trees we saw monkeys playing in the branches.

But most of the time, our travel on the sandy, unpaved, unmarked tracks was dull while we tried to avoid deep sand and mud holes. Again our stay at Kapanga was short.

We never realized we might have to tour the Congo before settling down at our assigned station. Round trip mileage to Elisabethville was about 1,000 miles.

SANDOA—LANGUAGE STUDY

From November 3rd to December 6th we stayed at Sandoa Mission for language study with Anna Lerbak, a Danish missionary.

Lunda is now a written language with story books, other literature, a very large vocabulary, a song book and the New Testament in print. In 1995 there's a complete Bible in Lunda.

Anna had prepared some good language lessons. Several kind Congolese helped us with our word pronunciation since Anna still had her Danish accent. The Congolese helped us with useful idiomatic expressions as well as explanations of culture with good manners.

The language structure and customs are quite different from those in English, Spanish or French. One feature of the Lunda language is "concord." Here'is an easy example of concord. "Chikumbu chinech chidi chikumbu cha Nzambi." This means, "This is the House of God." "Yikumbu yiney yidi Yikumbu Ya Nzambi," Means, "These houses, are the houses of God." Other features are the frequent usage of many prefixes, infixes, and suffixes. This means that some letters may be placed at the beginning of the verb (prefixes), inserted into the verb (infixes), or added to the end of the verb (suffixes). Intonation is extremely important. When pronounced one way the word "ngaku" means snake, with only a slight change in tone it means "grandmother."

This is similar to the Spanish expression, "Feliz Cumpleafio." Pronounced with the tilde "~" it will mean

"A Happy Birthday," without the tilde it means something like "Happy Rectum."

To aspirate means you breathe out when pronouncing a word. To unaspirate means you must breathe in when saying the word. Sometimes certain words can be aspirated or unaspirated without changing the meaning. Other words change their meaning drastically. All of these features meant learning Lunda is challenging, although not impossible. Our linguistics professor at Kennedy School of Missions told us if village idiots can learn the local language, so can missionaries.

At times we felt the village idiots were smarter than us.

We didn't master the Lunda language in five weeks, but we did absorb enough to begin our task of construction supervision and to converse with our household help.

One day, Bill Davis and I went to the Sandoa Govt. Dispensary to visit a Belgian amateur hunter. He'd gone on a lion hunt by himself, which was very foolish. His first shot had wounded and angered the lion. His rifle jammed and before he could clear it, the lion started chewing on him. It almost bit through his shoulder; then chomped down on his thigh to drag the man through the brush.

His tracker finally frightened the lion away. Lion and leopard bites are dangerous because they're predators and have decaying bits of animal flesh in their teeth and claws that can cause deadly infections.

Bill and I hunted many times, but never went after any lions. And we never hunted alone. On the 6th of December 1952, we returned to Kapanga and finally began our careers as missionaries. Within our first two months in Africa, we'd traveled 700 miles in an unairconditioned train behind a wood-burning locomotive and driven 1700 miles on unpaved, unmarked "roads."

BRIEF HISTORICAL NOTES ON KAPANGA AND MUSUMBA KAPANGA

The vast Belgian Congo was governed by Belgium through a resident Governor General and staff.
Incidentally, the Congo is almost as large as all US east of the Mississippi River.
In 1953, there were six provinces with Provincial Governors and staffs. Within these provinces there were many Districts with Administrators and staffs. Each District was divided into many Territories with Administrators and staffs. All officials and staffs were duly appointed by the Belgian government. No elections had ever been held in the Congo.
Kapanga was established as a State Post in the Territory of Kapanga, Sankuru District, and the Katanga Province. Four Belgian officials were stationed at the post: one Territorial Administrator, one Assistant Territorial Administrator, one agronomist, and an official who served as the local judge and jury. It had a combined radio telegraph station and a post office.
All European countries had a PTT (Posts, Telephones, and Telegraphs), a bureaucracy that held a government monopoly on these services.
As a mission, we were never allowed to have two-way short-wave radio systems. We did have short-wave receivers. A number of merchants built small shops and stores stocked with a few canned goods, cloth, used shoes,

bicycles & parts, matches, coffee, tea and simple hand tools. There was a jail and several other government buildings.

The shopping area was a motley collection of crude buildings on a clay street. These shops had no display cases or advertising. Goods were stacked quite haphazardly on flimsy shelving. Measuring devices were crude. The Congolese suspected rightly that some devices were not accurate. For instance, a meter (100 centimeters) of cloth appeared to be only 90 or 95 centimeters long. A liter (1,000 milliliters) of kerosene or palm oil was believed to be only 900 milliliters. Therefore, soon after independence in 1960, a number of suspected cheaters were treated rather harshly.

MUSUMBA

Kapanga Methodist Mission was built on a concession of land (128 acres) adjacent to Musumba, the ancient capital village of Mwant Yav, the Paramount Chief of the Lunda Confederation.

David Livingstone, missionary and explorer, crossed Africa from the Indian Ocean to the Atlantic Ocean in the 1860's. He traveled the existing slave trade route through Congo and Angola. This route followed the ridges that form the watershed between the Congo and Zambezi Rivers. Many tributary river and stream crossings were avoided by traveling on the watershed ridges. Livingstone passed more than 150 miles south of Musumba, but he mentioned it in his diary as an important place to visit on a later trip—one he never made. He wrote that the capital village of

Musumba would be an excellent place for a new Christian mission. His suggestion was realized years later with the arrival of John Springer.

Rev John Springer, later Bishop of Africa, visited Musumba in 1912. The Methodist Church started its mission work with the arrival of Dr. and Mrs. Arthur Piper in 1914. Rev. and Mrs. Thomas Brinton arrived in 1916 when their son, Howard, was six months old. Miss Marie Jensen came from Denmark that same year.

The Paramount Chief of the Lundas received tribute from at least twenty tribes stretching north to include the Basala Mpasu, to the northwest to Tshikapa in western Congo, to the west to the eastern areas of Angola, to the south to include northern areas of Zambia, and east to Tanganyika (now Tanzania).

The Lundas were good warriors, but primarily they'd traditionally maintained allegiances through intermarriages between their Paramount Chief and daughters of other tribal chiefs. In reality these young women were hostages and couldn't go home.

All of the tribes were afraid of the fierce, cannibalistic Balubas and Batatelas, warriors. The tribal warfare stories were gruesome

The Balubas cut the Achilles tendons of captives, often leaving them alive but totally helpless.

The Batatelas tied large bundles of dry grasses around captives and set fire to the grass. These are "war stories" as told by the losers in some battles. They may or may not be true because the battles were fought many years ago.

The Paramount Chief had many sub-chiefs and village head men plus important tribal officials in Musumba. Nswan

Murund was a woman known as Mother of the Tribe. An old man was the official oral historian and could recite tribal events for several hundred years of history. Another ancient man was still living but was unemployed. He'd been the tribal executioner before the Belgians conquered the area.

The Lundas had arrived in this area before 1600. Without written records, the history of tribes that moved around central Africa is not known with any accuracy. And no tribe south of the Sahara Desert had a written language.

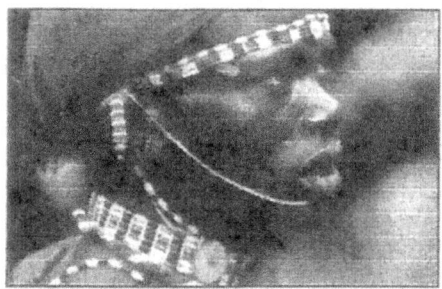

TELECOMMUNICATION IN CONGO

Musumba had a "talking drum." This drum a large, wedge-shaped, hollow segment of a special tree has a slit opening at the top. Each of the two sides of the hollow wedge has a different thickness. As the drummer hits one side, he produces a low sound. As he hits the other side, he produces a different sound. These two sounds are equivalent to Morse code (dots and dashes) used by telegraphers since 1840. It's also similar to the "ones" and "zeros" used in digital computers. The drummers used a code known only to chosen drummers of the tribes.

We lived across a valley from Musumba. After midnight we occasionally heard the deep, throbbing sound of a talking drum as it sent messages to distant villages.

How distant? When one Paramount Chief died after midnight, the talking drums spoke. Two-hundred miles to the south, in Northern Rhodesia, the local Lunda chief appeared at a missionary's home before breakfast. The local chief told the missionary the Paramount Chief had died and requested a ride to Musumba to attend the funeral and help select a new Paramount Chief. The death message traveled over two-hundred miles in less than six hours.

In central Congo, the Batatela used talking drums to send messages within the channels provided by tall trees along river banks. One tale advises some Methodist hunters were running out of ammunition. They sent a message back to the home station. That afternoon a man arrived with boxes of the correct caliber ammunition. The total distance was thirty-miles each way.

Only the drummers can interpret the drum sounds because they are a secret code. In the old days the drums were most important. They were used to warn villages of invading warriors or other impending calamities. Talking drums were reserved for messages. They were never used for dancing or entertainment.

OUR FIRST HOME AT KAPANGA

In the Hosmer Hall dormitory at Hartford, we lived with approximately 400-square feet of floor space. Our apartment in Belgium enclosed not more than 600-square feet, plus a pleasant balcony. But our Grass Palace was 120 feet long by 30 feet wide providing 3600-square feet under a huge grass roof.

We literally rattled around in it. We arrived with only the hand luggage from our stay in Europe. The Grass Palace was furnished with chairs, tables, beds, a kerosene fueled refrigerator, wood cook stove and a few kerosene lamps. The floors were oiled wood three-feet above ground. The walls were whitewashed mud on sun dried bricks.

Ceilings were wooden slabs covered with a layer of earth to slow down the spread of flames if the grass roof caught fire.

No one had lived in it for six months. There were no supplies in the pantry and no food in the cupboard. Dr. and Mrs. Arthur Piper lived in the palace from 1925 until 1952. We inherited some ancient medical textbooks dating back to 1914, which provided interesting reading about diagnoses and treatments from that era.

One relic was a dental chair with a foot-pedal driven drill. Your imagination could make your teeth hurt just looking at that chair and drill.

Happily, Ruth Piper married Howard Hardee in January and moved out of her aluminum-roofed house to Doctor Hardee's residence. After some small renovations, we moved from the Grass Palace in early February and into her now empty dwelling.

The Grass Palace wouldn't be occupied again until Dr. Warren and Jane (RN) arrived in May 1954, before we completed building their residence. Not surprisingly, they bugged me every day until they could move out of the Palace.

AVAILABLE FOODS

At an elevation of 3,000 feet, Kapanga couldn't grow many of the tropical food products. These included sugarcane, coffee, coconuts, natural rubber trees and similar crops that require warm temperatures to mature. The following temperate zone crops wouldn't grow well either: potatoes, leafy vegetables (cabbage, etc), apples and other fruits or vegetables that needed cool weather. We did have an abundance of mangoes, pineapples, bananas (dozen shapes, tastes and sizes), plantains, papayas, beans, tomatoes, native greens, avocados and citrus trees. Cassava roots were the main staple of the Congolese diet. Cooked cassava has the consistency of corn meal mush with fewer nutrients. An African relative of the jalapeno pepper is called Pili Pili. That seasoning lives up to its name. If used too heavily it will peel the top layers from your tongue.

COMMERCIAL ARTIST AND DRAFTSMAN

Phyllis' talents as artist and draftsman were much in demand when missionaries discovered her ability to sketch and draft good plans. At Sandoa, she made sense of the survey Willis and I did to locate the actual boundaries of that station. Back at Kapanga, she drew house plans renovating Ruth's former house for us. She found drafting board and supplies at an office supply store in the City of Elisabethville. Congo uses the metric system of weights and measures, so we had to buy metric rulers and architect scales. Actually the metric system is much easier to use than the chaotic "English" system of inches, feet, yards and miles.

She'd brought art supplies from Europe and bought more in Elisabethville. This was really a case of serendipity. We needed the art supplies when a famous artist visited us at Kapanga. During our two terms of service, she produced many plans and drawings for mission residences, schools , churches, hospital buildings, storage sheds, dormitories, Kapanga mission land, a lumber concession, school material and maps of roads leading to several towns. No real accurate road maps were published. No highway signs were in place. Phyllis' hand-drawn road maps were given to many travelers. Her maps became highly prized, keeping drivers from getting lost.

BELGIAN CONGO CUSTOMS OFFICIALS

In mid-January 1953, our shipment of household goods from New York arrived at Dilolo. We had an interesting day with the Congo customs officials. {As you may have gathered by now, interesting is not generally good}. All shipments into the Congo required a signed customs declaration listing each item, its original value and a statement as to whether it was new or used. Fortunately for us, we'd very scrupulously completed our lengthy declaration. All new items were subject to various tariffs. Used items were subject to no tariffs.

Unfortunately, some American missionaries entering the Congo a few months before us listed many new items as used or of little value. This improper declaration greatly displeased the Belgian Congo customs officials. {In our travels we've found Belgian and British customs were honest. Some other countries, best left unnamed, have customs officials who were difficult and in one case dishonest}.

Being the next American missionaries through the Dilolo point of entry, we became the unsuspecting target for those unhappy Belgian Congo customs officials. We were required to unpack every single item from every carton, barrel and box. We unwrapped all the individual pieces for a close look and inspection. That large customs shed was soon strewn with our possessions. Several officials checked and verified every piece against our declaration, but found no discrepancy. We paid their customs tariffs and spent the rest of the day putting all of our things back in place for the long trip back to Kapanga.

At 4:30PM we were loaded and headed up the trail to Sandoa. We didn't make it.

About 9:30PM the truck lights went out when we were in the middle of a long plain where lions had been seen recently. We slept fitfully in the cab. Our two male helpers were on top of the load. The area is about 4,000 feet above sea level. Consequently, the nights are cold. However, the cold didn't seem to intimidate the multitude of mosquitos.

Early Friday morning, we worked on the truck, got it started and limped in to the Sandoa Mission. After some more repairs we drove on to Kapanga.

On Saturday we cleaned the house and unpacked most of our household goods. About 11PM we fell into a comfortable bed, which felt much better than the small cab of a truck.

THE SOCIAL EVENT OF 1953

Howard Hardee and Ruth Piper were married in our local mission church on Jan. 24th. Ruth was born and spent most of her childhood at Kapanga. Her African name was Muteb, which was given to her by the Paramount Chief Mwant Yav Muteb at her birth.

All Lundas really thought she was their child. She spoke the language with absolutely no accent. She knew all the games, colloquialisms and customs of the Lundas.

Ruth's good friend and pastry chef, Kay Eye, came from Central Congo to bake the wedding cake and other desserts for us. Several other Methodist missionary families arrived. The Lunda and Basala Mpasu dancers performed many times.

Other guests produced lots of smoke with a long series of blank rounds fired from their muzzle loading guns. This was a local sign of great happiness. Ruth's Lunda friends brought many gifts and made long congratulatory speeches.

Many years previously Dr. and Mrs. Piper built a small cottage eight miles away in a beautiful location overlooking the valley. Howard and Ruth went there for their honeymoon.

On the way they found a fallen tree blocking the path. Howard and Ruth soon found African help to clear the track. Within a few days, they were back at work. Patients kept getting sick or injured. No other doctor was available.

SECOND HOME AT KAPANGA

As soon as Ruth and Howard returned from their honeymoon, we helped Ruth move to the Hardee residence and vacate her house.

We didn't wish to prolong our stay in the huge Grass Palace. Our second home had one bedroom, indoor bathroom, living room, dining room and an attached kitchen with storage area. No more rattling around and walking a football field length to pick up a book or grab a bottle of Coca Cola.

Attached to the back of the house was a brick structure supporting steel barrels containing our supply of water. One barrel was partly exposed to a fireplace so we could enjoy hot water occasionally for our baths. All water had to be carried, by a human carrier, from the spring which was about half a mile away. This house had a good corrugated aluminum roof that felt safer than tons of dried grass overhead. It wasn't immune to creatures. During the second week, we encountered a snake in the warm kitchen. Quickly it became a dead snake in the kitchen.

Our new home was located on the brow of a hill that sloped downwards for about ten miles to the Lulua River. A few yards away from the house, an open air teahouse (gazebo) with table and chairs provided a marvelous and unobstructed view of the wide valley. It was a great place to watch the violent tropical thunderstorms as they formed in the wide expanse of the valley below us. During the next three and a half years, we spent pleasant hours in the teahouse as we enjoyed meals and entertained guests.

On one really memorable occasion, we entertained some of the workmen. They were familiar with ordinary corn. Popcorn was a new experience. They heard the loud pops and watched with amazement as these kernels exploded into fluffy white balls. Just more of white man's magic.

COCA COLA IN CONGO

Being typical Americans from Georgia, we looked for Coca-Cola. But it was unavailable in bottles. Cans didn't exist yet. The only bottler was two countries away and no Coca-Cola was shipped into the Congo. Luckily, we found premixed Coca-Cola syrup was available in gallon jugs. Carbonated water made using a seltzer bottle pressurized with a tiny cylinder of carbon dioxide gas would give us the fizz. On April 9th our first delivery of three gallons of syrup arrived. Our spirits were lifted by a glass of ice cold Coke.

ORGANIZATION OF THE METHODIST CHURCH

In order for non-Methodist readers to understand our life as missionaries we wish to explain some of the organization of the 1952 model of the Methodist Church and its mission fields at the time we were overseas.

There are only four levels of Conferences in the Methodist Church organization. Local churches are called Charge Conferences, consisting of one or more congregations.

The Charge Conferences are united into an Annual Conference. One or more Annual Conferences are united in a Jurisdictional Conference. All Jurisdictional Conferences are united into a world-wide General Conference, which convenes every four years.

General Conference is the legislative body for the Methodist Church and approves the Book of Discipline, which governs all official activities within this denomination.

Foreign mission fields are organized in a slightly different way. For example, missionary activities in the Congo, Angola and Mozambique were united in a Central Conference under one bishop. Congo had two annual conferences. Each conference had a Field Committee that was authorized to vote on every missionary as he or she completed a term of service. If you didn't learn the local language during your first term you didn't return for a second term. Field Committees exist only on mission fields. Our Southern Congo Conference had been established years earlier by the Methodist Episcopal Church (northern US). The Central Congo Conference had been established in the late 1800's by the Methodist Episcopal Church, South. In 1939 they became part of the Methodist Church as the three branches of Methodism united.

Both of us were commissioned as missionaries and subject to appointment by the resident bishop each year when our own annual conference convened. All ordained ministers were automatically voting members of Annual Conference.

Lay missionaries, including wives of the clergy, were not members. According to the Book of Discipline, the voting membership of each annual conference must have an equal number of clergy and lay members.

Within the US, this balance of membership is not a serious problem, but overseas the quantity of commissioned lay missionaries greatly exceeded the commissioned ordained missionaries.

At Kapanga in 1953 we had six commissioned lay missionaries, but not one commissioned ordained missionary. According to the Book of Discipline, our station should have no voting representative at the annual conference. Lay missionaries didn't like that at all and so informed the resident bishop.

Missionaries are not meek and mild, if they were, they wouldn't have become foreign missionaries. Many of us were strong willed, outspoken and obstreperous. As a result, I found himself as one of a few laymen ever assigned to the Bishop's Cabinet. This group advises the Bishop in making difficult decisions about who will be given what task(s) and assigned to which mission station.

ANNUAL CONFERENCE—1953—KAPANGA

Our Southern Congo Annual Conference in July 1953 involved about 100 missionaries and Congolese who had to be fed and housed at Kapanga. No motels or restaurants existed within 150 miles.

School wasn't in session, so we used their classrooms. Our diary for 1953 has few entries because we spent most of our time planning menus, ordering and obtaining many supplies, including gasoline in fifty-five gallon barrels. Kapanga had no gas station. Then we entertained up to fifteen guests at every meal in our home because missionaries brought many children.

We were required to attend conference and committee meetings. Budgets were presented for construction projects and Phyllis' school work. We provided mechanics for vehicle maintenance. Congo roads are hard on cars and trucks. After conference attendees left, we washed towels and linens. Accounting for various food usage was difficult. Sugar and flour came in 100-pound bags. Food came in large cartons of canned goods. How much was needed for the conference? How much for our personal use? How much was given to other missionaries when they had need? Was anything stolen in transit? We spent hours calculating the consumption of food and supplies. All costs of transportation had to be included.

There were a million other details that required some attention. Not the least vexing was the typing and mimeographing of conference proceedings. Our mimeograph machine was old and difficult to operate. Master sheets were expensive. Word processors and photocopiers didn't exist. We'd brought a small portable typewriter. We are touch typists but we had no correcting tape or fluid. If you made any serious mistakes you re-typed the page.

Our first year as missionaries was filled with activity that wasn't directly related to spreading the Good News of the Gospel of Jesus Christ, our real reason for coming to Africa.

GEORGE AND INKY

In late summer we acquired our second pet, a baby monkey whose mother had been killed and eaten by hunters. He was a very tiny male and had to be bottle fed for a while. Lois Piper gave him the name, George.

He joined our black cat, Inky, and they played together. For a few months he roamed free in the two tall trees around our house. He grabbed a short stalk of sugar cane, carried it up on the aluminum roof and made a terrible racket dragging the stalk over the corrugations. We have a delightful movie of Inky and George playing around the yard.

However, after he pulled all the clothes-pins off the line and let clean linens drop on the ground, we built a cage for him. From his cage, he could look over the valley towards the river. When huge eagles soared on the thermals, George got hysterical, even though he was safe in his cage.

Some might believe it odd that domestic cats existed in the Congo, but history reveals the Egyptians revered them and science indicates domestic cats go back through human history nearly 12,000 years. Where there are people, cats follow.

George had been given to us by Madame Forrest, wife of a local Belgian official.

On Sept. 1st, she was holding a gasoline lantern over her husband as he siphoned gasoline into the tank. The gasoline fumes ignited, the lantern exploded and she was burned badly. Our hospital didn't have emergency facilities adequate to save her. Madame Forrest died the next day. Some missionaries prepared her body for burial. Our mission carpenters made a coffin. I helped place the body into the coffin. In the hot tropics that wasn't a pleasant task. We used fragrant frangipani flowers to mask the odor. Although she was a Roman Catholic, none of the priests or nuns would come onto our mission during daylight hours. In those days, there was a great gulf between Roman Catholics and the rest of Christendom. Madame Forrest was buried next day in the Catholic Mission cemetery. She left a widower with four small children. She was a charming woman and a good friend.

HEALTH HAZARDS—SMALL AND GREAT

Heavy rainfall and lots of sunshine create a lush tropical growth of trees, brush and grass in the Congo. These conditions also create an ideal environment for a vast array of health hazards.

One small insect, jiggers, bite into your skin, lays eggs and drops off. These eggs turn into large larvae that produce itching and pain as they grow larger. These jiggers are not life threatening, but are extremely painful.

On April 18th, Phyllis had two removed from a toe and immediately felt better. Much later I had one on the heel of my right foot. You do not die; you just hurt!

Hoping to minimize attacks and decrease the duration of malaria, all of us took daily doses of Aralen before we arrived in the Congo. Aralen suppressed the malaria parasites, but couldn't completely eradicate them. There were plenty of anopheles mosquitos that spread the three most common types of malaria. Cerebral malaria (blackwater fever) is the most serious and causes death. The other two can cause death if not treated. We had symptoms of malaria for nearly fifteen years after we resigned in early 1960.

The bites of tse-tse flies were very painful, but far worse, they often carried the sleeping sickness disease. Ruth Hardee contracted this illness, but thankfully, fully recovered.

Most of the sluggish streams and ponds contained flukes that get into human livers and create havoc. Other tiny organisms caused schistosomiasis, which is best left not described. A wide variety of intestinal parasites (tapeworms, etc.) existed. Various fungi could grow in warm, moist parts of the feet.

In 1995, I had traces of a fungus in one toe nail.

An unpleasant, but not fatal affliction that often arose from bacteria in food and water was diarrhea. A disease with similar symptoms was amoebic dysentery. That disease can be hazardous for adults and extremely hazardous for small children because it causes such very rapid dehydration.

Carnivorous animals (lions, leopards, and crocodiles) were plentiful. Phyllis accompanied me on a six-day antelope hunt at the village of Chala. While following a game trail we heard a cry of pain and a terrible scream. A few yards later, we located a dying antelope with a broken neck. On a small hilltop less than 100 yards away we observed a pair of frustrated lions. They turned and disappeared before we could shoot.

Our only encounter with a live leopard occurred late one evening on a road trip. This large leopard loped out of the bush alongside the Volkswagen and trotted in our headlights for a few minutes. Then he sauntered off into the bush. They are graceful animals.

Dr Bitsch-Larsen and I killed a crocodile in the Lulua River. Immanuel sent the skin and skull to a museum in Denmark.

Snakes of all sizes, shapes, color and length were abundant. Some were long, thin green snakes that dwelled only in tree tops in the dense jungle.

On that hunt near Chala, we saw the remains of a twenty-one foot python. The snake had died in a fast-moving dry-grass fire. That's why we could approximate its length. Pythons that big can, and do, eat humans. As written elsewhere, I had a close encounter with a hooded cobra while hunting near Mwini Dikamba's village. The extremely deadly mambas, black or green, were never seen.

DEATH COMES TO MISSIONARY FAMILIES

Our friends, Max and Anita Ritter, were teachers assigned to the school at Wembo Nyama in our Central Congo Conference, several hundred miles from Kapanga.

They used a totally different route in the Congo as they went to and from their stations. We never got to visit central Congo. The Wembo Nyama station had a large dispensary staffed with missionary doctors and nurses.

In 1953, Max contracted bulbar polio at Wembo Nyama. They were not able to fly him to a major hospital. Without an iron lung to help him, he couldn't keep breathing. He died in a few days at the age of 27.

Anita was pregnant, so they sent her home to America with their first son, Mark. A few months later their second son, Eric, was born.

Three years later, his grandparents were driving on an icy road in a heavy snowfall. Eric was seated on his grandmother's lap in the front seat. No one had seat belts or child restraints in those days. The car slipped off the road into a deep ditch. Eric was killed when he flew through the windshield.

So much tragedy in her young life.

Anita married a high school friend, Dr. Robert Fenstermacher. Later they came to the Congo as missionaries and were evacuated from Kamina, Congo with us in 1960. At the proper time, we'll speak about that year as refugees. Anita has written a heart tugging story about her life with Max and his death, which we have included in the section ODDS & ENDS.

Burleigh Law was building a mission hospital at Wembo Nyama in Central Congo scheduled for completion after Kapanga.

We were much more advanced in the hospital construction at Kapanga, so Burleigh Law made a long trip in order to get some helpful hints. We shared opinions on how to build a reasonably modern hospital with manual labor in a bush location more than 100-miles from a railroad or building supply store. About twelve years later, Burleigh was shot to death by rebel soldiers. His widow, Virginia, wrote a splendid book about their life in the Congo called "Appointment Congo". We have a copy and assure you, it will make you laugh and cry, sometimes at the same time.

Two other missionaries were killed in the Congo. In the 70's Dr. Glen Eschtruth and his wife, were serving at the hospital we built at Kapanga. A group of rebels, or bandits, came to the Kapanga territory. They were looking for trouble and brought it with them. After a heated discussion with Glen, they took him as a captive, then transported him away from the mission where they shot him to death.

Stan Ridgway was a pilot of one of our planes. Some other Congolese, with more firepower than brainpower, captured him for a petty reason, and then they killed him. We never met Glen or Stan.

Some would say all four men were martyrs. We knew Max and Burleigh and we aren't positive they would agree to such a lofty designation. Both were much too realistic and aware of their own shortcomings. We think they would say that they simply answered the call by God to go into the world as missionaries. All of us were required to leave valid copies of wills with the Board of Foreign Missions.

We knew we might not return. That was part of the covenant that we made with our Lord. We were not trying to be Saints with a capital "S." Although some missionaries were surely saints spelled with a lower case "s." On the other hand, some of us were just missionaries to the best of our abilities without worrying about being saintly at all.

PERSONNEL CHANGES AT KAPANGA--1954

Many personalities went away, while others were arriving.
The Willis Piper family created a big void when they left in January. Willis and Dot were not commissioned as missionaries but served under a contract. They began their service at Mulungwishi, Congo, where Willis constructed several buildings at that big educational center. They moved to Kapanga in order to build a residence for single women missionaries. Dot's mother stayed with them for a while. At 80-years-young, she was a delight. She enjoyed our bush life, comparing it to her childhood: outhouses, wood stoves, kerosene lamps, etc. The Willis Piper's last Congo assignment was at Katubwe, a joint educational project (high school) for both the Presbyterian and Methodist missions.

Willis was a pleasant enough character who'd been a ship yard welder during World War II. One of his stories involved a very clumsy welder who was working above Willis. When that inept welder dropped one steel tool that landed near him, Willis had a few strong words for the topside welder. When the second tool came clanging down, Willis moved his torch and then welded the tool to the ship's structure. If it happened again, Willis said he'd weld the welder to the ship's structure. Willis' language was a bit more colorful than we have written here. No more tools were dropped!

On the mission field Willis was content to do a great job at his construction projects and learn enough Swahili to get by. Not for Dot, she soaked up the languages, Swahili and Lunda, like a sponge. With a great curiosity, she was interested in all phases of our mission work: hospitals, schools, church, and African religious beliefs. Willis died years ago, but at 80, Dot is doing well in 1995.

The Danish Methodist Church has supplied Congo Methodism with excellent missionaries ever since Miss Marie Jensen arrived at the Kapanga station in 1916. Tove Jensen had been a nurse at Kapanga for years.

Dr. Immanuel and Valborg Bitsch-Larsen, and their six children, arrived on January 21st. Their family quickly doubled the local missionary population. Those children made our lives brighter for several years. Like all missionary children, they were multi-lingual: Danish, English, French and several local languages. Children had a great advantage over adult missionaries. Kids weren't afraid to make verbal mistakes. They endlessly repeated words and phrases until their African playmates told them they were speaking correctly. Adults hate to acknowledge their mistakes; kids learn from mistakes and keep on learning the words.

Our linguistics professor at Kennedy School of Missions was basically correct. Everyone can learn any language because the village idiots can do so. However, adults do not find learning another language is easy. It is hard work and requires endless patience. Most of us give up too soon. On the contrary children persist and learn almost any language easily and quickly.

As the New Testament says, we must "become like little children" in order to master a foreign language.

Immanuel was an experienced tropical medicine physician from his previous assignment in Central Congo at Wembo Nyama. He was skilled also in his second love—hunting big game.

For us, hunting was a primary source of meat, it wasn't a recreational sport. Any trophy horns or tusks were of minor interest. Rifles in the Congo were large caliber in order to safely kill the big wild animals. African elephants can weigh more than 8,000 pounds and stand ten feet tall. Hippos weigh at least 3,000 pounds. Cape buffalo weigh up to 1,300 pounds. Roan antelope weigh 1,200 pounds. The minimum caliber rifle was a 375 H & H Magnum Winchester Model 70.

Other missionaries had 10.75mm Austrian rifles and 458 Winchesters. One of the many English missionaries in Northern Rhodesia (Zambia) used a double-barreled, single-trigger, 577 caliber rifle. That weapon was deadly at both ends. It was extremely effective at killing elephants or buffalo. But its recoil on the hunter was horrendous.

Modern rifles and shotguns were controlled by strict regulations. Each legal resident missionary adult could possess one rifle, one shotgun and one handgun. Only one missionary owned a handgun. He carried it on a hunt just once, then left it at home because it was heavy and useless. Congolese were restricted to smooth-bore muzzle loaders using only black powder. Modern ammunition could only be purchased with an annual permit that limited the number of rounds you could buy every year. Re-loading of used shell cases was prohibited. Immanuel purchased a new Winchester, and kept the old one in Valborg's name.

Valborg never hunted, so I bought that old rifle, which is with us today. As the mother of six children, Valborg kept busy at home. She was a great asset to other activities on the mission station. Many years later, after all children were grown, she went to medical school and was awarded an M.D. degree. Both are now practicing physicians in a rural area of Denmark. They served again for a short time in Africa during 1995. We met them at a Congo/Zaire Missionary Reunion in 1992 at the Asbury College in Wilmore, Kentucky and again at the Lake Junaluska reunion in 1995.

Thelma Montgomery, a single missionary, arrived to live in the new women's residence and assume responsibility for Congolese girl's advanced education. Girls were expected to be engaged at puberty and married soon thereafter. In accordance with ancient tribal customs they were limited to the cultivating of gardens, chopping wood, cooking food, hauling water, keeping house and producing as many children as possible. Their education, if any, stopped at 12 or 13. Higher education was a waste of time and money.

However, as Congolese men achieved higher educational levels, (pastors, teachers and nurses), they wanted better educated wives.

Therefore, Thelma managed to recruit six teenage girls, keep them single, and educate them to finish junior high school. Other girls were later recruited as nursing students. Previously ALL nurses and teachers had been males. Upon graduation, every girl was sought after for marriage. Traditions change, but slowly.

Thelma was fluent in the Swahili language. Her African name in Swahili was Mama Mwila because the Congolese had great difficulty in pronouncing either Thelma or Montgomery. She'd been trained to do literacy work using the Frank Laubach system.

Phyllis and Thelma collaborated in literacy classes, mostly for the older women who'd been kept out of schools. In the early days of mission activity, the parents of Congolese girls didn't allow any girls to go to school.

SHORT TERM MISSIONARIES

Our Board of Missions established a short term program of mission service for recent college graduates. In Africa they were called A-J's, in Japan they were J-3's, and at home US-2's. Al Whelchel had been our first A-3. In 1954 Bill Harvey came out as his replacement. Both did very good work.

Bill returned to the States, went to seminary and eventually became a District Superintendent. At Kapanga Bill was called Mwant Dibu, Chief Palm Tree, because he was tall. Marvin Wolford served as an A-3 at Sandoa. Years later he worked with the Wyclife Bible Translators, returned to Congo and translated the entire Holy Bible into Lunda. President Kennedy patterned the original Peace Corps after the A-3 program.

BILATERAL PTERYGIA

Bilateral pterygia is an eye ailment you do not want to experience. I began to feel pain each time I blinked my eyes. Dr Bitsch-Larsen saw some granules were forming on the surface of each eyeball. I thought they were granules of ground bits of glass because my eyes hurt so badly. We traveled to the Congo government hospital at Elisabethville. There we were very fortunate to find a Belgian ophthalmologist who had his degree from Columbia University Medical School in New York. Once a week for three weeks the doctor injected hyaluronidase directly into the pterygia. Only local anesthesia was used in the eyes. I always believed hyaluronidase was close kin to the fuming hypergolic fuel NASA used in rockets. As the injections took effect the pain increased. However, at the end of three weeks both pterygia were dissolved and the pain soon stopped. Those pterygia have never returned. Our ophthalmologist now tells me there is only a very slight indication where the pterygia were removed.

BEAUTIFUL BUTTERFLIES

Several times during this term of service, Phyllis went hunting. She didn't stalk big game but the butterflies were abundant around our lantana and other shrubs. She made a butterfly net out of mosquito netting. We have her catches on our walls today.

WAYWARD WATER TANK KIT

You can live comfortably without electricity, paved roads and other evidences of modernization. Existing without running water is a sacrifice. Early in June we received word that a water tank kit for the mission had arrived, finally, at customs in Dilolo.

Howard Hardee had ordered the tank kit from England more than two years earlier. From the accompanying paper work, we determined it sat in Portuguese Angola customs for at least eighteen months. At last, the spirit moved the Portuguese and they moved the tank kit into the Congo.

Years of service in Africa taught us one lesson: Patience! With our trusty truck we moved four tons of steel from Dilolo to Kapanga.

We chose a spot and poured four suitable concrete foundations for the steel legs. That tank really was a kit that required "some assembly." {Stop laughing} When finally assembled it held more than 5,000 gallons of water at an elevation of eighteen feet above ground level. That kit contained: four steel legs, twelve steel cross braces, twenty flanged steel sheets (4 ft x 4 ft), a water level indicator, some large bags of bolts and buckets of sealing mastic for caulking the seams. All flanged sheets, legs and cross braces were pre-drilled with holes for the bolts. Therefore, no welding was required. The only tools we needed were: a drift pin for aligning the bolt holes, two wrenches to tighten the bolts and a block and tackle for hoisting the steel into place.

For a supply of water we laid a two-inch galvanized steel pipeline to the pump at the spring. Dr. Piper built a concrete tank around the mouth of the spring and put a cover over the tank in order to keep contaminants out of the water. That spring water had always tested as potable. We installed a small, gasoline-driven engine with attached pump to lift the water about seventy-five-feet up and into the new tank.

One old Congolese patient sat around the tank site for weeks while he muttered repeatedly: "If Nzambi (GOD) had wanted water up on the hilltop HE would have put it up there! "That pessimistic old patient was one of the first persons to draw water from a faucet after we pumped water into the tank. He made no more long trips to get Nzambi's water at the spring.

PATERNAL LOVE

In the men's ward, I encountered another old man. He wasn't a patient but was at the bedside of his sick teen age son.

Memories of the tender, loving care the sick boy received from his father remain vivid today (1995). In Congo all food was always traditionally prepared and served by women. Never by men. This good father broke that tradition. Kneeling by the hospital bed was this grizzled, gray-bearded, old hunter who would have been much more at home in the jungle. Here he was awkwardly, tenderly feeding his son. Obviously, there was a strong bond of love between them that is best described in the 13th chapter of 1st Corinthians.

ANNUAL CONFERENCE—1954—KANENE

Kanene is one of our very oldest mission stations. No missionaries were permanently assigned there in 1954. Partly for personal reasons, Bishop Booth convened the 1954 Annual Conference at Kanene, although it is a long way from anywhere.

As young missionaries, Bishop and Mrs. Booth served at Kanene. Their two-year-old son died and was buried there. As the missionaries and Congolese gathered for the conference, it became evident we needed meat. We were in Luba territory, a language none of us understood. Through translators, we sent out word that we needed a hunter and trackers.

Within a few hours, a very tall, handsome young man approached politely. "I understand that you gentlemen need some assistance in hunting for meat. I can help you!"

We were astounded and shook our heads in great disbelief. He was speaking faultless English. We soon learned he'd served as a policeman in Northern Rhodesia (Zambia) where he had learned to speak English and to use modern firearms. Using his knowledge of English and skill as a hunter near Kanene, his home village, we soon had a supply of antelope meat for the hungry conference attendees. The Lord gives "manna" in mysterious ways.

LAKE MUNKAMBA

All Congo rivers, tributaries and lakes swarm with carnivorous crocodiles—with the exception of one small lake.

No license was ever required to kill a crocodile. They were considered to be dangerous vermin. Many men, women and children were killed each year by crocodiles when people went to streams to get water or wash clothes.

But Lake Munkamba was delightfully free of crocodiles. The lake covers at least 100-acres. It's located many miles north of us in the Presbyterian mission area.

Several of the Presbyterian families and a few Methodists built vacation cottages on the banks of the lake. No commercial vacation locations existed in Congo.

We spent a pleasant week there while Bishop and Mrs. Booth were present.

A final mention of carnivores is an account of an event between one lone fisherman and one big crocodile. A Congolese fisherman limped into our hospital at Kapanga. The calf of his left leg had been shredded by a crocodile bite. The man had walked fifty-kilometers (thirty miles) without so much as a whimper. We would have died outright, but the Congolese fisherman had a phenomenal ability to bear pain.

He'd been wading in some shallow water collecting his basket fish nets. After that crocodile grabbed his leg, the man beat on the snout of the beast until the crocodile let go. Then he walked to our hospital.

PIPER MEMORIAL HOSPITAL

As we approached completion of the main hospital structures, we ordered a bronze plaque, *Piper Memorial Hospital*, from the foundry at the Union Miniere smelter in Elisabethville.

After Mobutu became absolute ruler of Congo (Zaire), he decreed that all people, places and buildings in Zaire must have Africanized names. As a subtle subterfuge, the hospital was re-named *Samuteb Hospital* by the local Lundas.

Dr. Piper was the father (*Sa*) of Ruth, first white missionary child born at the Kapanga mission, whose Lunda name was *Muteb*. All Lundas knew that *Samuteb* meant Dr. Piper.

On November 8th 1954, we enjoyed a happy day as we dedicated the hospital. Government officials, a Roman Catholic priest, local merchants, Bishop Newell Booth, many missionaries and a host of Congolese were present. The Congolese performed dances, held archery contests, sang celebration songs, beat drums and put on a marvelous play about how local "witch doctors" practiced medicine before Dr. Piper came.

Jason Sendwe, Assistant Doctor, demonstrated how a witch doctor could draw pain out of a patient's abdominal area. Our little houseboy, Diuru, acted as a patient while lying down on his back. Jason recited incantations, danced around and used a real feathered fish hook fetish to extract the evil spirits causing the pain in Diuru's stomach.

Jason's father had been well known as a Baluba witch doctor, Jason knew the proper techniques. We think Jason's son, Edouard, became an engineer in the US.

A group of workmen, complete with costume and headdress, acted out the extended consultation required to find out which spirits were the problem. There were bad, evil spirits and there were good, benevolent spirits. Which was now present in the patient? In a practical way the witch doctors and other Lundas had many home remedies that worked well. They knew how to use various leaves, fruits and roots to heal wounds and prevent infection.

CONSTRUCTION CHALLENGES

Arthur and Maude Piper walked into Musumba and Kapanga in 1914 after six weeks on the trail. Kayeka had been praying for a doctor for twelve years. Here came the answer to his prayers. Kayeka's story is so wonderful we included it, in detail, as we know it, in the section called ODDS AND ENDS.
We never met him; he died a short time before our arrival.
Dr. Piper began to practice medicine under a mango tree. Mrs. Piper set up housekeeping in a grass roofed hut and helped her husband. They continued their work for the next thirty-eight years; always living in grass roofed houses.
The mango tree was replaced with a grass roofed dispensary and clinic. Years later it was expanded. A corrugated metal roof replaced the grass.
Candles were the only source of light at night. They were soon replaced by kerosene lamps, which were replaced with good pressurized gasoline lanterns by Coleman or Primus. Dr. Piper never had a surgery type electric powered operating light.
Walking trips were speeded up a bit using bicycles in the early years, until the mid-1920's when they brought in one of Ford's Model T's.
The roadways gradually changed from rough tracks through the bush and over the hills into roads.
The smaller streams were crossed by sturdy wooden bridges and larger streams were provided with new ferries.

Many side roads were added in order to reach out into all parts of the territory. This improved travel system made it easier for the local population to come to the hospital. Therefore, the patient load increased each year.

This heavier load impacted the medical staff, but had no effect on the hospital food service. There was none. All patients were fed by relatives for two reasons: (1) the various clans and tribes had totally different food taboos, and (2) the fear of possible poison in food.

Death by poisoning occurred at least into the 1970's when a rival poisoned the reigning Paramount Chief. The old dispensary and new hospital have always provided kitchen sheds, but relatives still prepare all patient's food.

Medicine and medical supplies were scarce until after the Second World War. No dependable roads or transportation services, public or private, existed until the late 1930's.

During the Great Depression of the 1930's, the major nations of the world had severe economic problems and stopped most imports.

Soon the colonies in Africa were suffering because they could sell no raw materials. Ship sinkings and the submarine war at sea hindered or destroyed shipments from 1939 to 1945. Almost all construction material (cement, steel, window glass, nails, paint and tools) was difficult to obtain. High cost of transport was a heavy financial burden. After World War II, the Belgians developed the primitive tracks into real roads with good ferries where needed. They created government sponsored truck routes for freight, packages and mail. Radio-telegraph stations were built at most post offices, including the Kapanga Post Office. All major cities had full service banks.

Ford and General Motors established many dealer and repair facilities. A large cement factory was built in Katanga Province. Prior to the building of that plant, all cement came hundreds of miles from South Africa or the Rhodesias. Large building supply stores were established in Elisabethville and Luluabourg.

However, Kapanga was at least 125-miles away from any of these economic improvements, except the local radiotelegraph station. We did use it frequently.

For our mission construction projects, we had to hand press clay into bricks and fire them in a wood burning kiln. Tall mahogany trees were thirty miles away, near Kambundu. More than thirty-five sawyers spent years cutting down those trees, digging saw pits, manually crosscutting the trees into boards and carrying the boards on their heads several miles to the road. Large trees grow in fertile valleys near streams; roads are built on the ridges to avoid stream crossings. Bridges were difficult to build in rural area and expensive to maintain.

Missionaries Jim and Geneva Pottenger arrived at Kapanga in March 1948. He drew plans for the 200-bed hospital that had been approved for the station. Soon he gathered construction material. Several hundred-thousand hand-made bricks were fired in several kilns. Good sand was found in the banks of a nearby stream. Forests were located near Kambundu and the previously mentioned sawyers were recruited.

Tools for masons, carpenters, brick makers and all their helpers were ordered. In 1950, Jim died suddenly at Mulungwishi on a trip. He was 33-years old. His wife, Geneva, continued to be a missionary. We were diverted from Sarawak to Kapanga. While waiting for us to complete the Kennedy School of Missions and mandatory Ecole Coloniale in Brussels, the mission hired Leon Holt as short term construction superintendent.

Howard Hardee, MD, reluctantly agreed to direct the construction and be the only physician in the territory at the same time. Either task was a full time project at least.

After we arrived on the mission, we had sixty or more workers. We employed ten carpenters and helpers, thirty masons and their helpers, fifteen sand and rock diggers, several all-purpose employees and three auto mechanics who were our truck drivers.

At Kambundu we dealt with thirty to forty sawyers who were cutting down the large trees for lumber. All employees on the mission were paid once each week. The sawyers were paid for each cubic meter of lumber that we bought at the truck. Sometimes not all of the fallen tree was cut into the lumber that came to the mission. Some villagers had wood chairs and furniture. Incidentally, we never had any powered tools for any of our construction related tasks in our first term. Early in our next term (1957-1960) we bought a gasoline-driven cement mixer because the manual mixing of concrete is maddeningly slow and inefficient.

X-RAY

In January 1955, the Congo freight haulers, M.A.S., brought nineteen, heavy, wooden boxes containing one x-ray machine. The Women's Division had purchased and shipped this great medical apparatus. After carefully unpacking all the crates, we started reading the instruction manual. The factory in the US had enclosed the manual for a totally different machine. The manual that arrived with the x-ray equipment was useless. An urgent cable to the New York mission office brought a second copy of the same incorrect manual from the factory. Thankfully, the factory originally sent a large electrical schematic in one of the boxes. It included some limited notations about assembly and operation of the machine that we actually received. I was an electrical engineer and familiar with complicated electrical schematics and drawings. We quit trying to get the correct manual from the manufacturer. I learned enough to put the parts together and operate the x-ray properly. Later, I was able to teach the physicians and others to use the fluoroscope. As noted later, we never had air conditioning at Kapanga, so we never bought any x-ray film or developing capability.

We built a suite of rooms for the x-ray and erected a thick concrete wall directly in the path of the x-ray tube when used as a fluoroscope. No sheets of lead were available. We had used concrete as shielding. We bought no X-ray film or developing accessories because they were terribly expensive. X-ray film has a very quick expiration date when not kept cool. Developing is almost impossible without cooling by air conditioning, which we would probably never have at Kapanga.

Therefore, the doctors only used the fluoroscopic features to see broken bones and other internal injuries. No Congolese would stand in front of the fluoroscope until I went first. When they saw the clear outlines of the bones in his hands and forearm they were amazed.

Many Congolese were treated with the knowledge the doctors gained from fluoroscoping an injured area. Gunshot wounds from hunting accidents were common.

For electric power we installed a 25 KW Onan generator set. This set provided electricity for the x-ray. We had a smaller 5 KW generator set for the modern German made operating lights that we installed in the two operating rooms.

I became the radiological and operating light assistant. I was usually present when either was used, in case the power set failed or the x-ray machine needed adjustments. As the resident technician, I frequently sat on a high stool in the operating room and watched the surgery.

While Howard Hardee was doing a rare (for the Congo) appendectomy, Howard held up a mass of human plumbing. He offered to teach me how to do a "simple" appendectomy. I quickly replied Howard could do the human plumbing, I would take care of hospital plumbing.

Dr. Duvon Corbitt was talented with the scalpel. He knew precisely where all veins and arteries were located; he knew how to avoid them. His surgery drew almost no blood. This slight loss of blood was most important, because we had no apparatus for blood transfusions.

Our scalpels had replaceable blades. Being far away from surgical supply houses and often short of cash, the mission resharpened scalpel blades. In fact the task of sharpening scalpel blades came to me because I was a real "engineer," and knew all about technical details.

The real reason was sharpening is a tedious task that doctors didn't want to do.

I wandered into the maternity ward delivery room as a woman was giving birth. I never made that mistake again. I decided to leave obstetrics to obstetricians and midwives.

Our hospital had several wards and buildings. There were wards for men, women and children; a surgery wing with two operating rooms; a maternity wing with two delivery rooms; a building housing the pharmacy-storeroom and x-ray; and a chapel building.

We later added a school for the nurses and a dormitory for the students; and many other buildings.

The open air cooking shelters were never changed during our two terms of service. These shelters were not really kitchens but simply protection from rain.

All our doctors were so skilled and compassionate that many missionaries came long distances to Kapanga for operations. These operations ranged from major surgery like hysterectomies down to less major surgery for the removal of tumors on breasts.

Specimens for the pathologists were sent to Johannesburg, South Africa. A number were sent, but all tested negative.

A number of missionary children were born at Kapanga because of the excellent care given to the expectant mothers. All were normal births. However, head and chest surgery was never attempted because we had no suitable source of anesthesia, no resuscitation apparatus and no heart monitors.

We had no capability for any dental care. Kapanga missionaries had to travel northward to the Presbyterian Mission at Lubondai. They were in the process of establishing a dental school for Congolese. Elsewhere we have written about one wonderful trip to the dentist that was taken by me, Al Whelchel and Valborg Bitsch-Larsen.

AFRICAN CAPE BUFFALO

The African Cape Buffalo may be of the same general species and look similar to the water buffalo of Asian countries. Any other similarity stops right there!

The Asian Water Buffalo have been domesticated as work animals for centuries. To our knowledge, no one has ever come close to taming a Cape Buffalo, although two or three colonial powers tried.

Every Cape Buffalo we encountered in the Congo was mean spirited, tough to hunt, and dangerous. Their forehead and skeletal structure around the eyes contained about four inches of thick dense bones.

Using a 416 caliber Rigby rifle, an English hunter had shot a Cape buffalo in the front of the head. That bullet, heavier than my 375 slugs, bounced off like a tiny 22 caliber slug. It didn't make a dent, but it did greatly anger the buffalo. The next shot was more prudently placed.

A 1,200 pound buffalo will yield many pounds of delicious, tasty and tender lean meat. Because of the tsetse fly (sleeping sickness), cattle can't be raised successfully in most of Congo. Congolese raised some sheep and goats.

You had to be very hungry to eat them, they were tough. Pigs were invaded by trichinosis, intestinal worms that render the meat inedible. Chickens were devastated by coccidiosis.

Kapanga is one hundred miles from the nearest butcher shop. Unless we hunted wild game, we had no meat on the table. Hunting wasn't a sport, but was a necessity driven by hunger.

Big buffalo were a real prime target in spite of their well-earned reputation. There are many varieties of antelope in the Congo, but no antlered wild animals like deer. Antelopes range in size from the dik-dik at less than twenty pounds to the giant Derby eland weighing up to 1,600 pounds. Many antelope were rare and protected by game laws. Usually we hunted the reedbucks and similar medium-sized antelope.

Once we tried to eat elephant meat, but it's like chewing on an old boot. An elephant moves constantly in order to eat enough to stay alive. The tenderloins of hippos were tasty.

In late January 1955, Immanuel and I went to Mwini Dikamba's village west of the Lulua River to hunt buffalo.

Congolese boys always roamed savannas and jungle. Often they wrapped bundles of dry grass around their bodies. From twenty yards away, they were invisible in tall grass. They'd recently seen signs of a buffalo herd. We were hunting in the dry season which meant that the soil was hard. A herd of buffalo didn't leave any tracks that were easy to follow.

Mwini Dikamba was a skilled tracker and located a few signs. Being untrained white men, we could see the signs only after he patiently explained to us how to read them.

On the second or third day we tracked the herd into a valley with tall trees and dense undergrowth. As we neared the stream, we heard a loud noise similar to two heavy, hard objects colliding. Leaving the porters and our supplies behind, the three of us proceeded cautiously.

In a few minutes we walked quietly in the stream towards the sounds. Two large male buffalos were butting heads. They ignored us. There was no wind, so they didn't smell us.

One of the buffalo caught sight of us and ran up the slope. The other turned his anger on us and charged. Less than twenty-five yards of stream bed lie between us. With his massive head and horns down in protection of his chest, My first shot clipped a small chunk out of the right horn. This simply made the buffalo unhappier and he continued his charge. I stepped aside and shot the buffalo in the right hind leg, breaking it.

No heavy animals, buffalo or elephant, can walk (or run) on three legs. Antelopes of any size can hobble along. The wounded buffalo dropped in the knee deep water and kept trying to drag himself towards us, the enemy. Immanuel finished him off with a shot to the chest.

Being charged by a big, angry buffalo is a temporary cure for low blood pressure.

Immanuel had killed buffalo and elephant in Central Congo, so he let me have the horns. They measure about 34 inches at the widest point and are not too far from being eligible for the trophy book.

We never paid Congolese to go with us on hunts. We shared the meat as an incentive for them to find game, rather than escort us around in a paid tour of the countryside.

Fortunately, the Congolese preferred the internal organs, and we wanted the tastier steaks and roasts. This was an equitable distribution because the internal organs spoil quickly. Our trackers consumed them immediately in nearby villages. The body of the animals would keep fresh longer, until we returned home.

PERSONALITIES IN 1955

Howard Hardee returned for two weeks in March in order to sort through their possessions. He sold or gave away some things and asked us to pack and ship the rest to them in Tampa, Fla. He left their Ford station wagon with us. Packing was quite a challenge. They'd inherited or purchased a variety of crystal and other rather fragile items. The shipment would go by truck, train and cargo ship to the US. If you've watched any carriers load and unload cargo you know handling is often rather rough. Later, Howard wrote not a single item was damaged or broken.

On March 16th Bishop Newell and Mrs. Esma Booth arrived with Bishop Richard and Mrs. Lucille Raines. Richard Raines was resident bishop in Indiana and extremely interested in African missions.

He appears later in this story when I spent a week in Indiana with the Paramount Chief Mwant Yav Ditend. On March 26th, Al and Pat Broadhead arrived. Al was a male registered nurse. Pat assumed the task of bookkeeping for the hospital. She took care of their children which included home schooling for some of them.

On April 19th, Reverend Bill and Mrs. Doris Davis arrived with their children. Bill took over the church of the mission. Doris was soon involved in women's work and school. We first met Bill and Doris at Scarritt College in 1950. {All of us were there in order to be interviewed individually by the Personnel Committee of the Board of Missions}.

A month later, May 14, Dr. Warren and Mrs. Jane Freeborn arrived. Jane was a registered nurse. She and Warren spent the next month at the hospital with Dr. Bitsch-Larsen. Warren and Jane tried to cope with the Grass Palace. With more missionary families than quality residences, we'd installed the Freeborns in the Palace until I could complete the construction of their new residence. They'd arrived early enough to choose the colors of paint for the inside walls. They chose a chocolate brown for the bedroom, which made it dark without any electric lights. We think the next occupants repainted those bedroom walls.

Dr. & Mrs. Bitsch-Larsen left in late June, so we were back to one doctor until late September when Dr. Marc and Mrs. Amiee Jespers arrived at the station.

In November Dr. Ralph Dodge, Mission Board Secretary for Africa, came for a short visit. Ralph and Eunice served as missionaries in Angola for many years. Near retirement, he wrote a fascinating book called "*THE REVOLUTIONARY BISHOP.*

In fact, he was only a real revolutionary in the New Testament sense of the word; he wasn't a modern, political, bomb-throwing revolutionary. His book is an excellent account of the years that he and Eunice spent in Angola, at the Board of Missions as Secretary for Africa and as a Bishop in Africa.

AFRICAN NAMES

Because European names are unpronounceable for Congolese, they often gave us African names. Many

Africans have been given names that mean something or commemorate an event.

One of my workers was named Kambove Dilolo. His mother had been traveling on a train when he was born somewhere between the mining town of Kambove and the frontier town of Dilolo. Family names were not used. Each child received an individual name or names.

Anyway, Bill Harvey was given the Lunda name Mwant Dibu, Chief Palm Tree, because he was tall like the local palm trees.

I was first given the name Mwant Kasompu, Man Who Can Build Anything, because I built so many structures and the X-ray. The workmen wanted to name him Mwant Yav Kaumb. The men said Chief Kaumb had taken good care of his people and villages, just like I took good care of his workmen.

Phyllis had been named Maku Chisambu,"Woman of Peace," because she was always happy and acted as a peacemaker. Now the workmen wanted to name her Rukonkesh Kat, a deceased Lunda woman chief, because Phyllis was kind to women and children just as Kat had been.

One of the Belgian Territorial Administrators, Monsieur Sovet, was called Weeping Willow. At the ferry one day the ferrymen explained Weeping Willow changed his mind very frequently and put people in jail for petty reasons as a result. I didn't believe weeping willow trees could put people in jail.

In fact, Sovet was called weeping willow by the Africans for the similarity between Sovet and the tree. Many willow branches float on the surface of the river water. As the eddies of water go around, and back and forth, so do the branches. Sovet had changed his mind and his decisions frequently. The Africans had named him appropriately.

Most Congolese didn't know we spoke Lunda, as Belgian officials, merchants and the majority of Roman Catholic priests didn't know the language. They used only the trade language, Swahili, which is partially understood from the Atlantic (Angola) across Africa to the Indian Ocean at Kenya, where the original Swahili tribe lived. As Methodist Missionaries we were required to learn local languages.

A European journalist asked for an African name. Temporarily he was pleased with "Divumo Ditoku Dijim;" it had an authentic ring to the sound of the words. Then he discovered it identified his most prominent physical features, "large white belly," which he did possess.

When you are exposed to another language for the first time, be careful. Often the local citizens trick you into using some ridiculous words. In the Congo some common words were quite acceptable. Bwana means man, or sir, or boss. Bwana Makubwa simply means the "big" man or big boss. Ndona is a corruption of the Portuguese word, Dona, which is the feminine equivalent of Don, an honorary title of respect. Bunduki is the almost universal word for firearm. In the old Tarzan and similar movies the two words Bwana and Bunduki were frequently used, sometimes correctly.

ALL SNAKES ARE BAD &
                ROUND BOTTOMED DUGOUT

By August 1955 we'd learned much more Lunda and were still taking lessons. But we hadn't discovered the word for venomous or poisonous. We did know the word for bad.
When I went on another hunt near Mwini Dikamba's village I asked the tracker, "Which snakes are bad?"
With the utmost solemnity, the barelegged and barefooted man replied "All snakes are bad!"
His statement was verified later that day when I disturbed a sleeping cobra. As I arrived at a turn in the game trail, a large hooded cobra rose up one pace ahead and spread his hood. I froze, my rifle useless, pointed upwards in its sling on my back. The cobra was within striking distance and any movement might incite him to do so.
In our party of hunters, someone always carried a shotgun loaded with buckshot.
I quietly alerted Bill Harvey, who slowly stepped aside and killed the cobra with a blast from the shotgun.
My rifle would have been difficult in any case as it was meant for big game. Unless careful aim is taken, shotguns are useless against leopards and lions. They require shots to the brain for instant death.
One of our missionaries shot a lion through the chest with a 308 cal. rifle. The lion continued running fifty yards towards the hunter and finally collapsed a few feet away; just before the missionary collapsed.
On another hunting trip, Warren and Jane Freeborn accompanied us on a hippo hunt. We cared for a leper colony. Many lepers are so disfigured they can't garden,

fish or hunt. In order to feed them as well as possible, we hunted hippos. Weighing upwards of 3,500 pounds, one big male hippo provided meat for lots of undernourished Congolese lepers.

Warren and Jane were in one dugout canoe made from a large tree trunk. We were in a second dugout. These dugouts are not a stable platform if you stand up. It is much safer to sit down in the muddy water that seeps into the canoe. I had been hippo hunting several times and knew about their instability. Warren didn't—yet.

As the boatman propelled Warren's dugout toward the landing, he stood up and moved around a bit.

"It is a round-bottomed dugout," I shouted. "Do not stand up!"

It was too late. Warren had disappeared from our sight. All we could see was his right hand holding a very expensive, but NOT waterproof Leica camera just above the water level. Near the bank, the river was only about six-feet deep. A soaked Warren clambered up the bank holding his dry Leica at eye level.

To our knowledge, Warren never stood up again in a round-bottomed dugout while it was away from the bank of the river.

We got our hippo and fed the lepers. They each received a generous portion. We took the back tenderloins home. Each one weighed forty-pounds. They were four-feet long and in cross section the size of a dinner plate. The meat is excellent, similar to pork, but leaner.

FAMOUS BELGIAN ARTIST

On November 22nd, Dr. Marc Jespers' father visited his son at our station. His father, Floris Jespers, is a famous artist with works in the Belgian National Museum as well as other museums in Europe.

When he arrived he had no art materials. Temporarily he was quite frustrated seeing many scenes he wanted to paint. Phyllis brought out her supply of brushes, oils and canvas; within two hours he'd completed five paintings in the nearby village of Pambala.

One of Floris Jaspers Congo scenes

As a reward for her help, he offered Phyllis her choice of a painting. We now have treasured art originals by Phyllis, our daughter Cathy, missionary Colin Molyneux, and the Belgian artist, Monsieur Floris Jespers. We have no estimate of their commercial value, but we wouldn't sell them at any price less than a million dollars. Well—maybe a few hundred thousand dollars would tempt us.

HUNTRESS PHYLLIS

As countless wives have said to their husbands, "You never take me anywhere!" In this case she referred to our big game hunts. We had gone dove hunting together many times. She is quite skilled with a 16 gauge shotgun and killed her share of birds. This skill amazed our African friends because Congolese women never hunted with guns, or even with bows and arrows. Hunting was for Men Only.

We arranged to go on a hunt with our good friend, Mwini Dikamba, at his village. We arrived at sundown. Our gracious host prepared a delicious dinner with nsej as the meat course. This meat is clear and tender like veal. We learned nsej is really a swamp rodent. Mwini Dikamba gave us a large pan of warm water for washing faces and hands before the meal.

Early next morning we hiked out of the village towards the river about six miles away. After a long hike downhill, we shot one antelope. We started back uphill toward the village. The path grew steeper.

We became tired as we trudged uphill, waded across some small streams, and carried our kill.

Darkness comes quickly in the tropics. After dark, Congolese light torches of dry grass for a small amount of light on the rough pathway. Exhausted we stopped for rest more often.

We hiked fifteen miles that day and finally arrived alive around 9:30PM. Dog tired, we collapsed. We mixed a jar of strawberry jam with reconstituted milk and made milk shakes. Never, before or since, has any drink tasted so delicious.

Next morning, we shared the antelope meat with our good host and drove back to the mission. Strangely enough, Phyllis didn't ask to go on another antelope hunt until our next term of service.

I can't imagine why.

UNHAPPY CANNIBAL WITCH DOCTORS

Al Whelchel, Valborg Bitsch-Larsen and I needed dental work. It was only available at the Presbyterian station of Lubondai. They drove north from Kapanga and soon were in the tribal area of the Basala Mpasu.

Back in the early 1930's, this cannibalistic tribe had killed and eaten a Roman Catholic priest. The Belgian authorities sent soldiers from another tribe into the area and killed an entire village of 3,000 Basala Mpasu.

The Administrator told Chief Tolume if any more white persons were killed and eaten, the government would wipe out a larger village. The Basala Mpasu were uneducated, but not stupid; they got the message. From then on they captured and ate only Congolese; usually from another tribe.

They took to the extreme the Biblical saying "I was a stranger and you took me in."

My truck drivers wouldn't drive through Basala Mpasu country alone; they always required a white person with them. That year, there were nine cases of alleged Basala Mpasu cannibalism in the courts.

The Presbyterians lost one of their Congolese pastors in this manner. Some modern anthropologists blindly insist that "cannibalism" never existed, but that's a minority opinion not based on fact. They've never been threatened by angry witch doctors waving large sharp knives.

As the three missionaries, Al, Valborg and I passed through a remote part of the countryside, we encountered a large group of people heading off the road and into the bush.

Al and I spoke Lunda which is understood by the Basala Mpasu. Several of the people urged the missionaries to come on along with them. A quarter of a mile into the bush, they stopped in a clearing among many other people.

Almost immediately three exceedingly upset and angry witch doctors jumped around on the outskirts of the crowd. They were dressed in their witch doctor regalia, violently waving large sharp cannibal knives and yelling "Kill the white intruders! Kill them now!"

We'd inadvertently blundered into a funeral for one of the sub-chiefs. The witch doctors wanted to add new bodies to the fresh grave, still open.

Valborg was extremely frightened. All she saw were the sharp knives and she heard the angry exhortations. Her fear was increased because she didn't understand Lunda.

Al and I were a mite nervous, too. We both quietly and quickly, in Lunda, said we would leave immediately. Slowly, (it felt like an eternity) we backed up the trail and reached the vehicle.

Never again did any of us join any group of Congolese until we knew exactly what they were doing. During our second term, we paid three witch doctors, probably not the same ones, to perform for us while we took movies. The atmosphere at that paid performance, which we filmed, was much more congenial than at the funeral.

POLYGAMY

Men who were wealthy enough had two or more wives. Many of the Paramount Chiefs had numerous wives. Mwant Yav Muteb, Paramount Chief when the Arthur Pipers arrived in 1914, was said to have 87 wives.

Most of these wives were the daughters of subject tribal chiefs and were actually political hostages, property of the Chief as homage to his power.

One of my workmen, a little guy named Kanyik, had two wives. In a conversation with us, Kanyik solemnly stated white husbands were very lucky. Their wives did whatever they were told to do; they were obedient. He said he often had to hit his wives when he wanted water or food. I smiled but said nothing.

Phyllis stifled a grin and remained silent, as a good wife should do.

LITERACY

Frank Laubach, missionary to the Philippines, long ago developed a simple method for teaching any language to illiterates.

Phyllis learned this method and applied it to the Lunda tongue at Kapanga. As pupils, she had three of the most influential Lunda women. Mwadi was the Queen of the Lundas and first wife of Mwant Yav Ditend. Nswan Murund was the Mother of the Tribe. Rukonkesh was a delightful character who had a most influential position.

Once or twice a week they came to our house with their books and some writing material. Each had a young girl as her Lady-in-Waiting who carried these items. Royalty carried no burdens at any time. These women were thrilled as they progressed in their lessons and began to understand these strange symbols we call words. They didn't become scholars, but learned to read words and numbers. The gift of literacy is a marvelous gift to the illiterate.

WILLIS JR AND HIPPOS

Adult missionaries were honorary aunts and uncles to missionary kids in a very extended family. Willis Jr, approached me one day with a request.
Willis wanted to tell me a story, but didn't want it passed on to his mother. With reservation, I agreed to listen.
Along the banks of the Lulua River are animal trails the hippos use when going to and from the marsh land for food. As the river level recedes in the dry season, these huge hippos carve a passage down through the soft bank. This passage is just wide enough for one hippo. Once hippos enter they cannot turn around until they get to water level.
Willis and friends were lying down beside that path in order to grab a handful of three inch bristles from their tails as the hippos passed.
Willis had some bristles to prove his story. I kept my word. I didn't tell Dot Piper until many years later.

SECULAR TEACHING AND SCRIPTURE

The workmen had a great curiosity about the inventions and equipment that white men were bringing to Africa. They considered these things as "children of the white man's brain." During the first year or so they continually asked questions about motor cars, motor oil, gasoline, electric lights, paper, plastic, concrete, metals, money and glass.

There was never enough time to answer many of the inquiries during working hours. Eventually we took a gasoline-powered lantern to the carpenter shop after dark each week and gave a lesson on one subject at a time.

A workman would read a scripture and pray before the beginning of the lesson. Their favorite passage seemed to be the 8th chapter of Psalms: "What is man that THOU are mindful of him?"

Phyllis made some good illustrations and collected samples of money: bills and coins. We gave them the history of money, how it began as something small but very valuable like gold, silver and copper. We never explained the banking system because they had no experience with banks or checks.

Having grown up near oil and gas fields in Texas, I explained how crude oil was created by God. Man has gradually learned how to extract it, then refined it into kerosene, gasoline, diesel fuel, motor oil and lubricants.

Other subjects we covered were elementary lessons on automobiles, trains, airplanes and tractors. Some of the men had worked in the copper or manganese mines. They'd been exposed to lots of big equipment, but had no idea about how it worked. Our lesson about electricity was accepted on faith. We're not sure they comprehended what it is or how it works.

Basically we tried to teach them that God created the natural phenomena. Mankind has slowly learned how to use them. Humans do not really create anything. They discover the laws of God's Creation, apply them to the 100's of elements in the universe, and learn how to make things that are useful.

Humans have gradually learned to understand natural phenomena (lightning, etc) and the benefits they bring.

OLD STYLE PRISONERS

We don't remember when it happened, but on one of our trips we passed a column of Congolese prisoners herded along the roadway. All prisoners were men. Each man had a large iron collar around his neck. The first prisoner had a chain from the back of his collar to the front of the second man's collar, and so on. On that hot, dusty road, they weren't a picture of happiness. In addition to the chains, the colonial prison officials occasionally dealt out punishment with a long whip made from dried strips of hippo hide.

NON-METHODIST VISITORS

Our lives were enriched by several non-Methodist visitors.
On May 26, 1953 Mr. & Mrs. Colin Molyneux, AEB missionaries, spent the night with us. Theirs was a small, poor faith mission from England. They came south on their way to Sakeji School for mission kids in Northern Rhodesia (Zambia). In the late spring they traveled through again to take their children home for the summer. Colin was a talented water color artist. He had some beautiful water colors of the Congo landscape and jungles along the

river banks. He sold these water colors as a source of money for their mission. We bought several of them.

On June 16th we were surprised to greet a hitch-hiker. Lore Kegel, a middle-aged German woman, was soloing across central Africa in search of native artifacts for the museum in Zurich, Switzerland. She was catching any available rides. Congo had limited public transportation. Only two railroad lines and a few riverboat steamers on the Congo River and its tributaries carried public passengers.

In 90% of the 300,000 square miles, you had to bum a ride or have your own vehicle. Lore was a spunky woman traveling alone. There was very little danger. Violence in Congo didn't begin until Independence came in 1960, (leaving out the cannibals).

She knew English quite well. In one of her stories she explained how meat, usually unavailable, appeared in Bremerhaven butcher shops after a devastating series of bombing raids killed 40,000 persons. Hungry and starving, no one questioned the origin of the meat. Survival was more important than knowledge.

We were not totally neglected by news reporters either. In July 1953, a Mr. Edvard Andersen, reporter for *Politiken*, a Danish newspaper, was with us for several days. He took many photographs and asked a lot of questions. Although he spoke fluent English, he wrote the reports and articles in Danish. The Bitsch-Larsens told us the articles were fair and sympathetic to mission work. Many other writers of that era wrote rather disparagingly about "do-good" missionaries meddling in the lives of unsophisticated African tribes.

In early February, 1954, Walter Shepard and Pat Morison, Americans with the Presbyterian mission, visited our area for several days in order to look at our school work. Presbyterians have a congregational type of oversight with no hierarchy. All decisions were made by their presbytery as a group. They expressed a desire for our type of strong episcopal (bishops) leadership.

We told them on some occasions, we'd be delighted to send them our bishop—on long term loan. Occasionally bishops can be a bother.

During the first week of April 1955, three Belgian teachers came to observe our rural schools. Monsieur Maurice Jacobi and Rose, his wife, and Monsieur Emile Sauvage were working in the City of Elisabethville with fifteen tribes and languages. They encountered challenges we didn't have at Kapanga. All our mission school children had the same language.

EFFECTIVE VERSUS EFFICIENT

These two words are defined in *The American Heritage* dictionary as follows:
1. Effective - having the intended or expected effect, serving the purpose, and...
2. Efficient - stresses the ability to perform well and economically.

Returning to camp from a long, unsuccessful day of hunting, Bill Davis and I were carrying our usual heavy weapons, but no shotgun. Bill had a 458 caliber Winchester and I had a smaller 375 caliber Winchester. Both weapons are effective and efficient in killing large African animals such as elephant, buffalo, crocodile, hippo and antelope. On this hunt, we had walked all day and encountered no game.

As we approached camp, the tracker spotted a small flock of guinea fowl in a dusty clearing. The cock was standing on a small ant hill. Being tired and hungry, the tracker and porters begged Bill and I to kill it. We patiently explained to the men, we had no shotgun and rifles were not useful for shooting small birds. The men kept insisting, you have "bundukis." Bunduki is the Swahili word for any type of firearm.

Once again, the men complained they were tired and hungry, please kill some meat. Bill had a few soft-nosed cartridges that were useless on the big animals we were hunting. He loaded one into the chamber and fired. The bird's head flew into the air and the legs stayed in place. Only feathers and bits of skin remained on the anthill. Bones, viscera and the rest of the feathers were scattered over a square yard or so.

"Ak, Ak, Bwana, you were right," chorused the Congolese as they surveyed the scattered bits of bird. A 458 bullet is effective; the bird was dead. However, the use of a 458 bullet wasn't efficient. Nothing edible remained on or around the ant hill. Our trackers learned there is a real difference between rifles and shotguns, although all are bundukis.

Neither Bill nor I were ever again asked to use our rifles on birds.

1956——GOING HOME

Sometime during our first year in Congo, Phyllis exclaimed, "I want to go home to see Mother!"

Without thinking, I pointed to the northwest. "Your mother is over there about 8,000 miles." Momentarily, I'd forgotten about her real skill with firearms.

In late 1955, the Board of Missions scheduled us for furlough in early 1956. We had been gone almost five years. The mode of travel home was our decision. We chose to travel home by freighter across the Atlantic Ocean from Matadi, Congo, to New Orleans, Louisiana.

This was a wise decision. The long ocean voyage on the MV Del Oro lasted from January 23rd when we left the dock at Matadi, until March 3rd when they tied the ship to the Poydras Street Wharf in New Orleans.

We had thirty-nine wonderful days to do nothing but eat, sleep, read whatever we liked, visit strange seaports on the west coast of Africa, and attend no meetings.

We'd saved a little money and wanted a station wagon to be waiting for us in Atlanta. By correspondence with

Beaudry Ford in Atlanta, we arranged to buy a bright red, four-door 1956 Ford Wagon with a Thunderbird engine and a few accessories. Air conditioning was rare and expensive, so we didn't have it installed.

In December, we'd shipped barrels and boxes of our possessions by train and river boat to the Port of Matadi. We hadn't decided whether or not we would return to Congo. The hospital was basically completed and we wanted to explore the possibility of adopting children. No agency, including our own Methodist Children's Homes, would place children for adoption with missionaries who served overseas. Strange, but sadly very true!

LAST FEW WEEKS IN CONGO

Leaving for furlough is almost as hectic as the first arrival in Congo. Financial records of all construction had to be in order and turned over to someone. Phyllis had to plan menus and buy enough food to complete our stay. Worn tropical clothing had to be sold or given away. Our pets, George and Inky, needed new homes. We found a home for Inky, but let George go free in the jungle. Because of his friendliness with humans, he approached some hunters who very promptly shot and later ate him. They didn't know he was a pet, they thought he was a dumb monkey.

We wrote letters to our supporting churches, Board of Missions, families and friends. All three of Phyllis' sisters had married and are still married to the same lucky men in 1995.

Phyllis is a neatnik. She cleans every house we move into. She cleans every house before we leave it. With US passports, we needed no visas to enter the US. None would be needed at any of the ports we visited. Short visits into these port cities could be made with no requirements, except a valid US passport. As soon as the customs officials knew us by sight, they quit looking at our passports.

We received many gifts from our Christian friends: workmen, teachers and women whom Phyllis had taught to read with the Laubach System. Most of the gifts were simple in nature: gifts of fruit, flowers and handmade articles of cloth with exquisite, colorful patterns in embroidery. The girls made book bags in their home economics classes. We have several attractive bags that are well made and useful. Being dark skinned, the Congolese females can wear and carry vibrant colors that don't go well with white skinned missionaries.

For building the hospital, nurse's school and other facilities, the Mwant Yav Ditend awarded me a ceremonial, tribal crown. I never thought it prudent to ask if it made me eligible to be a polygamist.

KAPANGA—NEW ORLEANS
WITHIN CONGO—KAPANGA TO MATADI

Early on the morning of January 17, 1956 we were packed and ready to go home!
Bill Harvey and his girlfriend Nan Blake agreed to drive us to Luluabourg, our nearest airport. Nan was an A-3 missionary in Algeria, North Africa, who'd come down for a short visit to the real Africa. After a misunderstanding or

two, they became engaged, were married, created a family and have served many churches in Ohio.

One day Bill said he didn't understand how females could be so different. My only advice was to quote the French expression, *Vive La Difference.*

Along the way to Luluabourg, we passed one more time through the fascinating Basala Mpasu countryside. We made short farewell visits to the American Presbyterian Congo Mission (APCM) at Moma and Lubondai.

The Pax Hotel was a comfortable place for us to spend two nights. Luluabourg had a population of about 75,000 more or less, depending upon tax time. When Congo collected annual taxes, the citizens went to Angola for a short visit. When Angola collected taxes, their citizens became temporary Congolese.

With a commercial airport, railroad service, banks, post office, hardware stores, gas stations, auto dealers, building supply warehouses and provincial government offices, it was quite modern and well maintained.

In 1995, our friends tell us, it is a ghost town where nothing works, except violence and chaos.

Jim and Charlene Halverstadt, APCM missionaries, invited us to lunch. Jim was the business manager and treasurer for APCM. He'd been an officer for a major bank in Atlanta before becoming a missionary.

At the hotel, neither of us slept much, although the food and bed were quite satisfactory. Our efforts at sleeping were often interrupted by our emotions about going home.

We have heard it said anticipation is greater than realization. In our case, we hoped that wasn't true. We loved Africa and felt we'd accomplished some small measure of good work. But we longed to see families and friends again.

Next morning Bill and Nan transported us and our luggage to the airport. Piston-engined aircraft were still in use. Sabena had a DC-4 waiting for us. Flying above the clouds, we saw nothing of the landscape.

However, as we circled to land at Leopoldville, we were able to see the huge Stanley Pool on the wide Congo River. That pool is more than a mile wide, twenty miles long, and hundreds of feet deep. Millions of years ago the entire inland basin of the Congo River and all its tributaries (Ubangi, Lualaba, Kwilu, Kwango, Kasai,etc) was a lake in a saucer like depression. Although the basin covers more than 500,000-square miles, the torrential, tropical rains falling throughout the year eventually filled the basin to overflowing. Parts of the basin get more than six- feet (72 inches) of rainfall annually.

The huge Congo basin straddles the Equator. Therefore, the Congo River receives rainfall runoff every month of the year. South of the equator the rains generally come from October to April. North of the equator the rain falls from May to September.

The lowest point on the mountainous rim around the basin was in the Crystal Mountains between Congo and the Atlantic Ocean. Although these mountains are very hard rock, the tremendous forces exerted by the water rushing through such a small pass soon cut through that rock like a knife.

Today the walls along part of the river are vertical for hundreds of feet with no beach, riverbank or vegetation at water's edge. At times the river is only 1,300 feet wide.

Engineers have estimated from 10% to 25% of the total potential waterpower in the world is available in the short stretch of Congo River between Stanley Pool and Matadi. The difference in elevation is slightly more than 1,000 feet.

Prior to Independence in 1960, the Belgians had proposed building a dam in the Inga Gorge. From the electric generators downstream, they were going to build a network of power transmission lines to the mining areas of the Kasai (diamonds, gold) and the Katanga (copper, coal, tin, manganese, iron ore and uranium). The extraction and processing of these natural resources use a tremendous amount of electricity. New cities, towns, and rural developments are dependent' upon a source of electricity.

After independence a small dam was built and power transmission lines were connected from Inga Gorge to the mining areas near the town of Kolwezi on the Zambian border.

Sadly, the extreme political upheavals, riots, and tribal wars in the Republic of the Congo, now known as Zaire, have stalled that project. It has not been fully implemented and is very expensive to maintain. Additional prudent investments in infrastructure, like electric power, have been replaced by greed that demands instant income with no plans for any long range development planning. The damage to people and natural resources in Zaire after over thirty years of Mobutu dictatorship will be difficult to overcome.

HISTORY AND GEOGRAPHY

Our train ride from Leopoldville to Matadi was far more pleasant than the wild-west train ride across Angola in

1952. Our passenger car was comfortable and the engine was diesel electric. We didn't miss the soot and ashes from the two KDL wood burning locomotives.

After a ten-hour trip, we arrived at the port of Matadi where we registered at the Hotel Metropole. Matadi is not the hottest place on earth, but it is a "mite warm" as we say out in Texas. [The Empty Quarter, Rub Al Khali, in Saudi Arabia is the hottest]. There's a small shelf of low hills along the banks of the river but within a short distance the mountains rise high again. There is no breeze.

Matadi means rock in Swahili and these rocky hills don't erode. Henry Stanley returned to the mouth of the Congo River in late 1879.

Earlier in 1874-1877, he'd been the first white man to explore from the east, Zanzibar on the Indian Ocean, to the west, Atlantic Ocean at the mouth of the Congo. Many of his expedition were from the Swahili tribe and had gone down the Congo from source to ocean. On his expedition up the Congo in 1879 he brought some Swahili men again.

Stanley didn't realize it, but he was spreading the easily spoken Swahili language across central Africa from the Indian Ocean to the Atlantic Ocean.

More than 200 distinct languages are spoken by the tribes within the Congo River basin. By this, we mean these tribes speak 200 mutually unintelligible languages, with only a few words understood by any neighboring tribe. There are hundreds more dialects that are variations on these basic languages. Swahili soon became a trade language and the language used temporarily by all the Congo government officials.

In late 1879 Stanley prepared to build a roadway from Matadi to Stanley Pool, bypassing the impassable cataracts on the river.

King Leopold II, King of the Belgians, and their territories, financed the expedition which was expected to open the Congo basin to commerce. Stanley brought hand tools and some wheeled conveyances, but no powered equipment for moving earth or breaking rocks. One account writes he used newly invented dynamite and the other account says he broke rocks with sledge hammers.

In any case, he broke lots of rock and acquired the Swahili name "Bula Matadi", which means rock breaker. Because he represented the governmental authorities, the nickname "Bula Matadi" has been applied to every government official in the Congo since the days of Henry Stanley.

With a small band of Europeans and Africans, Stanley laboriously hacked out a ten-foot-wide rough roadway the fifty-two miles from Matadi to Isangila between March 1880 and February 1881.

From Isangila up to Manyinga, the Congo River is navigable for about ninety miles. Twelve more months were required to build a rough roadway from Manyinga to Stanley Pool.

Among other equipment and supplies they manually hauled overland the parts for a twenty-ton wood-burning river steamer.

At Isangila, they assembled the steamer for moving themselves and their supplies ninety miles upriver to the village of Manyinga.

There, they disassembled the steamer in order to haul it and their supplies, by human power overland to Stanley Pool.

Once again they assembled the little steamer and used it to explore the Congo River east of Stanley Pool.

In summary, they toiled for two-and-a-half years of hard labor moving that little steamer, workers, and their equipment from Matadi to Stanley Pool. A trip we made comfortably in ten hours.

In the 1890's the Belgians, under Captain Thys, spent eight years building a railroad to replace Stanley's makeshift roadway. The railroad was routed parallel to and south of the Congo River, going over much less difficult terrain. Stanley had chosen to go closely parallel to the meanderings of the river in order to utilize the 90 miles of navigable river.

Stanley's roadway opened the Congo Basin to exploration. The railroad opened the vast basin to commerce. Now ocean freighters could dock at Matadi. Freight trains could travel between Matadi and Leopoldville. Larger river steamers were brought in for use on the 2,000 miles of Congo River and its tributaries.

In 1908 the English completed the railroad from South African and Indian Ocean ports to the Katanga mining area. This was a part of Cecil Rhodes' dream to build a railroad from Capetown in South Africa to Cairo in Egypt on the Mediterranean. In 1930 the English and Portuguese completed the previously mentioned Katanga-Dilolo-Lobito railroad from Lobito on the Atlantic Ocean to the Katanga.

In the 1930's the Belgians built a railroad from the Katanga to the capital of the Kasai, Luluabourg, and on northward to Port Franqui on the Kasai River, which is navigable to Leopoldville.

Therefore, when we arrived in 1952, the Congo had excellent transportation to and from the rest of the world. This was tremendously important to missionaries. Good transportation made it more comfortable and safe to travel, while it enabled missionaries to receive supplies at less cost with less delay en route.

Unless you've lived in a country without dependable surface and water transportation, it is extremely difficult to understand how much transportation influences every aspect of your daily life and actions.

Living in America or Europe, we forget so quickly that much of the rest of the world does not have a fraction of the rail, highway and water transportation system we have available. We do not appreciate our "infra-structure."

MATADI

On the 21st the MV Del Oro had not yet arrived, but the stuff we'd shipped from Kapanga in December had arrived. When the Del Oro appeared in the river next day, we were able to identify it through our binoculars and take movies of its passage to the wharf. The freighter was 450-feet long, with a gross tonnage of 16,000 tons or so, but it looked like a rowboat in the huge expanse of river. Next day we obtained our tickets at the office of NAHV and went to the ship. They'd begun to unload tons of wheat flour as part of the import cargo. When asked, the Captain gave us permission to go on board and remain on the ship while they unloaded the imports and loaded the exports.

That medium-sized freighter carried a maximum of twelve passengers. Only two were on board for the round trip from and back to New Orleans. Mr. Flanagan was a bachelor who'd retired from work in Chicago. Mrs. Myers suffered periodically from severe migraine headaches and hoped to get some relief on the long peaceful voyage. We were the only new passengers who boarded the ship for the return voyage. Missionary families with children didn't use freighters because there was never a doctor on board.

On Wednesday, Jan. 25th, the Del Oro loaded the export cargo. We watched them load our possessions into the forward hold. At times it is best not to watch stevedores handle your stuff. They are not always gentle. One of the most interesting export items was 4000 tons of palm oil. We thought the quantity of oil would make a lot of Palmolive soap. Wrong! Palm oil was destined to be used for quenching hot steel ingots in steel mills.

Phyllis and Mrs. Myers visited the nearby freighter, MV Lubilash, where the Captain escorted them on a tour of his ship. Invariably we found officers and seamen were lonely and usually enjoyed visitors. However, they were often leery of missionaries and halfway expected to be accosted with the question "Brother, are you Saved?"

Being laymen and engineers, we made friends with our officers and seamen in more subtle ways, while quietly witnessing the fact we really and truly were missionaries. Our unique task had been to construct many school buildings, a hospital, residences and churches as our witness to God who'd called us to Africa. Street preaching and pulpit pounding sermons were not our way of dealing with people.

These two freighters, MV Lubilash and MV Lualaba, were named after major rivers in the Congo. Actually the

Lualaba River, as it is called in the Katanga, is the upper most part of the Congo River. The Lubilash River drains into the Congo River, but so does every other river and stream in the Congo basin of 500,000 square miles.

MATADI—LUANDA—LOBITO

For the shortest way home, the Del Oro would have sailed out of the Congo River and headed northwest. But it didn't. We took a 1,000 mile detour in order to unload and load cargo at two ports in Angola: Luanda and Labito.
The Port of Matadi is eighty miles upriver at the headland of that part of the lower Congo River which is navigable for large powered vessels. Before leaving the last of the crystal Mountains, the ship had to deal with one very dangerous situation.
The Devil's Cauldron was still there and will be for many millions of years in the future. This cauldron is created as the Congo River makes a sharp left turn, probably close to ninety degrees, and forms an awesome whirlpool. Going downriver, ships must stay on the right side of that powerful circling water. The big diesel engine of the Del Oro shuddered as it maintained the ship's course against the forces trying to pull it toward the deadly eye of the whirlpool. Sailing ships were never able to get upriver past it. With the fast flowing Congo current, the freighter sailed quickly down river after the cauldron. We passed wide flat expanses of reeds and papyrus in the adjacent swamps. Amongst this expanse of swamp and lowland is the steamy village of Barna. This was the port of entry for the Congo until steamships became powerful enough to navigate

safely by the Devil's Cauldron. After clearing the coastline the Del Oro turned and headed south for Angola.

At 7AM, January 27th we docked at Luanda. It was a beautiful old city that had been occupied by the Portuguese and the Dutch. The Portuguese explorers visited the area first in the late 1500's on their way to locate a route to the East Indies around the southern tip of Africa, Cape of Good Hope. They built a fort to protect the settlement which supplied their own ships with food and fresh water. In a few years, the Dutch explorers conquered the fort and built the beautiful Dutch Reformed Church, which we visited. Later the Portuguese returned and kept control of Angola until 1975. They converted the Dutch church to a Roman Catholic Church.

The roofs and outside walls of all buildings in Luanda were vivid pastel colors. Sidewalks displayed fantastic mosaics using colored tiles. Luanda is a very beautiful, photogenic city.

We made new friends, the Colemans and Blackburns, who drove us around Luanda while they explained some history about the city, the colony and their mission. Methodist and other Protestant missionaries were tolerated, but not encouraged. Their evangelizing activities were restricted. We visited the large Catholic cathedral and shopped for some souvenirs. The Del Oro unloaded its import cargo and loaded many tons of Arabica coffee. About midnight on the 30th we sailed south for Labito.

At night we sailed far out in the Atlantic and lost sight of land. Captain Owen, 1st Officer West, Mrs. Myers and Mr. Flanagan played a very competitive game of Scrabble. About 6 PM on the 31st of January the Del Oro docked at

Lobito. They unloaded the import cargo, continuing through the night. All next day the rain was heavy so we stayed on board. For entertainment we showed our slides to 3rd Officer Holm and Mr. Flanagan. When the unloading was completed, the task of loading many tons of manganese ore brought from the Katanga mines near Kasaji followed. Thursday, February 2nd, was bright and sunny.

We went downtown in order to shop for the beautiful Angola stamps (flowers and animals) and magazines. We discovered the Del Oro library had a few hundred books, but no magazines of general interest. Around noon they finished loading the export cargo. At 2:30PM we sailed out of Lobito, made a starboard turn and began the 1,500 mile voyage to Abidjan in the Ivory Coast.

LOBITO TO ABIDJAN

At sea, we watched Captain Owen, 1st Officer West, Mrs. Myers and Mr. Flanagan in another hotly contested game of Scrabble. Later we visited the bridge where 3rd Officer Holm explained the auto pilot that steered the ship on an accurate, economical course. The next day we were thrilled to watch a huge whale leap clear of the water and come down in a great belly flop. Water flew high in the air! The Atlantic Ocean off the west coast of Africa is part of the migration route used by whales going from the Antarctic to the Arctic regions. On Feb 5th we were at sea with no ships or land in sight. However, we were given a fascinating acrobatic show while a school of very large blackfish leapt out of the water as if they were playing tag.

BIRTHDAY PARTY

On the 6th the ship's cook baked a surprise birthday cake for Phyllis. I'd brought a card and a gift (handkerchief) from Thelma Montgomery.

We were on the bridge about 11PM when the Abidjan lighthouse came in view. Heavy fog rolled in and we anchored in the Atlantic just off shore. We could hear fog horns and ship's bells. Fog horns make a deep, mournful sound that interrupts sleep. When the dense fog lifted after daylight, we could see other freighters anchored near the Del Oro.

A French harbor pilot came aboard to guide the ship through a narrow passageway into their large inland lake harbor. After docking they loaded coffee, logs (four to six tons each) and bales of raw natural rubber.

At sea my tooth became inflamed causing a difficult tooth ache. We went ashore to find a dentist. A good dentist put in a temporary filling that lasted until we reached our dentist in Atlanta.

Next day we went ashore with the Del Oro's local agent, 1st Officer West, Mr. Flanagan and two seamen. They had drinks and food at a good bar/restaurant, while we ate. Mr. Flanagan was a good ambassador for the city of Chicago. The Africans asked each of us where we were from and where we were headed. When Mr. Flanagan said that he was from Chicago, they didn't recognize the name. They'd recognized New Orleans. He explained it was 800-miles inland from the port of New York.

"OH, way back in the jungle!" they exclaimed.

For the rest of the voyage, we heard very little about Chicago.

While in the port of Abidjan we did a little bit of shopping, but the shops were expensive. We did lots of free sightseeing. The town is quite heavily influenced by the French colonial authorities. Most of the buildings were painted in beautiful pastel colors and well designed for the tropics. There were many ships at the wharf. Next day we stayed on board for rest and my haircut by my personal stylist—Phyllis. While we were at the Kennedy School of Missions, a Hartford barber had taught the wives how to do men and boy's haircuts. Since 1950 I'd gone to a barber very few times. It has been much cheaper to get an excellent haircut from Phyllis. The ship loaded only export cargo because on the trip from New Orleans the Del Oro had already off loaded all the import cargos when it had stopped at Monrovia, Takoradi and Abidjan.

In late afternoon we sailed along the coast towards Takoradi on the Gold Coast (now Ghana). During the night we saw lighthouses, village fires and a dim outline of the coast. Again we were on the bridge when we anchored out in the harbor of Takoradi about 5:30PM, Feb 11th. There were too many ships and too few berths at the docks. For three days the Del Oro loaded huge mahogany logs four feet in diameter and thirty-five feet long. A few went into the holds, but most were chained to the decks on the topside.

We took one of the water taxis for a ride to the wharf and walked downtown. Watch out! All traffic drives English style in the left lane. If you look the wrong way you may get hit.

In Takoradi we saw many followers of Mohammed—Muslims, who didn't want to be photographed. Muslims aren't allowed to portray any human form in portraits, art, sculpture or photos. Only in very recent years have some of their religious leaders permitted personal photographs, movies and now videotapes. Islam spread from the Mediterranean coast south across the Sahara Desert with the Muslim trader's caravans. Islam does not have a hierarchy and has no missionaries as we know them. Each Muslim is expected to be a bearer of the news that there is but one God and Allah is his name. Mohammed was the final prophet. Islam has not made much progress farther south than the southern fringes of the Sahara.

The black citizens were subjected to centuries of slave traders. Some of these slaves were taken north and northeast. Other slaves were sold to tribal enemies who carried them to the American and European slave ships calling at ports on the Atlantic coast.

While downtown on the 13th we met Mr. McGinnis, an American Baptist missionary, who drove us on a tour of Takoradi and nearby Secondi. We viewed and took a photograph of his "Wedding Cake" church sitting on top of its own little hill. It looks like the miniature churches frequently used on wedding cakes in the 1950's. In the afternoon we went swimming in the Atlantic Ocean surf on the Gold Coast of Africa. We accepted a supper invitation from Mr. and Mrs. Paul Wiedman, Assembly of God missionaries. Afterwards we watched a movie at the British Council building.

Next day we visited the African Industries shop and sales room. We bought two small wooden elephants, a small ivory Ashanti royal stool, a silver charm stool and linseed oil. The oil was to be used on the large wooden coffee table which had a carved elephant supporting the table top. We gave this table to friends in Wyoming. At lunch we visited with James Clair Appiah, chief of the Fanti tribe. He'd been brought up by British Methodist missionaries and spent eleven months in the USA. As a farewell gift, he gave us a pair of local sandals, which we later gave to the Carnegie Museum in Pittsburgh.

About 7PM we sailed west for Monrovia, Liberia and arrived there about 3AM, Feb 16. Liberia was established in 1836 as an independent African country for former slaves who'd been freed in America. All their currency and stamps are issued in US dollars. The ship loaded many bales of raw crude, natural rubber and a few other products. Monrovia wasn't a prosperous city because the interior is underdeveloped. Firestone Rubber plantations and iron mines are the major developments. Our U.S. Methodist Church has had missionaries in Liberia for more than 100-years, but unfortunately the mission is far inland from the coast city. The ship aft of the Del Oro was loading a full cargo of iron ore which Liberia has in great quantities. They used a tremendous series of wide conveyor belts to load the ore. We left Monrovia and the African continent in the evening. Now we were truly on our way to New Orleans and Home. A sixteen-day voyage on the Atlantic Ocean, Gulf of Mexico and the Mississipi River would bring us to the Poydras Street Wharf in New Orleans.

MONROVIA TO NEW ORLEANS

As we left Monrovia the Del Oro was fully loaded and riding so low in the water the Plimsoll Line was barely visible. The Plimsoll Line is the top of the red barnacle resistant paint on the part of a ship's hull which is usually under water. If the Plimsoll Line is not visible, the ship is too heavily loaded and might sink in rough weather. For the first five days we didn't do anything but sleep, eat, read and watch the ever changing ocean. One day the sea was rough. Another day we passed near two ships and were told they were from England bound for South America.

On the sixth day, we went to the bridge late in the evening after Captain West retired for the night. Mr. Holm, 3rd Officer, had invited me to steer the ship. First, Mr. Holm showed us the strip chart recording the voyage as the auto pilot steered. It was a straight line. He took the ship off auto pilot and let me take the wheel for the next thirty minutes or so. There was a quartering sea with waves coming towards the starboard bow of the ship. After Mr. Holm placed the ship back under control of the auto pilot, he showed us the strip chart I'd produced. It was definitely not a straight line. The fully-loaded 16,000 ton, 450-foot ship was reluctant and slow to respond to my commands through the wheel. Consequently, the strip chart showed a somewhat jagged line for my efforts. Auto pilots are much more accurate than humans. Freighters cost more than a $1,000 a day to operate and travel as economically as possible.

Another day Mr. West, Chief Mate (1st Officer), explained the cargos that Del Oro carried to and from Africa. We included the list elsewhere.

The 25th of February was stormy with rough seas but we never got seasick because we took Dramamine every day. After supper on March 1st we went topside to watch for lights and passing ships. The Del Oro entered the Florida straits between Florida and Cuba. Within a few hours, we saw the lights of five ships going east and two ships going to the west. Ocean vessels have two white lights, one low toward the bow (front) of the ship and one high on the superstructure. By observing the lights, you know which way the ship is headed. We saw the light house beacon at Key West because the Florida Straits are narrow. In 1956 the USA and Cuba were friendly neighbors. Castro arrived on the scene in 1959.

Two days later at 4AM we saw the lighthouse beacon at the extreme southern end of the Mississippi River delta and the Del Oro dropped anchor close enough to see land. This was our first view of the good ole USA in almost five years. That glimpse of the scrubby marsh land looked great to us. We were ready for the crew to move the heavily-laden Del Oro upriver against the strong current of the Mighty Mississippi as fast as the big diesel engine would move. We were anxious to get to our families and friends once again.

A river pilot came on board and we started the slow trip up river against the strong river current. Spring thaw had begun so the river level was high and the water moved swiftly. All day we changed river pilots frequently without stopping because the Mississippi river is constantly moving mud and silt around in the channel between the levees. Each river pilot knows his section of the eighty miles of river channel. The short trip of eighty miles took almost twelve hours at an average speed of less than seven miles-per-hour.

We docked at the Poydras Street Wharf about 4:30 PM and were allowed to go ashore two hours later. After clearing our carry-on luggage through customs, we checked into the De Soto Hotel for some Louisiana food. Next day, March 4th, we toured downtown New Orleans. It took more than 24-hours to unload the huge pile of logs lashed to the deck. Those logs blocked access to the hold which contained our boxes, barrels and trunks. On the 5th of March we returned to the Delta Lines Office. We took possession of all our baggage, cleared it through customs easily and went out to the Hotel Roosevelt for lunch.

Only then did we let our family know we were back in the USA. We sent a four word telegram to the Lewis family in Atlanta:

"YOUR AFRICANS ARE HOME!"

At the railroad station we made reservations on the Southerner for 8AM, Tuesday, March 6, 1956. Twelve hours later we were in Atlanta once again. We'd been gone almost 5 years and we would soon found out how very much life had changed in the USA from 1951 to 1956.

HOMECOMING

Tears of joy were in evidence after the Southerner train (better known as Chattanooga Choo Choo) stopped at the Terminal Railroad Station in downtown Atlanta on a Tuesday, March 6, 1956.
Five years overseas is a long absence from families and friends.
Furthermore, we'd felt so isolated and far away.
Mail was slow. Telephone calls were impossible.
In 1995 telephone calls can be made easily to and from almost any location in the world. Back in 1956 the very first undersea telephone cable was placed in service between the USA and Europe. That cable, long since retired, could carry only the magnificent total of forty eight (48) voice conversations at one time. In 1995 undersea fiberoptic cables carry up to 48,000 conversations at one time.
Air mail service between the USA and Africa required a minimum of two weeks, often a full month. Surface mail and packages spent at least three months on ships, trains and trucks en route to Kapanga. Therefore, from 1952 to 1956, all exchanges of news between us and our families were dreadfully slow.
By contrast, when I worked in Saudi Arabia from 1982 to 1986, I could call home as fast as I could push twelve successive buttons on a touch-tone telephone. Travel to and from Dhahran required less than one day. Air mail letters arrived quickly. Travel and communication changed drastically in 30 years.

At the Terminal, Phyllis' parents, Claude and Thelma Lewis, were first in line to greet us. Not far behind were their three daughters. Each had a husband they'd married during our absence. Huber, Margie, and Huber Jr Parsons were there.

Elaine, daughter #2, married J.B. "Bill" Whitmore. Jessie, daughter #3, married J.F. "Frank" Stodgell. May Belle, daughter #4, married Guy Fish, Jr. Phyllis knew Guy, but not Bill or Frank. I didn't know any of them.

After a lengthy series of hugs, kisses, and exchanges of recent news, we picked up our luggage and walked out of the building. We'd been traveling for more than forty days.

Four years in a tropical climate hadn't prepared us for the raw March weather in Atlanta. Our clothes were thin cotton and our blood was "thinned" by the years of tropical sunshine.

Always the conscientious mother, Mrs. Lewis asked Phyllis "Where's your coat?" The answer was easy.

"Mother, I haven't owned a coat in more than four years."

Neither of us had any clothes except the worn tropical outfits we were wearing. We'd left our cold weather clothes in Brussels when we left Belgium in 1952. We needed none in Congo.

You can imagine the non-stop gossip and intense conversations that occurred among the Lewis family for the next five days. Our new brothers-in-law weren't sure how to interact with two foreign missionaries. Our vocation was evidently new and strange to the three young men who were a salesman, an electrician and an aircraft mechanic. They eventually accepted our eccentricity.

AT HOME AGAIN

From March 6th through March 11th we gave gifts to everyone in the family and showed them many of our souvenirs, artifacts, movie films and photos. Rich's Department Store was the place we both went to shop for clothes. Our missionary clothes weren't suitable for donation to charity.

Sunday morning we were dressed decently enough to attend church at Saint Mark. Our good friend, John Tate, was the senior minister who preached to us in the sanctuary where we had been commissioned. A host of friends welcomed us: J Tom and Martha Smith, Huber and Margie Parsons, Col Frank and "Miss" Agnes Groseclose, Mr. & Mrs. McRae, Mr. and Mrs. DW Brooks, Dawn Atkinson, Jean Luttrell, Ethel King and others. We enjoyed an Open House at the Parsons in the afternoon. More friends came by. It was great to be in Atlanta again.

The effectiveness of the Abidjan temporary filling in my tooth began to wear. Our dentist, Dr. Teague, took about ten seconds to decide that the remains of the tooth had to be pulled. He asked for, and received, permission to place the extracted tooth on display in the Dental School museum. There was no material left in the middle of the tooth, only four small vertical sections projecting upwards at each corner. Dr. Teague said that it looked like a Tiffany mount for a large diamond. He said he'd never seen a tooth with so little remaining in place. He said the French dentist had placed an excellent temporary filling in order to keep it painless for so long.

We headed out to check in with the Board of Missions as well as visit our family and friends and enjoy all the modern USA had to offer. Not used to such excellent roadways, I developed a severe case of car sickness as we approached Arlington. During our stay a local doctor prescribed Dramamine, which took two days to take effect. On Friday the 16th we left Arlington in fairly good weather. It did not last long.

Snow fell on us in middle New Jersey. By the time we arrived at the Lincoln Tunnel under the Hudson River, we were in a blinding snow storm. We crept along the streets of New York City (Manhattan) until we reached the inside garage of the George Washington Hotel at Lexington Avenue and 23rd Street. Snow continued to fall for five days. Traffic came to a complete halt. We have a photo of me on a narrow foot path cleared across Broadway. The snow is up to my belt.

Fortunately, the Board of Missions at 150 Broadway was near the hotel. Saturday and Sunday we walked to a few places of interest, the American Museum of Natural History and the Marble Collegiate Church (Dr. Norman Vincent Peale) among them. Monday we checked in with the Board office, collected mail and took our physical exams. Fortunately, psychological exams were not required for returnees.

During the week we visited the Board office every day to complete our physicals, report on our years of service overseas and collect our possessions shipped from Africa. We retrieved the 16 gauge shotgun and had it professionally cleaned so we could return it to Rod Morrissey. Even though we'd relaxed on the long voyage home and visited Atlanta for a while, we found metropolitan Manhattan a rude awakening to life in the USA.

At the Board Office, Dr. Ralph Dodge, Secretary for Africa, told us not do any church visiting or public speaking for at least three months. We needed to rest after a long term overseas.

At Haber-Fink Photo Shop we bought a new slide projector and large screen for the hundreds of slides we'd collected in Europe, Africa and at sea.

A visit to see the musical "Carousel" was delightful. We marveled at skillful performers at an ice skating show. What a change from Congo! A tremendous amount of African art was on view at the Segy Galleries. It made our collection seem rather puny.

On Saturday, March 24th we loaded the wagon and drove north on Lexington Avenue toward the Merritt Parkway east toward Hartford. Snow was falling thickly!

In Hamden, Connecticut we struggled off the parkway to buy and install some snow chains. Our southern tires had no grip on that snow and ice. For the next few days, we visited the Kennedy School of Missions and our friends in the Hartford area. Sunday we attended a Communion Breakfast given by the Methodist Men of Greater Hartford. Our own bishop of Congo, Bishop Newell Booth, was the speaker.

We dined with Rod and Margie Morrissey, showed them slides and, with sincere thanks, returned the shotgun to Rod.

We renewed our really great friendship with Mrs. Shellabear, who'd been so kind to us while we attended the Kennedy School of Missions.

On Tuesday, March 27th, we drove to Somerville Massachusetts, (near Boston) to visit Immanuel and Valborg Bitsch-Larsen, our own Congo doctor. He was doing special studies at the Massachusetts General Hospital. They found the Boston area to be much like their home country, Denmark, and felt at home.

We continued visiting friends and family over the next few weeks.

After a pleasant visit with Phyllis' relatives, we drove to Harrisburg in eastern Pennsylvania in order to visit Bob and Anita Fenstermacher. Anita had been with us at the Kennedy School of Missions and the Ecole Coloniale in Brussels. Max Ritter, her husband, died in the Congo in 1953. (see Odds & Ends) She'd married Dr. Robert (Bob) Fenstermacher, whose last name means "window maker."

We shared stories and showed our slides.

Two long months after landing at New Orleans, we finally arrived at Santa Rosa for a visit with Dad and Mom Little. They said that it was about time!

Meanwhile, we'd been thinking about our future actions. We wanted to adopt children, but no agency, not even our own Methodist Children's Homes, would place children with any missionary families who were going overseas again. In addition, the situation in the Congo was so unsteady, construction might be impossible for several years.

We decided to resign if I found a good job.

We finally returned to Atlanta on April 12th.

For a month, we unpacked, distributed gifts, shared souvenirs and renewed friendships. On May 5th we visited the First Methodist Church in Eastman as guests of Mr. & Mrs. Johnson. Eastman First Methodist Church supported us during our term.

We returned to North Avenue Presbyterian Church to chat with Dr. Broyles, who'd officiated at our wedding. At Saint Mark we spent many hours with dear friends. In College Park we attended the First Methodist Church with Charles and Sue Crawley. There we heard Catherine Parham, a fellow missionary in the Congo. She was a great teacher and missionary. The church has installed a beautiful stained glass window as a memorial to her service and witness.

We were tired, but slowly re-acclimating to American culture. Our friends were so interested in the Christian message in general and in our Congo missions in particular. We partially ignored the Board's request and spoke to youth groups, women's societies, Methodist Men, civic service clubs and even preached a sermon or two, while we were supposed to be resting. It came naturally.

At one of the meetings, a young man said he was quite interested in becoming a missionary, but he loved to travel. Having traveled thousands of miles in recent months, we told him he'd better love travel or he'd never be happy as a missionary. Every missionary we ever knew has logged thousands of miles each year using feet, bicycles, cars, trucks, trains, busses and airplanes.

In late August, I was hired by the Continental Oil Company (CONOCO) in Houston, Texas. They sent me to Frannie Field, Wyoming as my very first assignment.

CONOCO's regional engineer told me I'd first be assigned to Wyoming. Afterwards I would go on to Oklahoma, Texas and Colorado before receiving a permanent assignment. It's difficult to rent apartments for two to three months; most landlords want at least a six-month commitment, preferably a year.

We decided to look for a house trailer we could pull with our wagon to accommodate the situation.

January 1957 was so cold the thermometer never rose above 30 degrees BELOW ZERO for a full week. We had to install an electric powered head bolt heater in the engine block of the wagon in order to keep the engine warm enough to start. We managed to keep the trailer warm most of the time. However, our incoming water line and outgoing sewer drainage pipe froze periodically. Shopping for groceries was an ordeal we did infrequently.

Going out in the foul weather was a nightmare.

Our next assignment was for two months at CONOCO's Laboratory in Ponca City, Oklahoma. Enroute the weather was terrible. While we traveled through the Wind River Canyon in Wyoming we battled with snow drifting across the highway. Late one afternoon in Kansas we found ourselves in a sudden but severe ice storm with no place to stop. As it became darker and darker, we inched along on a slick, icy surface. As we drove around a slightly banked curve, the trailer slid down the slope across part of the lower lane. Finally we found an open motel and stopped until the weather warmed up a bit.

In Wyoming, we'd been corresponding with Kapanga missionaries who kept asking us to return and build some more structures.

Money was available but they had no builders. We wrote the Board of Foreign Missions and asked if they would take us back. When we arrived in Ponca City we received their one sentence reply: WHEN CAN YOU SAIL?

The Board asked us to go to the University of Oklahoma at Norman for psychological and psychiatric tests. Our old friend and fellow missionary Bill Davis had already written to the Board that he didn't need to take any such tests. One term in Congo proved he was crazy!

Neither the psychologist nor the psychiatrist had ever been out of the U.S. They said they had no real idea what you needed to be or know in order to serve well as a foreign missionary. Our answers to their Ink Blot tests, and other psychological tests, were based on our African experiences. As a result our answers puzzled them. Such answers didn't correlate to typical American experiences.

Anyway, they approved us as being normal.

Our answers to other questions also baffled them. They asked, "Why do you want to go back to the foreign mission field? Aren't there opportunities for service in the US near your families?"

Neither had the foggiest idea about a "Call from God."

May 31st I resigned from CONOCO. The Regional Engineer asked me how much salary I'd get at this new job. He was amazed when I told him it would be half the CONOCO salary. Oil companies were quite desperate for engineers and hiring them away from each other as the engineers completed training periods. He was flabbergasted when we told him we would be missionaries.

"What the Hell will you do as a missionary?" he blurted.

We are still trying to answer that question.

MISSIONARIES AGAIN

June 1, 1957, we began our second Belgian Congo term as "engineer-missionaries." Our US Passport Office requested your profession in the front section of the passport.

Our passports listed "ENGINEER-MISSIONARY." During the next few years more than one customs official asked, "Are you an engineer or are you a missionary?" Very few were ever convinced we were indeed both. However, they never refused us entry into any country. They probably considered our declaration of our profession as a strange American designation to be tolerated. To them it was not illegal, just illogical and peculiar.

Sunday, June 2nd, we spoke to the Sunday School at the small Berkeley Methodist Church in Denver. After visiting friends along the way, we returned the trailer to the dealer in Billings, Montana on June 6th. A few days later, we enjoyed our last trip to Yellowstone with our Lovell friends, Dick and June Wessel.

Sunday morning, June 9th, we both preached at the Lovell and Denver Methodist Churches. We spent the afternoon at Powell Methodist Church.

Rev. Ward and Fernan Barter raised enough money to purchase a truly magnificent Model 70 Winchester 375 H&H Magnum caliber rifle with case and telescope sights. That rifle put lots of meat on our table during the next three years in Congo. We lost contact with the Barters, but thirty-six years later, they appeared at our home in Bradenton. They were wintering in the central part of Florida and somehow found our address.

On our way to the Missionary Conference at Greencastle, Indiana, we toured Mark Twain's home in Hannibal, Missouri, and visited the tomb of President Lincoln in Springfield, Illinois.

Our week at the missionary conference was great. We were reunited with many fellow missionaries. Now that we were veteran missionaries, we fully appreciated the stories told by senior colleagues.

On June 23rd we visited John and Frances Kirchner (Frances is my youngest sister) and family at Fort Campbell, Kentucky.

On a visit to the fort, I went inside one of the Armored Division's battle tanks. It confirmed my belief that Navy service was preferable to service in the Army. Inside a battle tank, the space is crowded, cramped and noisy. Tank engines have a minimum type of muffler in order to get the maximum output. Noise is not a factor on a battlefield.

Leaving Fort Campbell we headed southwest for a last visit with my parents in Santa Rosa, Texas. Along the way we visited Phyllis' Aunt Mary in Columbus and my Georgia Tech classmate, Farris Gibbs, in Meridian, Mississippi.

In Houston we spent a few hours with Shorty and Frances Little. Watermelons were in season and we ate our share.

On July 1st we arrived in Santa Rosa where we stayed until the 13th. We spoke at several church meetings and spent one day at the beach on South Padre Island. In 1957 it was a lonely uninhabited barrier island stretching 135 miles from near the mouth of the Rio Grande River northward to near Corpus Christi. Less than a mile of brackish water in the Laguna Madre separates the long narrow island from the mainland. In those days the island wasn't developed and had no permanent structures on its wide, beautiful beaches. In 1995, the south end is highly developed with motels, a convention center, restaurants, bars, clubs and beach cottages. It is now *the* place for college students to frolic on their spring breaks.

A MEDICAL PROBLEM

As missionaries we were always required to take a complete medical physical exam before going overseas. When the mission board doctor was told about my visits to Naval Hospitals for some possible kidney stones, he requested I have a cystoscopy at the Valley Baptist Hospital.
Unfortunately the urologist was a real sadist if I ever met one. He was rude and had no feeling.
The actual cystoscopy was performed in a frigid operating room while I was dressed in a ridiculously skimpy hospital gown which didn't provide any protection against the cold air. The instrument was a long piece of rusty galvanized pipe wielded by a very insensitive "doctor." As the examination progressed, the pain level reached such a height I believe I surely left a full set of my fingerprints imbedded permanently on the steel rails of that cold operating table.
The staff of the hospital kept me overnight for "observation."
Early next morning they said I couldn't leave because the "so-called urologist" had gone fishing without signing any release. I quickly told them they better call the Texas

Rangers if they wanted to keep me. I intended to get out of their hospital immediately.

In a few weeks we were scheduled to go overseas as missionaries. No absent-minded, poor-excuse-for-a-doctor was going to prevent or delay that sailing. The bill had been paid in full. There was absolutely no justification for keeping him any longer. They released me in a few minutes.

SECOND CYSTOSCOPY

About forty years later, our family doctor innocently suggested I go to a urologist for another cystoscopy. He was rather surprised at my strong, vehement, negative opinion of all urologists. In fact, I very flatly refused to even consider going to any "urologist" for any reason whatsoever. Our doctor assured me, in writing, that such tests had been improved. I reluctantly went and this time the cystoscopy wasn't fun, but it didn't involve any of the pain and suffering of the first one. This urologist was a real doctor. He and his staff were quite considerate. The cystoscopy was performed in his comfortable office on a padded table. Again, the test was negative.

Many more tests have been performed in later years for urinary and prostate conditions. X-rays, ultra-sound exams and Protein Specific Antigen (PSA) tests have all been negative. Ultra-sound exams are not painful but are rather awkward because the physician inserts the sound source wand into the lower colon in order to get it close to the prostate and urethra. The exam seems to take forever but is actually completed in twenty minutes. X-rays are painless and the PSA test involves nothing more than a small sample of blood drawn from a vein.

MISSIONARY DEPUTATION
—JULY 21 to SEPTEMBER 22

This is an account of our missionary visits to churches, which is known to missionaries as deputation. A succeeding section will detail our non-deputation activities for the same period of eight weeks. Time spent in the USA by missionaries was called a furlough in 1957. However, a missionary furlough has no resemblance to any military furlough. Army personnel on furlough are free to do what they wish to do, or do nothing.

Missionaries on furlough do much deputation, which is more like work. Between July 21st and September 22nd we spoke to many groups at sixteen locations in two states. We think there were more, but sixteen is all we recorded in our diary:

1.   July 21...We spoke at Park Street Methodist Church near Atlanta, with our dear friend Jimmy Moore as pastor.

2.   July 28...Traveled to Eastman First Methodist Church to speak to several groups. JB Hutchinson, pastor.

3.   August 4...spoke to the Young Adult groups at Saint Mark Church in Atlanta.

4.   August 11...Full day at Decatur First Methodist Church near Atlanta. I preached at both morning services. That packed sanctuary was expecting a missionary sermon. What they heard first was a short "story" about our literacy work. Supposedly, Phyllis taught a cannibal chief to read

and write using the Laubach system. He wanted to write a book. When we asked him for a title, he replied "*How to Serve Humanity.*" The first small snicker broke out towards the back of the sanctuary. It quickly spread as the remainder of the congregation caught the real implication behind the title.

The rest of the sermon was serious and the congregation agreed to support us for our next term. They gave us a large portable battery-powered Zenith shortwave radio. The radio was great because we were able to listen to news from BBC in London and the Voice of America. In the afternoon, we met with the local Commission on Missions. In the evening we had supper with and spoke to the Methodist Youth Fellowship.

5.   August 18...Morning, Returned to Decatur First Methodist Church to speak to the Keystone Bible Class, about 100 men.

6.   August 18...Evening, Spoke to the congregation of Saint Paul Methodist Church, Atlanta, where our friend Jimmy Moore was now pastor.

7.   August 21...Returned to Park Street Methodist Church. Spoke at Prayer Meeting at 7:30PM.

8.   August 25...Lewis Davis, My best man at our wedding, invited us to his church, Acworth (Ga) First Methodist Church. We spoke to the MYF at 7PM and congregation at 8PM.

9.   Sept 1 & 2...Returned to Thomasville (GA) First Methodist Church where Weyman Cleveland was pastor. Weyman was a brother to Mike Cleveland, who baptized Melton at St Petersburg First Methodist in 1962. At Thomasville we spoke to the Sunday School, morning

service, afternoon Methodist Youth Fellowship and the evening service. We stayed with Dr. and Mrs. James Reid in their beautiful southern plantation home. This church again faithfully supported us during our second term.

10. Sept 8...St. Petersburg, Florida—spoke to the morning congregation at Saint Luke Methodist Church. At 6 PM we met with the Methodist Youth Fellowship at First Methodist Church.

11. Sept 9...Phyllis spoke to the Women's Society of Christian Service (WSCS), Wesleyan Service Guild and the Commission on Missions at St. Petersburg First Methodist Church.

12. Sept 11...Phyllis spoke to her Aunt Alice's circle of the WSCS at Saint Luke Methodist Church.

13. Sept 15...Return to Atlanta. At 10 AM we spoke to the Hill Bible Class of more than 100 men at Saint Mark Methodist Church. At 6:30 PM we shared our experiences in Congo with the combined Methodist Youth Fellowship and Young Adults at Saint Mark Methodist Church.

14. Sept 17...Phyllis spoke to the general meeting of the WSCS at Saint Mark Methodist Church.

15. Sept. 18...Showed slides of our first term in Congo to the Mid-Week Prayer meeting at Saint Mark.

16. Sunday Sept. 22...at the morning service Saint Mark gave us money to buy a Volkswagen when we arrived in the Congo. They'd earlier given us: a manual adding machine from Mr. Harold Carithers, a self-winding Swiss watch that lasted 25 years, and a beautiful Bible from the WSCS.

NON-DEPUTATION ACTIVITY—
JULY 21 to SEPTEMBER 22

As additional evidence that missionary furloughs are not at all like military furloughs, we now present a partial list of the non-deputation activity that occurred during those same two short months:

1. Medical and dental: three visits each to the dentist for x-rays, cleaning and fillings. Visits to doctor for physical exams, also polio and tetanus shots.

2. Packing household goods: bought 8 used 55-gallon steel drums with lockable lids. Cleaned out chocolate frosting and shortening. Painted outside of drums and bought padlocks. Then purchased and packed: clothes, shoes, kitchen utensils, linen, housewares, pots, pans, Kleenex, Kotex, toilet paper and much more. Made complete detailed lists as we packed. Shipped the drums and baggage to New York.

3. Sold the wagon to an auto dealer in Atlanta. Much paper work involved: title transfer, tag removal, cancel insurance and deposit money to pay off the loan on the wagon.

4. Renew Passports and get Visa.

5. Spent one full day helping Guy and May Belle Fish move from Atlanta to Marietta.

6. Celebrated Bill and Elaine Whitmore's wedding anniversary.

7. Were interviewed and photographed by a reporter from the *Atlanta Constitution*.

8. Toured central Florida with family: Bok Tower at Lakeland. Great Masterpieces (mosaics) near Lake Wales.

9. Numerous meals and parties with old friends, new friends and family.

10. All day excursion, with family, to Lake Allatoona, near Atlanta.

11. ROY WARREN...Phyllis' Uncle Roy owned one of the largest real estate firms in the Atlanta area. He gave us money to buy a large Gestetner duplicating machine (mimeograph), which was sorely needed in Congo. Photocopiers didn't exist. One day we were sitting in Uncle Roy's downtown office when we saw a big helicopter hovering over the state capitol area. Uncle Roy said the governor had stolen everything else now he was trying to steal the gold leaf covering the dome of the capitol. In the late 1800's, Georgia had gold mines and a US Mint at Dahlonega. Gold leaf on the capitol dome is pure Georgia gold.

12. Phyllis' parents were planning to leave Atlanta and move to St. Petersburg for retirement. They were gone for several days. We explored the large, full basement of their home. Among other items, we found May Belle's old, rusted tricycle. May Belle, the youngest child, was 18. Claude Lewis did his own painting around the house. Some of his paint brushes were covered with dried paint. They could have been used for large hammers. But you get an idea of what we found. We spent two full days gathering old stuff and moving it to the sidewalk. Fortunately, the trash collectors came by before the Lewis' returned. Claude Lewis grumbled a bit about the good brushes we discarded. Thelma Lewis was rather pleased we'd decreased the amount of possessions they now had to pack and move to Florida.

We were already anticipating, with pleasure, the two weeks sailing from New York to Matadi, Congo with no responsibilities and no meetings, except for meals on the ship.

With reservations on the Belgian Lines freighter MV Lualaba for Friday the 27th, we had less than four days of frantic activity before boarding time. We checked into the George Washington Hotel late on Monday afternoon.

At the Board of Missions office we spent time as follows:

1. Purchasing Office for material and food to be bought and shipped to Congo.
2. Advance Special Office—First Churches in Thomasville, Decatur, and Eastman sent almost $5000 for our work.
3. Financial Office—settle travel expenses, tickets and travel money for going to Congo.
4. Africa Office—conferences with Melvin Blake about our work to be done in Congo.
5. Shipping—they required detailed, typed lists of everything we'd already sent to them for forwarding to Congo, and for insurance purposes.
6. Legal Office—executed our wills and left the originals with them.

In our spare time we had meals and conversations with several of our fellow missionaries. Louis Johnson, Central Congo, would go with us on the Lualaba. On Wednesday we went downtown near Wall Street where we bought a Kodak 35mm camera and equipment at the Haber and Fink Photo Shop. Our old first-term camera didn't take slides very well. At 3 PM on Friday, September 27, 1957, we boarded the freighter MV Lualaba in New Jersey and sailed past the Statue of Liberty soon afterwards.

VII. BELGIAN CONGO/ REPUBLIC OF CONGO
(1957-1960)

PREAMBLE

This term of service was so turbulent we cannot describe adequately all situations and events in Central Africa. Some of our memories remain vivid to this day. These were easy to write down, but other memories remain elusive. Our diaries show long gaps with blank pages when we were busy existing and not writing. As active Christian missionaries we could proclaim our religious message. At the same time we felt obligated to refrain from meddling in Congo politics. We couldn't tell the Congolese who to vote for because we were friends with the Belgian colonials, Roman Catholic missionaries, numerous merchants (white and black), and many of the Congolese in a variety of tribes and political parties. Some of our local Roman Catholic priests didn't refrain from meddling and suffered the consequences later. Eventually they were disliked by almost everyone, including the political parties and candidates they supported publicly.

What we have written is a tiny part of what happened. Our account includes only what we saw and heard, plus what we read or heard on the radio. No English language news organization {*TIME, NEWSWEEK, US NEWS & WORLD REPORT*} had any reporters who were knowledgeable about the Belgian Congo. The French language news reporters were no improvement, with one shining exception. A Belgian magazine called"*Pourquoi Pas?"*

[WHY NOT? in English] published many articles that accurately reflected events in Congo. They were a steady source of current events within the colony.

One intriguing French word used repeatedly was "effervescence." The spelling is identical in both French and English. However, after being translated into English and reading between the lines, the code word really meant "turmoil." It aptly described the political and economic conditions in Congo from 1957, when we arrived, until 1960, when we were flown out as evacuees. Conditions since 1960 can best be described as a state of "*beaucoup d'effervescence*," or in English "terrible turmoil." These later conditions, 1960 to date, are not described, we were not there.

To our knowledge, no book or long article, in English or French, explains life in the Republic of Congo/Zaire from 1960 to date (1996). Many articles were written about various events in the mid-60's and mid-70's. Missionaries have written books and personal accounts of their service in the Republic of Congo/Zaire. However, the writers had the same challenge we have faced. It is difficult to have any accurate knowledge about what really happens in a vast, diverse country. News gathering and interviews require knowledge of the 200 languages. US and UN personnel wrote some long articles and books years ago but the authors had very limited actual knowledge about their subject.

We've written two accounts for the same period of time—our second term. First, we have written about the people and events as encountered in our missionary life from 1957 to 1960. Second, we wrote about the political events that influenced our life and all of Congo from 1957 to 1960. Eventually, the political events impacted our missionary world enough to culminate in our flight out of Congo.

Incidentally, the United Nations declared 1960 the International Year of Refugees. It was very appropriate for us in the Congo. We have assembled these accounts from our own incomplete diaries, Guest Book, memories, writings by other missionaries, news sources and our letters as kept by Phyllis' mother, Thelma Lewis.

Our Congolese friendships included long personal acquaintances with Jason Sendwe, later one Prime Minister of the Republic of Congo; and with Moise Tshombe, a President of the Republic of Congo and the only President of the Republic of the Katanga as they tried to secede from the Republic of Congo. Sendwe was killed near Lake Albert and his body thrown to the crocodiles. Tshombe died while a prisoner in North Africa. He had a slight history of heart trouble. We suspect his final cardiac arrest wasn't due to an internal cause. Sendwe and Tshombe ended their lives as bitter political enemies but both were our friends. They are representative of the many divisions that split Congo. There were never just two sides in the Congo, rather almost as many sides as major tribes existed.

This chapter has been difficult to write and brought much sadness to our hearts. Congo [Zaire] is rich in natural resources: iron ore, gold, diamonds, manganese, copper, tin, cotton, palm oil, rice, sugar cane, corn, peanuts, etc.

In human resources the Congo [Zaire] has many talented individuals: preachers, teachers, nurses, doctors, political leaders, merchants, technicians, fishermen, army personnel, farmers, engineers, etc. The infant Republic of Congo should have become a great and prosperous nation sometime after 1960.

Unfortunately, the current (1995) long-time dictator of Zaire has been greedy, ruthless and oppressive for over thirty years. He's utilized ancient tribal animosities to keep his iron grip on the country as he bleeds it to death.

Tshombe told us in late June 1960 that black politicians in independent Congo would be more dangerous and damaging than the white colonials had been. Moise Tshombe died unexpectedly in 1968 as Mobutu gained complete power as a dictator by using threats, bribes and guns.

Mobutu's story is outside the scope of this account. He will be mentioned several times, but we don't have sufficient knowledge to write his sorry history. Someday, perhaps someone will write that book.

Now we return to a chronological account of our second term in the Belgian Congo.

HOBOKEN—CAPE VERDE ISLANDS—MATADI

The Belgian Lines freighter MV Lualaba was similar to and just about the same size as the Del Oro.

On board were a few more passengers: several US citizens of Portuguese ancestry traveling to the Cape Verde Islands, two Roman Catholic nuns from Canada and our friend, Louis (Pat) Johnson, returning to central Congo.

After leaving Hoboken, New Jersey, on September 28, 1957, we soon said goodbye to the Statue of Liberty. Next day we sailed into Hampton Roads (Norfolk), Virginia in order to load more cargo. As we left Hampton Roads, the ship encountered heavy rains that quickly turned into a full-blown Atlantic gale. For several days the freighter, big as it was, tossed about like a cork.

On the 6th of October, Captain Corbay escorted us on a thorough tour of the ship. We went into the spacious engine room where we asked why two shiny fifty-five gallon barrels hung on a bulkhead. He smiled as he informed us the "barrels" were spare pistons for the enormous diesel engine. From the engine room, we walked aft in a narrow passageway that contained the huge steel drive shaft that turned the large propeller. These guided tours are never possible on cruise liners. Such tours make voyages on freighters much more interesting.

On the same day, Phyllis became sick with blotchy red spots appearing on her upper body and face. As usual the Lualaba carried no doctor. Captain Corbay radioed the port authorities at Port St. Vincent, Cape Verde Islands, and requested they have a doctor meet the ship when it arrived next day.

A Portuguese physician did come on board and examined Phyllis carefully. He gave her medicine to take immediately. He gave Captain Corbay some small vials of medicine to be given to Phyllis in two injections over a period of four days. At least one officer on every freighter is trained to give injections by hypodermic needles. The doctor assured Captain Corbay the disease causing the spots wasn't contagious. He said she'd be free of them within 24 hours. As it turned out, they disappeared the next afternoon.

If the disease had been contagious, the captain was prepared to leave us under the doctor's care in Port St.

Vincent. There we would have waited for the next ship headed for Congo, or back to the States. Captain Corbay accepted the doctor's prognosis and allowed us to stay on board.

The Cape Verde Islands are a small group of islands way out in the Atlantic Ocean near the coast of Africa. From our own observation, they had a bare minimum of arable land and a scarcity of trees. Ironically, in Spanish and Portuguese the name Cape Verde means "Green Cape."

This is similar to the name for the island of Greenland, which is not green at all but is pure white when seen from a 747 airplane flying at 45,000 ft. On the 8th of October we left Port St. Vincent and sailed near other rather barren islands that were part of the Cape Verde Islands.

On this voyage, Captain Corbay was more sociable than Captain Owen of the Del Oro, who was friendly but often ate by himself and kept busy as master of the vessel.

After leaving the Cape Verde Islands, Captain Corbay spent lots of time with his passengers, including breakfast on the 14th. We crossed the Equator again. This time we were part of King Neptune's Court and not victims. Our victims were the two young (early 20's) and shy Canadian nuns, Sister Marie de St. Honore and Sister Marie Monique. It was evident they'd heard some stories about this Baptism of the Equator. They were visibly uneasy about getting through their initiation. The summons, in French, by King Neptune sounded ominous and included allegations of various misdemeanors. Pat Johnson, Phyllis and I dressed in the most outrageous costumes we could scrounge. Actually, the worst treatment for the two sisters occurred when we provided them with one slice of *dry* bread and a *small* glass of water, while the rest of us enjoyed a huge, sumptuous meal in their presence. They were quite relieved when the ceremony was over.

In truth, they were pleasant company when we chatted with them during the voyage, at mealtimes, under normal conditions. Their maternal language was Canadian French which was close enough to our Belgian French.

As we were neared the African coast next day, the captain informed us the Congo fresh water current can be measured 200 to 500 miles out in the Atlantic Ocean. This distance varies with the amount of rain that has fallen in the upper Congo River basin. As noted earlier, the basin receives more than six feet (72 inches) of rain in some areas annually.

The first river pilot came on board in the early afternoon. We docked at Matadi late that evening after our second trip through the Devil's Cauldron on the lower reaches of the Congo River. We have never wanted to contemplate what could happen if a shop's engine failed and was drawn into the "eye" of that enormous whirlpool. We never dared ask if any ship had lost power in that cauldron, either.

Do not think about "What If?" Accept "What Is."

Note: Sailing vessels had no chance against the eddy and several were lost before ship captains were aware of the Cauldron's existence.

MATADI—LEOPOLDVILLE—LULUABOURG

Jaqueline, a pleasant young woman from the Agence Maritime Belge, came aboard and stayed with us all day on October 16th. She assisted us in getting new identity cards and import permits for our guns (one rifle and one shotgun). We began the documentation for our customs declarations concerning the rest of our baggage. After the Lualaba unloaded our baggage from the hold, we cleared it through customs and transported it to the railroad station. Early on the third day, we left the ship and cleared our hand luggage past a customs official easily; at 6AM he was half asleep. A ten-hour train ride brought us to Leopoldville where we spent the night at the Leco Guest House. Leco was an acronym for Librairie Evangelique du Congo (Evangelical Publishing House in Congo) which printed most of the Protestant literature for our missions. At the Leco Guest House we had dinner with our delightful friend, Dr. Carrie Sprague, a physician for the American Baptist teaching hospital at Kimpese, west of Leopoldville.

In the downtown area, we bought some African created artwork. Several colorful paintings are with us to this day. Using a block of dense wood from an ironwood tree, an African artist had carved the almost full scale head of an old African man. It is a remarkable likeness, probably of museum quality.

We made Sunday reservations with Sabena to fly on another DC-4 to Luluabourg while our baggage traveled by train, riverboat and truck to Kapanga. The flight encountered heavy rain and much lightning. But that wasn't the most interesting part of the flight!

A few minutes before we were scheduled to land at Luluabourg, the aircraft began to travel in a circular pattern. This seemed odd to us because with maybe two or three landings each day, arriving aircraft shouldn't have to wait for a clear runway.

Our captain came on the loudspeaker with the information we would begin climbing quickly for a while. Fasten all seat belts. The plane climbed up to ten or twelve thousand feet, then it nosed over in a steep dive. A few thousand feet from the ground, the pilot pulled the nose up in a steep turn. We heard a loud clunk from the underside of the aircraft.

The crew hadn't been able to get the landing gear down either hydraulically or mechanically. They'd used the climb, steep dive, sharp turn and gravity to get the landing gear down into its proper place.

If that maneuver hadn't succeeded we would've made a wheels-up, belly down landing on a field with extremely limited rescue and fire-fighting equipment. We never dwelled on the possibility of a DC-4 belly landing in the Congo.

A good meal and pleasant night at the Au Bonne Auberge Hotel calmed our nerves.

BANKING SYSTEM IN CONGO

The Banque du Congo Belge had branches in every major city. We believe they used a system developed by the US firm, National Cash Register. At the end of every banking day, they prepared and sent us a complete record of all credits and debits to our account for that day. It was an excellent system that allowed us to balance our check books against their records with ease. Never before or since have we found any better system.

LULUABOURG AND THE BLACK BEETLE

The next day we located the Volkswagen dealer and looked at his small stock of "Beetles."

Everyone was black. We asked for another color. He quickly informed us that proper missionaries MUST drive black cars. Henry Ford would have been pleased. While building some 15,000,000 Model T's, Mr. Ford had always proclaimed that you could have it in any color you wanted as long as that color was always "black."

Further discussion with the young salesman appeared useless. We chose a black Beetle which had bright red leather upholstery: $1,500.

For our readers who are too young to know about the original post-war Beetles, we will describe one. Beetles were two-door coupes with manual 4-speed transmissions and a heater (why in the Congo?). But they had no other accessories, features or options. They had no automatic transmission, no radio, and no power anything. They had an air-cooled four-cylinder 42 horsepower engine in the rear end. The engine had absolutely no pollution control devices, no cruise control, a very simple carburetor and a directly connected steering wheel which contained a dinky horn. There were no shock absorbers and minimum springs. Of course, there were no seat belts and no air bags. The tiny trunk (luggage compartment) was under the front hood. This space also contained the eight-gallon main and one-gallon auxiliary gas tanks. There was no gas gauge. This neat arrangement meant the gasoline tanks were just forward of and above your knees. In case of a severe head-on collision with a larger vehicle, the driver and passenger were likely to receive a shower bath of raw gasoline.

However, in spite of its multiple idiosyncrasies, the Beetle, also known as "the Bug" was fabulously popular around the world.

With their small size and light weight, Beetles easily averaged 30 to 35 miles per gallon in the Congo. This economy was important to us because regular gasoline sold for at least $1.00 dollar per gallon in 1957. In the USA, gasoline cost thirty cents ($.30) per gallon in 1957. The auto tag was permanent and stayed on the vehicle until the vehicle was scrapped. We did pay an annual tax based on the horsepower of the vehicle. Our salesman helped us obtain a Belgian Congo driver's license. As we mentioned earlier, Belgium had no driver's license requirements but the Belgian Congo did require licenses to drive.

KAPANGA

Congo roads hadn't improved, so we spent the usual nine hours on the 100-mile trip from Luluabourg to Kapanga. Along the way we visited the Willis Pipers at Katubwe, the Joe Spooners at Moma and the open air Basala Mpasu tribal market.

At Kapanga we were greeted by Warren and Jane Freeborn, Bill and Doris Davis, Al and Patricia Broadhead, Tove Jensen and Carroll French.

A host of Lunda friends came to welcome us back. At the Kapanga government post we duly registered our identity cards, driver's licenses, the Beetle and gun import license. Then we obtained hunting licenses.

A small comfortable two-bedroom house was available, but it needed renovation. For six months we lived in it, while we removed an inner wall, added steel casement windows and improved other areas.

Unlike our arrival in 1952, no language study was needed and no long trips were necessary.

In a few days, Al Broadhead, male missionary nurse, relinquished all construction projects to me. Al returned to full-time to service at the hospital, district dispensaries and leper colony.

I was soon involved in construction and remodeling work. Phyllis was assigned to work with girl students at school and do bookkeeping for the business accounts at the hospital.

I did more remodeling on the Davis residence, put a new roof on a store house and installed steel windows frames with glass panes in the new nursing school dormitory. There were any number of various smaller jobs around the hospital that took a lot of time to locate and plan.

Once again, we were more than a hundred miles from building supply stores. Even the smallest items, like nails, required weeks to obtain. Obtaining special items often required months because they might have to come from South Africa, Europe or the USA. In order to enter the Congo, they required import licenses and payment of customs duties.

The remodeling of our own home required about six months as we did it by increments while we lived in the mess. At one time Phyllis and our houseboy, Diuru, worked at removing the old lime whitewash on our walls. That task was successful, but not very pleasant nor very easy. Phyllis resolved never again to attempt to remove old white wash. Just put a new coat of whitewash over the old coat.

While we were remodeling the house, we built a small garage for the Beetle. Hot tropical sunshine and heavy rains can quickly shorten the life and decrease the usefulness of vehicles. We had to do our own maintenance and care of autos. There were no car washes or service stations or repair garages within many miles. Car care was entirely the responsibility of the owner. The nearest dealer was more than a hundred miles north of us.

Two long trips were eventually required.

One day we received a telegram telling us a shipment for the hospital had arrived at the border town of Dilolo. I went with the truck to clear the shipment through customs. While in Dilolo, I bought barrels of gasoline and kerosene. We couldn't buy much fuel in Kapanga, only a barrel or two when one of the merchants had some in his stock temporarily.

On a side excursion at Sandoa Mission, I went hunting with Marvin Wolford. Marvin killed a large reedbuck and I killed a smaller one. We transported the hospital supplies to Kapanga.

A short while later, a trip to Luluabourg was slightly more exciting. The gas line to the truck engine sprang a leak. Leaking raw gas in the engine compartment cannot be tolerated. Of course, the leak occurred far from any garage or mission. Kabash, our Lunda truck driver, and I stopped the leak with a thick glob of heavy soap which was held in place by a Band-Aid. This mechanical first aid worked until we got to a garage in Luluabourg.

ELUSIVE ELAND

In Africa, one of the largest and rarest antelope was the big eland. There were a few small herds between Kapanga and the Angola border. South of Mwini Dikamba's village, the Congo government created a game reserve of several thousand acres around some large natural salt licks. Several of us received permits to hunt eland outside the reserve.

In late November, Warren Freeborn, Bill Davis and I spent three full days walking across the beautiful savannas near Mwini Dikamba's village. We never did see an eland on that hunt or any other. Those eland were smart enough to know they were safe inside the reserve. We determined this because our tracker kept insisting the eland were just "piswimp palemp." But we didn't want to be fined or sent out of Congo. By the way, "piswimp palemp" meant the eland were just a little bit far away to the south. This told us they were in the haven of the reserve.

END OF 1957

As a fitting finale to 1957, the household goods and supplies we shipped from Matadi on October 16th arrived at Kapanga on Christmas Eve. Unpacking those barrels and boxes for the next few days provided us a Merry Christmas indeed.

CHURCH CONSTRUCTION

When Bishop Lloyd Wicke, of Pennsylvania, visited our station, he was greatly impressed with a need for permanent roofs on churches. Grass roofs become dry and catch fire easily.

But first a bit about his arrival on a dark and stormy night.

When the missionaries gathered after dinner he said, "Tomorrow, I want to treat you to lunch at a restaurant!" There was a stunned silence as we tried to suppress our smiles. He'd just traveled over 100 miles on dirt roads as he got farther and farther away from the nearest restaurant.

Our Bill Davis gently reminded him of that fact. Bishop Wicke was a good sport and retracted his invitation; he would eat with us.

In our serious discussions about church expansion in the Congo, we told him the best plan should include a requirement that the Congolese Christians build the mud brick structures. They could also cut any trees needed for the lumber needed for rafters, church benches, and door jambs. After the local congregation did all that work, with readily available rural Congo resources, then the American churches could provide money to buy the permanent aluminum roofing. This is so expensive the local church can't afford it. He readily agreed.

When he returned to Pennsylvania, he raised enough money to buy steel framework, rafters, purlins and roofing for the large Musumba church. Additional money came to us for permanent roofs on smaller churches, including the first one completed by the pastor and congregation at Chala.

Months later, in August 1958, a steel erection crew from the Congacier company brought the framework from Luluabourg. They soon erected the steel columns on concrete pads we'd poured in place. They erected the steel rafters, connected the rafters with purlins, and attached the aluminum roofing on top.

Meanwhile, the Musumba congregation had made tens of thousands of kiln dried bricks for the walls. The Paramount Chief, Mwant Yav Ditend, made the first few bricks with his own hands. This was most unusual for a Paramount Chief; who does absolutely no manual labor. But he wanted to show his people how important the church was going to be for him. At that time he wasn't yet a Christian.

Bill Davis obtained money from churches in the USA to buy a small stained glass window to be placed above the altar. Belgian artisans created a colorful window showing Christ holding a Congo lamb.

Again, a case of one-ups-man-ship with the Roman Catholic Church across the dusty plaza. They had no stained glass windows.

Another US church contributed money for a tall steel cross to be erected in front of our church. Our Congolese pastors requested it be a bit taller than the wooden Roman Catholic cross across the plaza. Our cross was taller.

MISSIONARIES***COMING AND GOING*** 1958

E. Stanley Jones, famous Methodist missionary to India and a prolific writer of Christian books and magazine articles, visited Elisabethville, Jadotville and Kapanga in January. He was a self-disciplined person. His daily schedule included established time for undisturbed meditation, prayers, exercise and reading or writing. This didn't diminish in the least the fact that he was a pleasant person. When he talked with you, he gave you his undivided attention. What you said seemed to be important to him. In person he was exactly the same person you observed in his sermons and books.

Other famous people whom we've known were not always the same in private as they were in public. E. Stanley Jones returned to Congo in early 1960 when he conducted some of his famous Ashrams. We will write about his Kapanga Ashram when we get this account to 1960.

Dr. Warren and Jane Freeborn left in February for a well-earned homecoming. They'd spent one year in Belgium at the School of Tropical Medicine, and several years at Kapanga Hospital. Warren returned to a medical practice in Indianapolis where they adopted a delightful little baby girl Susan. They never returned to Congo.

Backing up a few years, let us tell you about their arrival at the Kapanga station. Like other missionaries, they had taken advantage of the short distances in Europe and traveled to Paris. When Doctor Warren was telling us about their trip, he used complex medical terms in describing one Paris location they visited. He implied they were observing "patients" who had lithe lower posterior lumbar development, excellent muscular coordination in movements of the torso, lengthy formation of lower extremities, pleasing cranial adornment, well rounded mammary glands, et cetera. In fact, they had not been to a medical convention but had watched the girlie show at the world famous Folies Bergere.

Roy and Esther Smyres spent time with us in late February. We'd met Roy during the Missionary Conference at Greencastle. He was a remarkably effective speaker because he mixed his great sense of humor with a deep Christian faith. For about 20 years he served with the Board of Foreign Missions. Many years later he wrote an excellent little book *The Thoughts of Chairman Smyres*, with the sub-title "Chairman, under God, of his own life and thoughts." This book presents a collection of two or three page thoughts Roy remembered from his long life of Christian service.

It is a take-off on the infamous little red book the Communist Chairman, Mao Zedong, required all "good" Chinese communists to buy, read, and practice. It was the Chinese communist "bible," as they had no god.

Dr. John and Helen Wengatz, a couple of retired pioneer Angola missionaries, arrived in March. They spent several months visiting and enriching our Congo mission stations. Their vivid stories about life many years before in primitive Angola made us appreciate the life of relative luxury we were leading in 1958. From their accounts, and other missionary friends who served in Angola, it soon became quite evident the Belgian colonial authorities were much easier to work with than the Portuguese colonial laws and authorities.

A good friend, Ed LeMasters, spent three months in a jail in Portugal because he'd simply read from the pulpit some of St. Paul's writing as recorded in the New Testament. The Portuguese were so paranoid they considered St Paul's writings to be seditious and politically inflammatory. Another major difference was the fact Portugal allowed, even encouraged, their retired colonial men to remain in Angola or Mozambique. Retired Belgian colonials couldn't reside in the Congo. Portugal was poor, small and crowded, so the government encouraged retirement somewhere else.

At that time Portugal was ruled by an eccentric, absolute dictator, Salazar. One of the early ball point pens leaked in his shirt pocket and ruined the shirt. He immediately prohibited the importation, sale and possession of ball point pens. When we traveled across Angola in 1952, we had hidden the few pens we owned. It was said Salazar would indeed fine you and/or put you in jail.

Our fellow Methodist missionaries, Dr. Hugh and Marjorie Deale, visited us during June. Hugh was the dentist at our Minga Station in central Congo. Hugh told us the same story our Presbyterian dentists shared with us. He could usually find more cavities in one missionary's mouth than he could find in the entire population of a Congolese village. We ate desserts and candy too frequently and brushed or flossed our teeth too infrequently. Our Congolese friends chewed the ends of a stem from a wild shrub then brushed their teeth with the frayed ends. They could find and use this shrub even when we were on hunting trips. Incidentally, it was amazing what edible products the Congolese trackers found when they went with us on hunts. We carried most of our food, except meat, and they carried very little.

In July Arne and Greta Reinar spent a few days with us. They found it quite a different life style from their home station at Mulungwishi. That station has its own railroad depot and is only a few miles from the large city, Jadotville. They had most of the modern conveniences with access to many shops and stores. They found Kapanga isolated and somewhat primitive.

In 1960 we'd use the Reinar's green Volkswagen to travel from the Congo to Kitwe, Northern Rhodesia. The Reinars had already left Congo and returned home. (How did THEY get a green Volkswagen?)

WHITE AND BLACK TECHNICIANS

In the field of technical training, the Portuguese decided long ago Africans could not, therefore, should not, be trained as technicians. As a result all skilled jobs in Angola were reserved for Portuguese citizens. This led to the curious situation where only Portuguese were telegraphers, railroad mechanics, train conductors and locomotive crewmen. When the trains arrived at the Congo border town of Dilolo, the black Congolese crews took over the same, or equivalent, equipment and operated all trains within the Congo. Most of the skilled mechanics, electricians, telegraphers, technicians and equipment operators at government posts and in the huge mines were black Congolese. A similar incongruity existed at the border railroad crossing into Rhodesia. All Rhodesian train crews and skilled mine workers were English or South

African. White crews would bring the trains to the border where the black Congo crews would takeover. In our conversations with them, neither the Portuguese nor the English could see any inconsistency in their beliefs about African abilities.

SOCIAL EVENT OF 1958

On August 2, 1958 the number of single missionaries at Kapanga was reduced by two. The number of couples was increased by one. Tove Jensen, RN, long term Danish missionary nurse, married Carroll French, agronomist (farmer) from Nebraska, in our church. When missionaries married in the Congo it became a unique mixture of laws and cultures. Belgium required a civil ceremony in order to make a marriage legal. Any church ceremony was optional. In the Belgian Congo, the laws were slightly different. At one time the colonial officials also required written parental consent before any couple could marry. Age wasn't a factor. The couple had to produce the written consent of their parents, if alive. There were some other legal requirements. Carroll and Tove became engaged on February 28th. It took five months to complete all the required paper work before they could be married. The Lundas had their own set of traditions about marriage. Their weddings required a series of ceremonies that lasted for three days or more, involving both extended families. Tove's Danish heritage added some features. Carroll's American culture brought other traditions, such as the wedding cake and reception. Mixing all these laws, customs and cultures produces a most interesting event.

Tove worked for many years in the maternity ward, women's ward and girl's school. The older Congolese women brought traditional Congolese wedding gifts. They accompanied them with a long lecture to Tove on how to be a good wife. Their advice must have been relevant because the result has been a successful marriage for Carroll and Tove. Now they have children and grandchildren. In recent years Tove has reluctantly given up her Danish citizenship to become a US citizen. At heart she is still a Dane.

OUR LETTER TO CHURCHES IN USA—1958

"In humbleness and awe, not understanding at all, we read and reread that Christ left all the glory of heaven to live as a man that we might learn how to live, and dying, he bore our sins. By trusting in Him we live in eternity. In Him, Christ, we have found life! Our hearts sing and we tell of his love. Listen, the hills and rocks praise him for his goodness and mercy.

Our mission station is small, we are only four couples who have answered God's call..........but we are still human and pray constantly that the "beauty of Jesus" may be seen in our lives.

We want to share with you some of the things that happened in Kapanga district recently:

****Over 600 new believers have entered the classes of preparatory membership

****15 village congregations have paid their own pastor's salary this past year. Two permanent village churches have been constructed this year. Two more are under construction. Bricks are being made in three other villages, two for churches and one for a class building.

****All the nurses at the hospital tithe. They were the first group. Teachers started tithing two months ago. Workmen plan to begin tithing next month.

****Our school teachers have pledged to try and lead more students to Christ by example of their own lives.

****People in our church congregations are asking for work to serve God, we now have more Sunday School teachers.

****In Musumba, the capital of the Lunda Tribe, the congregation has been busy making bricks to build a new 50-foot by 80-foot church. Mwant Yav Ditend, Paramount Chief, went down to the brick kiln and with his own hands helped to pack mud on the kiln before they began firing it. What a wonderful day!

{Note: As royalty the paramount chiefs never do any physical labor. He never carries anything, except a ceremonial item.}

Thank you for all your prayers and gifts to make this mission a more effective witness for Christ in this vast land.

Harry & Phyllis

MISSION TO CHURCH

From July 20 to 27, 1958, we attended the Annual Conference in the city of Jadotville. It is not necessary to write much about the annual conference. It was a repeat of other routine conferences, except for one new item of business.

Bishop Booth presented his proposal that the time had come to change our legal name. Our Mission Methodiste should become the Eglise Methodiste au Congo, Methodist Church in the Congo. After rather extended talks and discussions from missionaries and Congolese this change in status was approved and sent to the colonial authorities. Some Congolese were reluctant because they feared a possible loss of missionary support and finances from the Methodist Board of Foreign Missions. Some of the missionaries simply didn't believe the Congolese were ready to assume responsibilities. However, the bishop was correct. Very soon all district superintendents and pastors of all our churches were Congolese. Ordained missionaries were supporting personnel in the local churches, schools and teachers in the seminary.

Within two years the Congo would be abruptly thrust into independence. Within three years. the bishop would be a Congolese. Our good pastors were men like Jacob Kambilo and Joab Mulela, who'd been trained by John Springer. Others were Andre Nawej, Jean Mij and Pierre Kachandj, who'd been trained by Dr. Piper, John Brastrup, Anna Lerbak, Marie Jensen, Irving Everett and Thomas Brinton. All of these pastors lived long, useful lives as witnesses to the *Good News*. We also had Bible women who walked to tiny villages to talk about Christ. Some couldn't read, but they memorized much of the Lunda Bible. They effectively influenced life in the villages.

OTHER EVENTS IN 1958

The Corbitt doctors, Duvon and Phyllis and their family, arrived in February 1958. Duvon and Phyllis earned their M.D. degrees from Vanderbilt University in Nashville at the same time. They came to us with two small children, a girl named Jeannie, and her younger brother, who was baptized as Duvon III but known as Danny. Duvon was a highly-skilled surgeon and Phyllis was a general practitioner or family doctor, they were a tremendous asset. Making clay bricks by hand had become very expensive and cement became cheaper. In February we made concrete blocks with hand molds. Each concrete block was equivalent to eight bricks and walls could be built quicker. We never used clay brick again. From April 20th to 26th Phyllis, I and Kabash drove the big truck to Elisabethville to obtain supplies and buy a Volkswagen ambulance. When Phyllis went on trips she shared in driving the truck. She became very skilled at driving our heavy truck with its multiple gears. She learned the truck went through mud holes easily.

The Volkswagen ambulance was used frequently by the hospital. But it wasn't sturdy enough for Congo roads. Eventually it blew the engine apart and died. In May, the Davis station wagon developed engine problems we couldn't repair. We loaded it on the old green truck and the three of us lumbered to Luluabourg. The truck cab was small and not air-conditioned. Part of the time, Phyllis rode up in the station wagon and enjoyed a great view of the country side. In Congo, the tall elephant grass growing alongside the roadway kept you from seeing more than a narrow view up and down the path.

While I was driving a truck load of lumber on the road from Kambangu to Rubwiz, a Congolese man, Muhong, came barreling down the hill on a bicycle. We could see him, but he couldn't see the truck. I pulled to the side of the road as much as possible and stopped. Muhong never looked up until he slammed his bicycle into the front bumper. He suffered head injuries, a broken left arm and broken left leg. Fortunately, I had two carpenters with me. They quickly loaded the injured man into the truck and took him to the hospital. His family wanted to collect "personal injury" damages from the mission. Administrator Van Damme went to the site, interviewed me and the two carpenters. The Administrator was satisfied the man had unwisely run into a parked vehicle. Therefore, no damages were due. Duvon Corbit treated the patient, set both broken limbs and drew some liquid from his skull in order to relieve pressure on the brain. This is the only injury accident I had in 55 years of driving.

From November 3rd to November 13th we used the transit and steel tape to measure the angles and lengths along the nine (9) sides of the mission land concession. We placed concrete markers at each turning point. The original markers had been trees, rock outcroppings and other natural locations. Some had simply disappeared. Phyllis drew a map of the concession. We would use this map when we built the airstrip in 1960. The airstrip could not be located on the mission concession.

GIANT MUSHROOM

In the early morning of September 20th a shy, little girl appeared at our kitchen door. She carried a truly enormous mushroom that was over twelve inches tall and fifteen inches in diameter. We know the dimensions because we couldn't believe our eyes and measured the mushroom.

Our houseboy assured us it was edible and safe to eat. The little girl, about eight years old, told us they needed money. Her mother was sick in the hospital and in need of cash. Would we help them and buy the mushroom?

Of course, we bought it. For several days we ate delicious mushroom in every recipe we could find. We never saw another giant mushroom at any time or any place in the Congo. On hunts, we often found some mushrooms in the woods and jungles that were normal size.

ANIMAL CONTROL

In the Congolese villages all domestic animals roamed freely because there were no pens or cages for any pet or livestock. This had been acceptable in the old villages. Definitely, it wasn't a satisfactory situation on the hospital grounds. To state it discretely, urine and excreta from sheep, goats, pigs and cows create an unsanitary environment.

Doctors Corbitt and staff created an animal pound. For a week they proclaimed warnings to everyone. The fine was 50 francs (about three day's pay) for each animal that was impounded.

On the first day they caught seventeen animals. We bought one of the unclaimed goats for 400 francs and gave it to the animal control officers, our workmen.

Stray animals disappeared.

TRAVEL IN 1959

In late February, we went to Sandoa where Dean Freudenberger demonstrated a very small gasoline powered tractor for possible use in Congo. A group in California was quite interested in extensively testing this prototype tractor for good service and suitability.

They hoped to build a few in the USA, then build them in a factory in Africa. Planting, cultivating and harvesting crops was totally manual labor, which resulted in small harvests per human hour of work. We started to write "man hour" but that wouldn't have been a true statement.

In the Congo, men chopped down the trees and cleared the land. Women used short handled hoes to prepare the soil, plant the crop, harvest it and prepare the food. Mechanization was a good idea. Two of our mission goals had always been to improve health and increase the local food supply. Nearly every mission station had an agronomist, or farmer, whose goal was to improve farming.

A trip to Luluabourg in May solved one of our real problems. Since the beginning of mission work in 1908, the stewardship of money had been done with manual bookkeeping methods. This involved laboriously posting receipts and expenses in bulky ledgers and into individual accounts using double-entry bookkeeping. Balancing these accounts and eliminating errors was tedious.

Jim Halverstadt, the business manager of APCM in Luluabourg, showed us a very fool-proof and simple Swiss system of double-entry bookkeeping. This patented system used carbon paper interleaves in order to make simultaneous entries in the general ledger and individual accounts. It worked!

We bought the system and saved hours of time. However, the system didn't solve our mechanical problems. The truck broke down as we were leaving the city. After four days in the repair garage, we left again and kept going to Kapanga.

From July 3rd to the 12th we attended Annual Conference in the city of Elisabethville where Bishop Booth and Bishop Springer were ordaining new pastors.

As a young man, Bishop Springer came to the Congo in 1908. He was so successful, effective and well known that for many years the Congolese Methodists called themselves

"SPLINGERS." They could pronounce an "R" by itself, but not in a combination of letters like "SPR."

A great many of his house-help, porters and students became teachers and preachers. They would have called him "Saint John" if such a title existed in their tribal languages. Some of their sons were ordained in 1959 by Bishop Springer.

After Annual Conference, we drove across the border to Kitwe, Northern Rhodesia.

Watch out Again! All the roads were paved, but traffic used the left lane, English style. A left turn was easy. To navigate a right turn required steering wheel turns that were against all your instincts and driving habits. Phyllis wasn't too calm as huge mining company dump trucks (10-tons) roared past her side of the car in the right (wrong?) lane.

Kitwe is a beautiful city of modern shops where we bought some things we couldn't obtain in the Congo. It was also the location of the Ecumenical Institute that prepared a lot of good Christian literature with African themes and illustrations. This made them much easier to re-translate into many local languages.

Quite often our own American and European cultures are impossible to translate intact. "Bread of Life" means nothing to a people who never, never eat any bread. "Ruku", cassava mush, was the Lunda equivalent of bread of life.

MEDICAL CARE

Rosemary Manchester and Betty Metcalf came to the Kapanga Hospital in late February. Betty had a minor operation and stayed a short time. Rosemary had a major operation so her recuperation lasted several weeks. She missed her husband and four children.

One day, Bill Davis had just shaved and put on shaving lotion. As he walked through the room, Rosemary stopped him from leaving. "Come back through here. I have not smelled shaving lotion in weeks!"

An embarrassed Bill complied with her request.

In spite of some rumors to the contrary, many missionaries were quite normal.

In March, Elsie Freudenberger came to the hospital for the birth of her baby. A boy, David Owen Freudenberger, was born at 6:30 AM on March 20, 1958.

In May the malaria bugs bit Phyllis, me, and Lindy Davis. Phyllis had the worst attack which lasted about five full days.

Chills and fever, alternately, kept her in bed most of the time. I had chills and fever for two days. Lindy Davis, less than two-years-old, had malaria badly enough to cause minor convulsions before recovering.

Usually common malaria is a nuisance. You feel weak for a few hours then the symptoms go away. However, cerebral malaria is painful and can be fatal. Thankfully, none of us had cerebral malaria.

In early November, Phyllis had an operation to remove a small growth from one breast. That specimen had to go to the city of Johannesburg to a pathologist. Congo and Rhodesia had no pathologists. In a few weeks the report came back negative. As we wrote earlier in this story, our life in Congo taught us one thing—PATIENCE.

VISITORS IN 1959

Bishop Gerald Kennedy, Rev. Wondenburg and Rev. Wesley Neal, California Conference, came to Kapanga. They were extremely interested in construction and maintenance activities. When they returned to California, they organized a work team of six men who came to Kapanga on July 3, 1960. The work team story will be told in our section on 1960. Bishop Kennedy was well known and respected in California.

When I and Paramount Chief Mwant Yav Ditend went to California in late 1960, the Bishop got them on a CBS talk show with Zsa Zsa Gabor, Jack Benny and Danny Thomas. That appearance is described in the Odds & Ends section.

Al Burlbaugh, civil engineer and builder, and Ray Watson, pharmacist, came to Kapanga from the Central Congo Conference. Al was interested in our construction techniques and equipment of the hospital. Ray was interested in the pharmacy and our school for nurses.

On June 17th we entertained the new Territorial Administrator, Monsieur LaLievre. He was a good man and a great improvement over several previous administrators. In 1960 he helped us with the airstrip by staying out of sight, officially, until it was almost complete. Our last visitor came when Monsieur Herbert and a crew from ConGacier arrived from Luluabourg to install a metal roof on the shop and garage at the hospital.

NEW MUSUMBA

In 1958, Mwant Yav Ditend had gone to the International Fair in Brussels as a guest of the Belgian government. After he returned he talked repeatedly with Duvon and me about two subjects. (1) His capital village of Musumba had several thousand inhabitants but absolutely no planning. (2) He had flown on convenient aircraft in great comfort and enjoyed that mode of travel more than vehicle travel on Congo roads.
First, he said he would provide any land needed for a new village if we would plan it, survey it and advise his people how to build it.
As Paramount Chief he was custodian of all land settled by Lundas. There was no private property. Duvon and I agreed to do what he asked.
However, our Bishop told them they could not spend any money because the project wasn't on our mission concession.
Mwant Yav Ditend asked Duvon and I to write the municipal regulations for New Musumba. As Paramount Chief he would issue and enforce them. That was all the challenge that Duvon and I needed.
Most of the missionaries were noncommittal or skeptical that they would get it done. In consultation with the pastors, teachers and tribal leaders Duvon and I drafted a list of regulations concerning anyone who wanted to build a house in this new Musumba.
That list is too long, but a summary will suffice.

MUNICIPAL REGULATIONS FOR NEW MUSUMBA
1. At least 100 lots would be surveyed and plotted
2. Sites would be designated for municipal buildings
3. Two sites for churches (Roman Catholic and Methodist)
4. Wide streets
5. Residence must be built of brick on rock foundations with metal roofs. Must have doors, windows and concrete floors.
6. A pit privy to be built on each lot
7. Children must attend school
8. Sick must go to the hospital (discouraging witch doctors)
9. Each lot must have fruit trees, bananas, flowers, & trees
10. Being a secular community church attendance was encouraged but not mandatory
11. Extended families were required to live in separate areas.

Each lot was awarded by drawing a number from a glass jug held by Mwant Yav in person.

When we left in 1960 about fifteen residences had been completed or were under construction. To the chagrin of local male chauvinists, a strong-willed widow woman completed the first house.

MISCELLANEOUS—1959

The pastor of the church at Chala village came to the mission with the information that an elephant was destroying their gardens. Elephants do like peanuts. This beast was trampling their peanut gardens as he pulled up the plants in order to get the peanuts. He had been destructive in a corn patch or two. Bill Davis and I bought an elephant hunting license for $100.

On the first day of the hunt we tracked him for hours but never got close. Before noon on the second day we were getting closer.

Following his tracks across an open plain we came upon an uprooted tree. That tree was at least a mile from any other tree. Evidently it had displeased the big elephant because he butted it, then wrapped his trunk around it and yanked it out of the ground, roots and all. We realized we were not tracking a small elephant. I could barely reach around the tree trunk, which means it was about twenty inches in diameter.

We continued following the highly visible tracks as they went down into a valley of tall trees and thick underbrush. Within a few minutes we froze as we heard a loud crash. Elephants often feed on certain tree leaves and small limbs, and less often on grasses. We heard him noisily stripping a tree. Although we could not see him, he was close enough for us to hear his stomach rumble as he ate. As these loud sounds continued, we moved slowly towards their source.

Suddenly the monkeys and all the birds in the treetops went deathly silent. That silence was an alarm signal to the feeding elephant. He quit eating! With no wind he could not smell us. With dense undergrowth he could not see us.

Being a very cunning animal, he began a methodical search for the intruders, who might endanger him. We barely moved a muscle, except to breathe quietly. He made a circle. Every ten yards or so he would butt a tree and make a terrible sound. He was determined to scare us off or at least locate us. He continued this circular path around the jungle. Finally he came around toward us. But all we could see were his big white toenails and the top of his head. The dense undergrowth of shrubs and vines hid the rest of him. We had no target for a good shot. We waited.

Suddenly he thrust his long trunk through the last shrub and opened his wide nostrils. As he inhaled, he smelled humans. (After being in the tropical jungle several days, we did have strong odors). In an instant he wheeled around and flattened a five foot wide path as he fled out of that patch of dangerous jungle.

We dared to breathe again! When he had stopped and turned around, his closest footprints were fifteen paces from ours. We measured that short distance and went back to camp because it was getting late in the day.

Next morning as we began tracking again, the trail looked like a bulldozer passed that way. His footprints in the soft jungle soil were large enough for me to put my two boots end to end inside one footprint.

Obviously he was a full-grown elephant and very smart. In mid-afternoon of the third day we were crossing a grassy plain when we thought we saw a tall termite hill. It wasn't. It was our elephant and he was in the open.

Again, there was no wind, as we walked slowly through the six-foot-high grass. Bill had a 458 caliber rifle. I had my 375 caliber rifle. Rapidly we shot him five times. He was wounded severely, but not fatally. He turned and ran across a small stream into a wooded area. It was late in the afternoon and we didn't wish to encounter a wounded elephant in poor light. We went back to camp and returned early next morning.

To prove how smart that elephant was, we found he'd taken temporary refuge in a small grove of trees on the next hillside. There he'd backed into the trees for a long wait while he watched his trail. He planned to ambush his tormentors. We knew he'd stayed there because most of the grass inside the clump of trees was trampled down. His stumbling tracks were easy to read all day but we never found him. Being late on Saturday we had to return to the mission. We never hunted on Sunday.

An African hunter found the dead elephant. He chopped out the tusks and brought them to Musumba. We paid him a reward. Bill kept one tusk. I took the other tusk. They were medium sized for 1959 and measured about 36 inches in length. Neither of us have tusks today. Bill gave his away; I sold my tusk.

We are positive the elephant was big because his footprints were twenty-four inches in diameter. He was a tall elephant because we found a horizontal tree limb he'd used to scratch his shoulders. The bottom side of the limb had mud and hair on it ten feet from ground level. We measured.

We're not sure when these following events happened as we failed to record the dates in our diary, but on other hunts we had close encounters with elephants, lions, hyenas and wild dogs.

Our African trackers always recommended, really they insisted, that we pitch camp on the plain. They insisted the plains were safer at night than the jungle or deep woods.

One early morning we got up and walked around the camp area. We quickly became alert when we discovered a pride of at least three lions had circled our camp during the night. A little farther out we made another discovery. At least two elephants had gone by while we were sleeping.

Hyenas and wild dogs are scavengers. They are not fast enough to kill the healthy animals that lions, leopards and cheetahs can. Elephants, wild dogs, hyenas, lions, and leopards leave sleeping hunters alone. We found out snakes never bothered us, either.

Frequently we found lion tracks near our campsites when starting out to hunt. On one memorable hunt I almost tried to run while still zipped up inside my sleeping bag. About 2AM a male lion wanted to let the neighborhood know HE was king of the jungle. He let out a majestic roar that sounded so close we thought he was in the midst of our camp.

Actually the lion was a mile away, but in the stillness of an African night the sound was blood curdling. We didn't sleep much during the remainder of the night. NO, you cannot run inside a zipped up sleeping bag. Anyway, I didn't know which way to run.

HOW BIG ARE ELEPHANTS?

To illustrate African elephants are really big we will recite a true story about one elephant and his encounter with a Ford station wagon on a Congo road.

Kapenda Tshombe, Moise's father, and his sons created a thriving Congolese business with many retail stores.

One night two of their employees were driving along an isolated stretch of road between Sandoa and Kapanga. Fog was thick in the low places. Visibility was limited to a few yards.

Lots of cotton was raised in the Katanga province and hauled to market on large trucks. A load of loose cotton was heaped in the open truck bed then covered with a gray tarpaulin.

As these two Congolese drove into a foggy valley, they saw this tall, unlit gray mound in the dim light from their headlights. They were driving a large Ford Station Wagon with a V-8 engine. Thinking it was a stalled cotton truck, the driver honked his horn loudly. The gray mound woke up, wheeled around and charged the noisy contraption that disturbed a sound nap.

That mound was an African elephant standing and sleeping on the warm sand of the roadway.

We do not know the exact sequence of events. We do know somehow the elephant jammed his tusks through the windshield and wrapped his trunk around the steering wheel to twist it. Broken windshield glass cut his trunk and angered him. He stomped on the hood so violently he tore the engine loose from its mounts.

Then the elephant backed up a bit and kicked the station wagon. This violent kick turned the wagon completely over as it landed on the tires again. We know this happened because there were elephant tracks UNDER the wreck. Meanwhile, the two Congolese were scrunched up under the dashboard. Eventually the unhappy pachyderm went away.

When our friend, Maurice Persons, came along next morning, he found two very frightened and almost "white" Congolese. The driver and passenger were speechless at first. Gradually they recovered enough to tell part of the story.

Before You Honk,
Identify Your Target!

ONE HAZARD FOR OUR SURGEONS

When operating in the abdominal or facial areas of Congolese women, our surgeons had to be very precise.

The local women had scar tissues in intricate patterns on their faces and abdomens. These markings were part of the local culture. The location, type and design of these scar tissues had definite meanings. They could not be altered without altering the significance. Therefore, our surgeons had to be very precise when suturing any incisions on the surface of the face or abdomen.

In case of error the women and their families would become critical of the surgeon's skill.

MEDICINE, PRAYER AND FAITH

Our mission doctors and operating staff always prayed with patients before surgery. One afternoon I met Duvon on the hospital grounds as he was making his late afternoon rounds among surgery patients.

Duvon was muttering to himself "I'm going to re-write some medical textbooks. They are wrong."

That morning he'd performed a hysterectomy on a woman. When he went to her bed she was gone. The nearby patients assured him, she hadn't died. Duvon searched for her. Only five hours after a major operation, he found her happily chopping food for her supper. He told her to get back in bed. She replied he'd removed her pain and she was well, "Thank You."

With no torn sutures and no bleeding, she continued chopping wood and preparing her meal. Duvon came away mumbling about how faith had healed her.

A miracle? Ask any woman who has had a hysterectomy. Does prayer heal?

After an operation any part of the body that was removed was put on display outside the operating room. This proved to the family and friends the operating team had removed something "bad".

One testicular tumor weighed 20 kilograms (44-pounds). That man had greater mobility afterwards. In fact, he soon danced and shouted with joy at his new freedom. Our doctor said the tumor had probably been growing for five years. Who knows why the man had never come to the hospital. With that size tumor, he could no longer move a single step. We brought him in on a load of lumber.

On another occasion, Duvon operated on a man for a hernia, which were common in Congo. They are dangerous because if they become strangulated they will kill you.

With spinal anesthesia, the patient was awake while he intently watched the surgery. He could see it by looking into the small mirrors of the operating light. Duvon knew the man was a local witch doctor because of the unique pattern of scar tissue on his abdomen.

Duvon decided to tease the man by saying that a witch doctor could not perform such surgery, could he? No answer was forthcoming.

Physicians find out what illness you have; then they decide how to cure it. African witch doctors specialized in the WHY. Why did you get sick? Why did your child die? YOU had displeased some god or spirit. You must pay the witch doctor to appease the evil one.

DR. ARTHUR AND MRS. MAUDE PIPER

When the Piper Memorial Hospital was dedicated and opened for service in 1954, the Pipers and Miss Marie Jensen hadn't been able to attend. All had retired prior to the planning and approval of this modern hospital. They were anxious to see it.

In 1959, they scheduled a visit to Kapanga. Miss Jensen arrived on November 6th. Mwant Yav Ditend and a large group of elderly Lundas warmly greeted her. Some had been her students; all had been her friends for years. They reminisced about her arrival on foot in 1916 and marveled at her arrival by plane and auto in 1959.

A week later, Dr. and Mrs. Piper arrived. Dr. Piper had received a chief's crown from a previous Mwant Yav. Now it was to be Mrs. Piper's turn as Mwant Yav Ditend awarded her a crown. A stream of older nurses arrived to talk about the early days. They were eager to show the veteran doctor their new hospital.

When Dr. Piper entered the first operating room he was overwhelmed at the sight of the big operating light. He never had electricity during thirty-eight years at Kapanga. His eyes sparkled as he watched the skilled Congolese nurses assist Dr. Duvon Corbitt in an operation.

In the laboratory, Dr. Piper had tears in his eyes when he saw the modern microscopes and other lab apparatus. The X-ray was something he'd dreamed about but never had in his day.

All three were very pleased and grateful as they read the big bronze plaque *Piper Memorial Hospital* beside the entrance doorway.

Next day the younger Congolese nurses performed an excellent reenactment of the original arrival of these three missionaries: the Pipers in 1914 and Miss Jensen in 1916.

After a few more days of non-stop conversations with old and new friends the Pipers left. Congolese and missionaries knew they wouldn't see each other again on earth.

On November 24, 1959 the Pipers wrote a letter to their "Friends in America" from Kapanga Mission station. The following are two paragraphs from that letter:

"What a wonderful experience we are having in this place which was our home for so many years. (Editor- 38 years) We are seeing all the wonderful changes which have taken place since we left here in April, 1952.

Our hearts were stirred to the depths as we saw the wonderful new 200-bed hospital equipped in a modern way, as few hospitals in Central Africa are. It is now being staffed by Dr. Duvon Corbitt and his wife, Phyllis, also a physician. And by a group of variously trained Congolese workers."

PRIZE POSSESSIONS

In early September we received word that the Broadhead family wouldn't return to Kapanga as expected. They had left some of their possessions in storage on the station. I packed these things for shipment.

Meanwhile, the political situation in Congo deteriorated each week. After talking it over, we decided to send some irreplaceable souvenirs, gifts and photographs home with the Broadhead shipment. We packed and shipped two steel barrels filled with souvenirs and photographs.

At that time none of our fellow missionaries sensed any need to ship anything out. Although Congo had some troubles, our fellow missionaries believed it would muddle through the problems.

Three months later the Congo situation was visibly worse. Two other missionaries agreed it was prudent to ship irreplaceable items out of Congo. The Corbitts sent three large boxes and the Frenchs one box. We shipped two more steel barrels and a foot locker.

If we hadn't, we would have lost most of our prized possessions. In July 1960, we'd fly out of Congo with only forty pounds of luggage.

EVENTS IN 1959

In January 1959, we'd started a formal apprenticeship program on the work crews. The older skilled workers had gone away as young men to work in the mines or industries in large cities.

Our most experienced truck driver/mechanic, Mutombu Nyangula, was a Luba from Tshikapa. He was with us in order to receive medical treatment for an early stage of leprosy. He was a skilled mechanic and a very pleasant person.

Several workmen had gone away to the city in order to work in the mines, smelters, or other industries. One of them had been an electrician's helper. Another had worked in a garage. But the younger men were not going away to the cities. Many stayed in Lunda territory.

Therefore, with no trade schools anywhere in the Congo, we had no source of technicians or workmen. We started the apprentices with months of training in masonry, carpentry and simple automotive mechanics.

This program continued until Independence in 1960, when all such activities ceased with our evacuation. A few of our mission stations have resumed the training of masons, carpenters, electricians and mechanics. It has not been easy. Sporadic fighting and government intervention have been a continuous problem.

Steve and Mark Davis joined the church on Sunday, January 18,1959 after being baptized by their proud father, Rev. William D Davis. Their mother, Doris, and younger sisters, Susan and Lindy, watched the sacrament with pride. On February 18th I was in Luluabourg on business when I met a fellow missionary. After dinner we sat on the balcony and enjoyed two Schimmelpennich's cigars. This is the only "forbidden fruit" I enjoyed during his two terms.

AIRSTRIP MWANT YAV DITEND

Mwant Yav Ditend's second dream was to build an airstrip near Musumba. The Belgian Congo government refused to build an official airstrip. Therefore, the Paramount Chief wanted to build one with local labor. However, he didn't know how to design and build it. He just wanted to use it and quit traveling on those miserable roads.

Duvon and I wrote or talked with pilots in the Congo and elsewhere in order to get tentative specifications for an airstrip. They determined that the maximum slope should be three to five percent from end to end. Preferably it should have no slope from side to side. For prestige purposes, the chief wanted it wider and longer than the nearest government airstrip at Sandoa in Tshokwe tribal territory.

We settled on 100 meters wide and 1,000 meters long, or about 330 feet wide and 3,300 feet long. Using my surveyor's transit, we found a suitable location across a small valley from Musumba. With one end of the site adjacent to our mission station, a hangar could be built on mission property. On January 14, 1960, we finished surveying the four sides of the future airstrip and cut a path along each side.

Mwant Yav Ditend called in his chiefs, sub-chiefs and advisers, the Atubung. As the group walked along the long side of the future airstrip, the Paramount Chief stopped from time to time. He assigned a section of airstrip to each chief or sub-chief. Each of them was required to bring in enough "volunteer" labor to cut down huge mango trees, clear stumps, cut down the tall grass, remove shrubs and clear the entire surface down to the bare clay. They were to keep working until I was satisfied with the airstrip.

They only had their own equipment: hoes, axes, shovels and wheelbarrows. When they started it looked like a swarm of ants.

Duvon and I were afraid these unpaid and volunteer workers would be mad at us. On the contrary, these workers were happy they were increasing the status of the tribe and their Paramount Chief.

Working until the middle of April—ten weeks—they cut down and chopped into pieces the tall mango trees. They grunted, heaved and rolled pickup size chunks off the airstrip. Smaller trees, palms and large shrubs were removed.

In addition to Mwant Yav Ditend's desire to ride airplanes rather than cars on rough roads, we had an urgent reason to build the airstrip. The rainy season from September 1959 until the end of the year brought torrential rains in the Katanga. In February and March 1960, the ferries across the Lulua were out of service due to flooding. The roads east and south flooded at several bridges. We couldn't get freight or visitors into Kapanga and we couldn't travel out of the area. We couldn't receive any Mail!

We seriously needed an airstrip.

Women and children carried off tons of grass for roofs. The only machinery was a small bulldozer for two weeks in February.

We moved a number of palm tree trunks. I found someone used the palm trunks to ferment palm wine. Several men said the wine makers would be unhappy. I replied if the winemakers complained to me, I would report their illegal activity to the Bula Matadi.

No one ever admitted being the winemaker.

The bulldozer leveled tall termite hills and built a roadway to the airstrip. For hours one day little Lindy Davis rode in the driver's seat with me as I leveled rough places near my house. Lindy was only two-years-old and her mother wasn't eager to see her on that big, snorting monster. Lindy loved it, of course. As she was freely perspiring in the hot sun, I asked her if she wanted to get off.

She grinned as she shook her head "No!"

On March 10th the Vice Governor General of Congo visited New Musumba and the airstrip. Prudently, he didn't ask and wasn't told that neither project had been approved by the government.

They were local projects. On April 1, 1960, I acquired aerial photos of the Musumba area. I marked the location of the airstrip and turned it in for official approval.

That process was lengthy and was never finished before the Belgian Congo became the Republic of Congo.

We doubt the Republic ever completed the approval, either.

On April 18th the first Sobelair commercial aircraft, a twin engined Cessna, landed on Mwant Yav Ditend's airstrip with Bishop Springer and Moise Tshombe as passengers. Bishop declared on his first trip to Musumba in 1912, he'd walked for seven weeks. He liked the two-hour flight much better. Tshombe came in order to make numerous political speeches and visit family. The Paramount Chief was his father-in-law.

A NEW HOBBY FOR CONGOLESE—POLITICS

The indigenous populations of central Africa had never known democracy. Many tribes chose their leaders, they weren't hereditary. A few of their elders had a voice in the choices.
Starting in late 1959, they were allowed to vote. Tshombe took to politics naturally. We understood enough Lunda to appreciate him. He was intelligent with the ability to choose words that were appropriate to his audience and didn't make unrealistic promises about independence.
He promised work, taxes and government authority. Other budding politicians were promising freedom from taxes, authority and an abundance of every good thing for all citizens. They were unrealistic and reaped a whirlwind.

MISSION LIFE IN 1960

E. Stanley Jones arrived on January 21st in order to lead us in an Ashram. This is a full, five-day period of prayer, meditation, Bible study and sharing experiences. All missionaries and about thirty Congolese pastors, teachers, nurses and tribal leaders participated.

Dr. Jones was amazed that Congo was scheduled for Independence without one college graduate and with very few high school graduates in charge. Tribal animosities troubled him because tribal and religious quarrels had resulted in tremendous bloodshed when India became independent in 1947.

His main theme was "You can choose your actions, but you cannot choose the consequences!"

One evening he had all the missionaries tell our ancestral backgrounds. Our Congolese friends always assumed white people were simply one tribe, known to them as Yindeli.

Now they learned that among only eighteen missionaries, we had fifteen "tribes" and languages represented in our immediate ancestors. This fact astounded the Congolese.

On the 28th we were privileged to drive E Stanley Jones to the airstrip at Sandoa. We had him to ourselves for a full day and most of the next day. It was an honor to escort him. We would meet him again ten years later in Pennsylvania.

The government started a university for Congolese in 1958. The entrance exams were tough. Our potential Lunda applicants had a good knowledge of French, but were weak in science.

Duvon Corbitt started teaching chemistry and I started teaching physics in French. We started classes at 6AM in order to weed out all but the most serious students. These classes continued until independence.

As independence approached, the local Congolese leaders became intensely interested in finances and bookkeeping. Previously they'd been interested solely in their salaries. They knew nothing about financial records. For three weeks Phyllis taught bookkeeping and elementary financial records to several local leaders. Soon it dawned on them that getting and spending money wasn't easy.

How much could you expect to receive in taxes? Where did you spend it? How did you create a budget that was realistic?

These men didn't have a clue about how to answer any of these questions. But they knew that in a few months, some or, all of them would be government officials in the Republic of Congo. The more serious were almost in a panic.

In the past they could blame everything on missionaries and government officials (Bula Matadis). Now they would become Bula Matadis!

EARLIEST AIRPORT ARRIVALS

As recorded earlier, the first commercial airplane landed on April 18th. One passenger, Bishop Springer, would be in our Musumba church a week later to baptize the Mwant Yav Ditend.

They had first met when a Paramount Chief of 1912 sent his warriors to lead the Rev. John Springer to Musumba.

Mwant Yav Ditend, Paramount Chief, 1960, was one of those warriors.

On the same day a small APCM plane piloted by John Davis and John Miller brought Wally and Ruth Henk, Methodist missionaries at Katubwe, to Kapanga. After independence arrived in early July, we needed Wally Henk. He was evacuated from Luluabourg to Kamina Air Base. He assured the US Air Force pilots there was a 3,300 foot runway at Kapanga. Our airstrip was locally built and had not been placed on government air navigation charts. Wally assured the pilots the airstrip was long and wide enough for a DC-3 to land safely.

On a visit in May, the new Commissioner of Sankuru District said, "You know the Methodist Mission, with Mwant Yav Ditend's help, built this airstrip and had the kindness to put it at the disposition of the government."

This is a rough translation of part of his speech. As you know by now, the Paramount Chief, and his "volunteer" labor built the airstrip. We merely designed it.

ONE LAST WORD ABOUT OUR BEETLE

One day in May, Iwas driving the Beetle along a sandy road with heaps of sand banked up just off the roadway. Suddenly the steering wheel turned freely without affecting the car's direction of travel. It was scary as the unguided Beetle drifted sideways into a bank of sand. The brakes worked.

The problem was quickly located. The vertical steering column was terminated with four flat metal fingers at right angles. Each finger had a bolt hole. The wheel control mechanism and tie rods were terminated in a similar fashion. A circular piece of tire fabric about 3/4" thick, with four bolt holes, had been placed between the two sets of flat fingers in order to create a sort of metal/fabric sandwich. Bolts had been put through the holes and tightened. Steering was controlled through this rather fragile tire fabric connection.

On our Beetle that fabric had split from bolt hole to bolt hole. Fortunately, we lost control of steering in a location where we could safely stop and not when going on to a ferry. We parked the Beetle in our garage on July 12th when we left the Congo. We have no idea what happened to it. For repairs we'd cut a piece of tire fabric out of an old truck tire and put the Beetle back into shape for safe driving.

 As late as December 1959 most of our fellow missionaries didn't read any French language periodicals.

The newspaper *L'essor du Congo* was optimistic and rarely reported any of the problems plaguing Congo. Only the magazine *Pourquoi Pas?* reported the incidents occurring all across the country and in neighboring countries. Our fellow missionaries believed the Congo wouldn't experience any serious troubles. The next major portion of this chapter gives an account of the increasingly violent events that occurred from 1958 through 1960. The rise in violence enhanced our belief the Congo was headed for a disaster after independence.

EMPIRES 1945 - 1960

It may seem strange to include a section on these empires. In truth the events in those empires from the end of World War II in 1945 until 1960 had a tremendous influence on events in the Congo from 1957 until 1960.

BRITISH EMPIRE
*** Greater India had been agitating for its independence for decades. Indian troops had served faithfully in the British Armed Forces. Thousands of Indians had been trained in universities, high schools and technical institutes. After much unrest greater India was granted independence in 1947. It was immediately split into three parts: East Pakistan, India, and West Pakistan. Within a few years East Pakistan became the nation of Bangladesh. East and West Pakistan were Muslim. India was mainly Hindu. Tribal and religious conflicts caused more than one million deaths and untold misery as millions of people were forcibly moved from one area to another. This pattern of violence and forced moves would occur frequently, but on a smaller scale, in most of the other empires as they came apart.
Early in 1952, Jomo Kenyatta, the "Burning Spear," began to inflame the Kikuyu tribe in Kenya, Africa. This quickly developed into the Mau Mau campaign of terror against other tribes and white colonials in Kenya. Robert Ruark wrote an excellent account of this campaign. The Mau Mau continued until 1960 when Jomo Kenyatta's political party obtained partial representational government from the British. Kenyatta was jailed from 1953 to 1961. Soon after he was freed, the British granted independence to the

Republic of Kenya in 1963. Thousands of blacks and hundreds of whites were killed in the years from 1952 until 1960.

Much information about the Mau Mau movement and results sifted into the Congo all those years.

FRENCH EMPIRE

*** At the end of the Second World War, the French Empire controlled Indo-China: Viet Nam plus Cambodia plus Laos. Immediately the Indo-Chinese began to demand independence for each of the three units. From 1947 to 1954 the French poured money and men into a futile attempt to maintain their control. In a large battle at Dien Bien Phu, Viet Nam, in 1954 the French Army was decisively beaten and surrendered. Viet Nam, Laos and Cambodia were free. For an excellent background reading on Viet Nam read Doctor Tom Dooley's books.

In North Africa, the area known as Algeria had been an integral part of France since 1848. Local fighting and skirmishes occurred frequently from 1947 through 1954. In that year both sides poured men and weapons into a full-scale war. This fighting continued for four years with heavy losses on both sides. In 1958 the newly elected President of France, General Charles de Gaulle, offered all French colonies a choice: membership in the French Union or total independence.

Algeria wasn't included because the French still considered it to be a part of France. In 1962 they finally gave up that illusion and granted independence to Algeria.

BELGIAN CONGO

*** The key year for Congo is 1958. By that date the British Empire in Africa was dissolving and the French Empire in Africa was gone.

As the Congolese became aware of these developments, they believed it was time for the Belgian Empire to disappear. This awareness was strongest among the many Congolese who were fluent in French, English or Swahili. A few were fluent in all three languages. Belgian and Belgian Congo officials didn't seem aware of this growing interest in independence within the colony.

The Belgian Congo Governor General published a book titled *Dominer Pour Servir*, Dominate in Order to Serve. He was too late and totally wrong.

ANGOLA AND MOZAMBIQUE

*** The Portuguese proclaimed they possessed African colonies for 350 years. They would keep them forever. "Forever" ended in 1975 when Angola claimed independence with assistance from the Soviet Republic. Angola is between the Congo and the Atlantic Ocean. It has been involved in civil war since 1975 date until now, 1995. The KDL railroad from Lobito, Angola to Dilolo, Congo was critical to the mining activity in Katanga. The Angola rebels knew this importance and quickly dynamited all railroad bridges. No traffic has used the KDL since 1975.

Mozambique on the east coast of Africa had little influence on events in the Congo. But it to claimed independence in 1975. Two years later, they also became embroiled in civil war.

"EFFERVESCENCE"

We shall write this section as a chronology of events that we know happened for the eighteen months from January 1959 to July 1960. It is incomplete.

** January 1959—There were serious riots in the capital city of Leopoldville with dead, wounded and destruction of property. In the mining center of Kolwezi there were clashes between the Lundas and the local government forces.

In Elisabethville and Jadotville there was so much tension gun shops were selling all the guns and shells they could legally sell. Tribal disputes and rivalries became open clashes.

**June 1959—Angry Congolese attacked the Belgian tax collector. He escaped by fleeing into Lake Albert in a native dugout canoe. Taxes were not collected.

**August 1959--Our Paramount Chief, Mwant Yav Ditend, was attacked during a riot in Kolwezi. At least eight men were taken to the hospital but there were no known dead. Later in August two Tshokwe chiefs rebelled against Mwant Yav Ditend. Chief Samusamb objected to more Lunda rule. Samusamb is an area that contains a sacred mountain. Chief Luputa rebelled and refused to acknowledge continued loyalty to the Lunda Paramount Chief. Other subject tribes were restless but not quite so open in their rebellion yet.

**September 1959—The Paramount Chief called a meeting of all Lunda chiefs and chiefs of subject tribes. He proclaimed he was the Paramount Chief and would continue to rule. There would be no more talk about this strange topic called "independence". Of course, the chief's speech was no more effective than the Governor General's book. Both of them failed to stay aware of and understand the political developments in Africa or the Congo.

Within nine months the Belgian Congo became the new Republic of Congo, later Zaire, and started down that miserable road it has been on for 35 years.

**October 1959—The mission hospital and medical school at Kimpese, near Leopoldville, was closed to new students. The mission school at Katubwe, near Luluabourg, was closed temporarily.

The stores and shops at Luluabourg were not ordering any new merchandise. They didn't expect to be open long enough to need anymore. In a few days there were more incidents. The government closed off the city and required a police permit to enter or leave the city.

At the Sandoa government hospital, the Congolese nurses refused to obey any orders from Dr. Bandoux. At Luluabourg the government motor freight line trucks could leave only with special permission from the Provincial Governor. Rioting, looting and gun fights broke out sporadically.

There was a story the government had used helicopter gunships. In Kasai Province, the Bena Lulua tribe armed bandits who raided and burned Baluba villages. The APCM missions at Mutoto and Mwaka were flooded with Baluba refugees.

The October 12th issue of *Time* came out with the lead article "Congo Reduced To Chaos." In a rare burst of accuracy, the magazine was reasonably correct.

At Dilolo we encountered a Belgian Congo secret police official. He confirmed in a subtle way our view that the Congo was effervescent and getting worse.

On October 22nd we heard a report that hundreds had been killed or wounded fighting in or near Luluabourg. On the last day of October a large riot occurred in Stanleyville with twenty-four known dead.

**November 1959—A Kapanga Territorial Administrator issued the official rules for local elections in the territory. These would be the first elections in the history of the Congo. Most of the local Congolese had determined to follow their own rules for elections. Their rule was a simple one: elect only men from your own tribe. This was the African equivalent to voting the "straight" party ticket in the USA.

**December 1959—Political parties for Congolese had been legalized a few weeks earlier. No political activity, by whites or blacks, had ever been allowed in the colony. If you did so you were jailed and/or deported immediately. Some missionaries had been refused re-entry visas for political reasons.

Jason Sendwe, a Baluba, created the Balubakat party in the Katanga. Moise Tshombe, a Lunda, created the Conakat party in the Katanga. The "Cona" stood for the "COnfederation NAtional", which was a union of many tribes in the Katanga.

Some Tshokwe tribal leaders at Sandoa wrote a letter to European Communists seeking their help. Belgian Congo officials intercepted the reply and had strong words with the Tshokwe's.

Josef Kasavubu, a Bakongo leader, went to Brussels and pleaded for delay of the local elections. He said there would be too much fraud, ballot box stuffing and riots.

At the frontier town of Dilolo there was agitation for Katanga to secede from the Congo. We heard that statement eight years before, when we first arrived in Congo. Soon fighting broke out from Luebo to Dibaya. Martial law was declared in Kasai Province.

Locally, Roman Catholic priests preached the Congolese should vote only for Catholic candidates. Our local government officials told them to stop, but the priests didn't do so.

**January 1960—The Belgian Government convened a "Round Table" in Brussels for the newly created Congolese politicians: Tshombe, Sendwe, Kasavubu, Lumumba, Gisenga, Kalondji, our Paramount Chief, and others.

Several were asked to preside over a session of the Belgian Parliament. Only Moise Tshombe did well. When asked why he could do so, Moise replied he'd participated in several Methodist annual conferences which use parliamentary procedures. As a Roman Catholic, the Prime Minister didn't have the slightest clue about the real nature of an annual conference.

Anyway, the Belgian Parliament was well aware of the deteriorating political situation in the Congo. They also knew the recent history of the British and French Empires, who had futilely tried to keep their colonies at a terrible price in money and men. Parliament voted to give the Congo its independence in six months, July 1, 1960.

**February 1960—The Congo Protestant Council ceased to exist. Any cooperation between Congolese churches could not be the same as relationships between foreign missions. There were student strikes at our Methodist station of Mulungwishi.

**March 1960—More troubles reported all across Congo.

**March 15—Five policemen from Mwant Yav Ditend's force were stationed at the hospital.

Effervescence was getting closer to Kapanga. Duvon, Bill Davis and I met with the Paramount Chief. Mutombu. Our Luba truck driver, said he was now afraid to eat in Musumba. He was afraid poison might be in the food.

The Administrator, LaLievre, discussed with us the great unrest becoming more evident among the Tshokwe tribe south of us.

**April 1960—At the Presbyterian (APCM) station of Katubwe the office was burned. Some missionaries were stoned by a mob.

At our station, the teachers told Doris Davis and Phyllis they had no more authority to sign any school documents. The teachers were in charge.

**April 4, 1960—Miss Marie Jensen left for Denmark.

**April 7, 1960—we made a wind sock for the airport using red and white cloth.

**May and June 1960—Our diaries, log books and guest book have blank pages. We have no records about happenings in Congo. That doesn't mean nothing occurred, but we were too busy to record anything.

**June 30 and July 1, 1960—The Lundas had a great "Independance" (French spelling) Party in Musumba. They displayed many new flags of the Republic of Congo. There were parades. Games of all kinds were performed. Dancers put on their best acts.

These citizens of the new Republic were not sure, but they expected this new state of independence to bring them prosperity with NO more taxes or harsh government rules. No Jails. No beatings with hippo hide whips. No arrogant Bula Matadis, that is, no arrogant government officials. Optimism abounded. It was a great day.

**July 3, 1960—A California work team of six men arrived. See entry for July 13th.

**July 4, 1960—The Paramount Chief celebrated the Fourth of July for us Americans. We didn't know for several days that the former Belgian Congo Force Publique had already revolted at their army headquarters in Thysville and across much of Congo. This Force Publique was an army with Belgian officers and Congolese soldiers. Revolts, fighting, looting, riots and burning flared everywhere in Congo as each local contingent revolted.

We had a contingent of twelve Force Publique men at Kapanga. The rebel leaders in Thysville and at the capital of Leopoldville sent urgent telegrams to all Force Publique detachments: "Revolt Now." Our telegrapher at Kapanga delivered the telegram to the Belgian Administrator who promptly disarmed all the Force Publique soldiers. We didn't know about the telegram for at least a week.

REFUGEES—1960

**12:30/Noon, July 9, 1960—On the regular English language news broadcast from Radio Elisabethville the US Consul advised all US citizens to leave the Congo immediately. He could not legally order us out. The British government can do so. The British Consul ordered all holders of British passports out of the Congo. As we left our house, we met Duvon and Phyllis Corbitt. Obviously they'd heard the same broadcast. We called to Carroll & Tove French and to Bill & Doris Davis. We went to the Women's Division house where the Freudenbergers were staying. Elsie was "expecting" any day.

Some of us were ready to comply with the request to leave. But how? Travel on the roads in all four directions was dangerous and we had no assurance our possible destinations would be any safer than Musumba.

NORTH: Luluabourg was in great distress and who knew what the intervening Basala Mpasa cannibals would do.

WEST: No one wanted to go toward Angola. There was no way to cross the Kasai River with vehicles. There were no ferries or border crossings.

EAST: The Balubas and Bena Luluas had been fighting each other for months across a wide area.

SOUTH: In Tshokwe territory, two of the local tribal chiefs had openly rebelled against the Lunda Paramount Chief. We spoke Lunda. Coming from Musumba we wouldn't be welcome. The frontier town of Dilolo had riots. The large mining town of Kolwezi experienced strikes and fighting.

At the moment we were safer in Mwant Yav Ditend's capital, Musumba. Anyway, after the arrival of the six-man work team, we didn't have enough vehicles to transport everybody at one time.

**Sunday July 10, 1960—We went to church and told our Congolese pastors our government had advised us to leave the country. They didn't believe this was necessary. Musumba was peaceful. But before the morning service ended, a stream of frightened refugees (Belgians and merchants) streamed in from the north and east. They brought stories about riots, gun fire, looting and burning of villages.

Two refugee Presbyterian missionary families, the Joe Spooners and the Robersons, came from the APCM mission near Moma. This station is in the midst of the Basala Mpasu tribal area. No one knew what this cannibalistic tribe would do when they were no longer subject to Belgian military threat.

Presbyterian missionary Eric Bolton and family came from Bibanga. Severe troubles were occurring in the vicinity of their station. A telegram came from Methodists in Elisabethville "Be prepared to leave."

**Monday July 11th—Joe Spooner and Eric Bolton got Joe's radio transmitter on the air. Eric broke into the Air Force Radio transmitting from Wiesbaden, Germany. Eric had been in the Air Force and knew what frequency bands they used. Then he moved to the frequency for the US Air Forces now at Kamina Air Base in Congo. Eric told the Kamina airmen we were not in immediate danger and we had sufficient food. But we did have fifty-six men, women and children on site. Some were refugees from far more dangerous locations. The Pipers, Goodrums and Stewart families came from Katubwe. Others came from more threatened locations.

Luluabourg was having severe riots, with dead and wounded. The USAF would fly to Luluabourg first on Monday in order to save the numerous US citizens who'd taken refuge there. Their own locations had been dangerous and now Luluabourg was becoming even more dangerous. The US Air Force spokesman stated the airplane for us would come on Tuesday. All of us were temporarily safe at Kapanga, but some needed medical care and assurance they were safe.

The Air Force kept its promise.

Tuesday July 12th—Wally Henk, already at Karnina, again assured the USAF that Kapanga did have a large airstrip, although it didn't show on the government air navigation charts. About 9AM a DC-3 from the US Embassy at Johannesburg landed.

A Lt. Colonel stepped down out of the airplane. He exclaimed "Who the heck built an Idlewild in the wilds of Congo? We saw your airstrip when we were thirty kilometers away".

Idlewild was the original name of the New York Airport now called JFK. The plane had been stripped of all seats and other unneeded equipment. There were no seatbelts.

POLITICAL CONVERSION

One of the newly elected local Congolese officials (Mbundj) had been extremely critical of missions and missionaries in recent months. After some serious thinking he came to tell us that someday he hoped the Republic of Congo would be strong enough to take care of its citizens as our missions had done.

LEAVING KAPANGA

About 10AM, thirty-one missionaries and children left for Karnina. All the refugee Presbyterians were sent first, along with the pregnant Elsie and her family. The plane returned after lunch. At 3PM, twenty-three missionaries and children left on the one hour and fifteen minute flight to Kamina. Bill Davis, the preacher, and Dr. Duvon Corbitt remained at Kapanga.

At Kamina refugees were corning in from all over central, eastern and southern Congo. Some came by vehicle and some by small planes. We were given space to sleep on the dance floor in the Officer's Club, Club Leoplod II.

**July 3 to 13—California Work Team.

We want to write a little bit about the team of six men who were a diverse and talented group. Unfortunately, their arrival occurred when the Congo was being torn apart. Neither we nor they knew this in time to postpone their visit. Anyway, a later arrival would have been worse.

Twenty years would go by before any more work teams were able to go to Congo (Zaire) and their stays were limited. Among our work team in 1960 there were men who worked with their hands. One was a master electrician for Disneyland in California. Another was one of the most skilled mechanics we ever met. In a few days he did great things with limited tools, mainly one large crescent wrench. Their leader, a preacher, helped our local pastors with good humor and great advice on how to be an effective pastor. The other three men had skills and enthusiasm.

As a group, they made an excellent impression on our workmen and our church leaders. With their many combined talents the group repaired and improved the performance of the equipment we had in our shop at the hospital. We realize this is an inadequate account of the six men who came to us at Kapanga. In person we gave them our heartfelt thanks and praise for their dedication.

Being in the wilds of Africa they wanted to see big game. One day we took all of them on an antelope hunt, or safari. Hunting in Congo requires a lot of walking, while carrying food, water, guns and ammunition. We were able to kill two antelope and give the men a glimpse of a big game hunt.

When we returned to the mission, they were tired but enthusiastic. These few days were so hectic that we recorded very little in our diaries or other documents. From our memory we have mentioned a few things that happened. Now we will resume the daily accounts.

**Wednesday July 13—At Club Leo we were reunited with many of our Presbyterian friends who'd been evacuated from Luluabourg. They spent at least one night at a hotel in Luluabourg while rebels fired guns through the windows. The missionaries were flat on the floor behind brick walls. Belgian paratroopers arrived and escorted the missionaries and local citizens to the airport.

Kamina Air Base became jammed with Americans, British, Portuguese, Belgians, and other nationalities. Our Methodist missionaries arrived from the Central Congo stations. Many of them had less than an hour to pack and leave.

As we met our friend, Anita (Ritter) Fenstermacher, we observed she was wore a raincoat and walked stooped over as if carrying a heavy burden. We asked what was wrong.

[Incidentally, we never wore raincoats in Congo. The high humidity made you perspire so much you became soaked. It was better to get wet from the rain and dry off quickly.] Anita replied with only 45 minutes notice, she hadn't had time to think clearly about what to take. She emptied her pockets packed with sterling silver wedding gifts. While laughing, she said she could really use some of the necessities she'd left on the station.

Many sizes of aircraft were seen at Kamina. They ranged from the Boeing 707 and USAF Globemasters through the DC-6's, DC-4's, DC-3's, Cessna's and Pipers. One 707 departed for a non-stop trip to Europe with 300 passengers, about twice the normal load. It seemed to use every inch of the 11,000 foot runway as it belched dense clouds of black smoke.

Belgians and Portuguese were going to Europe. American and British citizens were going south to Rhodesia.

On the first day, the big planes flew in the daylight. This was a serious mistake. During daylight hours the hot weather created high cumulus clouds with thunderstorms and high winds. As a result of the turbulent flights, many passengers got airsick. With all weather navigation instruments the large planes changed their schedules to take off in early evening with smoother flights at night.

Without the night instrumentation, the Cessnas and Pipers continued their daylight trips into small airstrips and dodged the bad weather as best they could. They removed many missionaries and colonials from harm's way.

**Thursday July14th—At breakfast we met Monsieur Mineur, Sobelair pilot, who brought the first plane into Kapanga. He'd been trained to fly by the USAF in Texas.

Now he was busy flying the Belgians out of small airstrips. Our Kapanga Belgians had flown out with him. The Sandoa Belgians chose to wait a while.

THE LONG WAY FROM MUSUMBA TO ATLANTA—
1960

We are beginning this section with our departure from the airstrip at Musumba (Kapanga), rather than from Kamina Air Base. This allows us to write one continuous story about the journey from our home in Congo to our home in Atlanta.

**Tuesday July 12—Fifty four (54) missionaries were evacuated from Musumba to the Belgian Air Force Air Base at Kamina, Congo. The six-man work team from California was part of our group: Rev. Wesley Skidmore, Perry Shipman, Ellis Sexton, Wesley Buttermore, Floyd Duncan and Charles Bradd.

Two missionaries, Duvon Corbitt, MD, and Rev. Bill Davis, remained on the station.

Mwant Yav Ditend, and the Lundas, swore that not one drop of missionary blood would be shed in their tribal area.

**July 13 & 14—At Kamina Air Base we lived on the dance floor of the Officer's Club. The Belgian Air Force took care of our primary needs and fed us as well as they could. They did an excellent job. After all, we were not expected.

The US Air Force was in charge of evacuating US citizens. They brought planes and equipment from all over Europe and eastern USA. Their commanding general was at Pope

Air Force Base in North Carolina. We later met General Box and gave him a big "thank you."

At a meeting in Kamina, the USAF Lt Colonel announced that women, children and sick would be evacuated first.

Obviously, he had never encountered missionary wives. Quickly, they emphatically informed him we would go as families! They were not leaving their husbands. Therefore, complete families with children went first, then childless couples and singles. The Lt Colonel said "Yes, Ma'am."

By this date we had reports that several Protestant and Roman Catholic missionaries had been killed or wounded or jailed. One Protestant woman missionary fled into the bush in lower Congo where the Congolese Christians concealed her for almost six months.

We heard that Mwant Yav Ditend had flown to Leopoldville. On the way, rebel soldiers at Bakwanga had fired at his plane. Bakwanga was one of the major centers for diamond mining. Congo supplied most of the world's supply of industrial diamonds in those years.

July 15—9:30PM One-hundred-eighty-three evacuees boarded a USAF Globemaster for a three hour flight to Salisbury, Southern Rhodesia. As a cargo plane the aircraft had no seats or seatbelts. We were so crowded the passengers took turns standing up for a stretch. That metal floor was cold and hard. Elsie Freudenberger was on one stretcher. On another stretcher was the only non-US citizen, a wounded Belgian.

Our Rhodesian hosts were efficient and hospitable. At a Royal Air Force officer's club they fed us hot soup and good food. We were south of the Equator with the seasons reversed from the USA. July is the middle of winter.

Salisbury weather was frigid. They gave us cots and blankets for sleeping in an old military barracks.

**July 16—Methodist missionary Hunter Griffin arrived to take us to Nyadiri Mission Station, about 25 miles. All mission stations have guest quarters, but Nyadiri was flooded with refugees. We slept in an outside store room that was cold. The church had a welcoming service for Congo missionaries.

Ray Watson and his wife arrived with two boys and a baby girl. The girl's grandparents had sent a most beautiful collection of clothes and accessories for the baby girl. These packages arrived a few weeks before evacuation. Having less than an hour to pack, the Watsons had these gifts fresh in their minds. They grabbed all the clothes and gifts. In Rhodesia the parents and boys had nothing. They had no clothes, no shoes and Ray had no shaving kit. The baby girl had a complete wardrobe.

Phyllis wasn't well and Dr Bitsch-Larsen gave her some medicine.

**SUNDAY July 17—We attended church service with a strong mixture of relief at our evacuation and sadness at the terrible news coming from Congo. Rebel soldiers and sympathizers were killing Congolese intellectuals, nurses, teachers and preachers. They also tortured and killed rival political leaders.

Hunter, Dr Bitsch-Larsen and I took the four Bitsch-Larsen girls to Salisbury. Next day the girls flew home to Denmark with Anna Lerbak. The two boys stayed.

Phyllis could barely talk and felt badly.

**July 18—Hunter and I went to Salisbury on a shopping trip for personal items and food. At the ice cream plant we bought a five gallon container of ice cream. That was a treat for everyone from Congo. We had rarely eaten ice cream in three years.

Hunter and I met the Willis Pipers who were leaving for Mozambique on the 21st in order to go home by ship.

**Bishop Booth arrived to share with us his news about Congo. He had been there for a few days. We discussed possible futures for Congo missionaries.

**July 20—There were more discussions between missionaries and our bishop. Each missionary situation had to be evaluated. All the ordained missionaries, doctors and nurses were chomping at the bit to go back to their stations. Schools were in chaos! Could mission teachers go back safely? No one knew.

Transportation and building supplies were impossible to obtain. It was decided that the Littles and most other builders would go on early furlough.

But first our episcopal leader, Bishop Booth, was determined to first schedule our annual conference in Elisabethville.

**July 21—I obtained a Rhodesian chauffeur's license and a hunting license.

We had to keep busy because annual conference could not be convened until August 4th.

Hunter and I, along with several older boys went hunting for Kudus. We saw one, but killed none. Kudus are a large antelope with long, gracefully curved horns.

The landscape east of Nyadiri is beautiful and dotted with huge rock outcroppings called "kopjes." On those clear winter days the magnificent Nyanga Mountains could be seen on the eastern horizon, at least twenty-five miles away.

July 22—The United Nations troops began trying to take control in Congo. Their four years in the Congo stirred things up as much as they calmed the situation.

We think they knew very little about Congo or Congolese. Friends and foes were impossible to determine because alliances and allegiances changed frequently. A multitude of languages contributed to the problems of security and food. The United Nations didn't do very well.

Our own US State Department leaders were misinformed and were no help. Several inadequate books were written about UN activities. We will write no more about the UN or US in Congo after 1960.

The bright highlight of the day came when we received a telephone call from Phyllis' family in St. Petersburg, Florida. We needed a lift to our spirits.

July 23—We had a wedding shower for the soon-to-be Stanley and Joanne Maughlin. They'd been engaged to be married in Central Congo. Joanne brought out her wedding dress. Stanley brought out his wedding suit. They didn't have much else with them. Their fellow missionaries showered them with Rhodesian gifts.

Phyllis still not feeling any better.

July 24 & 25—Attended church and visited with old and new friends. Anything to maintain our sanity. All news out of Congo was getting worse. Unfortunately, facts, rumors, and fiction were impossible to separate.

July 26—The wedding took place. Joanne was a pretty, red-haired bride. Stanley was an excited, handsome groom. Their marriage has lasted. We met the Maughlins again in

1992 during a Congo/Zaire missionary reunion at Asbury College, Wilmore, Kentucky.

**July 27, 28, 29—We existed, but have no records or recollections about what happened.

**July 30—We went to the Methodist Building in Salisbury in order to get plane tickets for the Henks, Davis' and Littles. We would fly to Ndola, Northern Rhodesia, then drive across the border to Elisabethville for annual conference.

**July 31—Visiting friends and saying goodbye as some left for home.

**August 1—Henks, Davis' and Littles flew from Salisbury to Ndola, then took two taxis for the short trip to the border town, Kitwe. We spent the night at the Ecumenical Institute.

**August 2—Shopping in Kitwe and waiting for transportation.

**August 3—We drove the WDCS Volkswagen from Kitwe to Elisabethville. At the border crossing you shifted from left lane driving to right lane driving, or else. Fortunately, the little Volkswagen had the steering wheel on the USA side.

Bishop started annual conference that afternoon. Shops, stores and public facilities in Elisabethville had been damaged, looted and/or burned. Our large Methodist Church and other mission buildings had not been damaged.

**August 4,5,6,7—Annual conference, we have no idea what went on because we'd been told we would go home as soon as the conference was concluded.

At 3PM, Sunday, Moise Tshombe, President of the Katanga, addressed the conference. His soldiers, and the new

Katanga flag, were everywhere. We stayed in a missionary residence and sat on the floor behind shuttered windows. There was occasional gunfire at night.

August 8—Drove the Arne Reinar's green Volkswagen to Kitwe and left it at the Ecumenical Institute. The Reinars had gone home. We purchased tickets to Salisbury. Howard and Libby Brinton drove us to the Ndola Airport. Left at 8:30PM and arrived at 11PM.

We were able to get a room at the beautiful Meikle Hotel for the most comfortable sleeping facilities we'd had in a month. Salisbury was a modern city. Many former British Empire colonials were retiring to Southern Rhodesia because that part of Africa has a comfortable climate and fertile soil.

August 9—Phyllis lost the Tissot watch we'd bought in Elisabethville. We bought beautiful Congo stamps and other small items. Republic of Congo francs were worthless outside Congo. We have the stamps in our collection.

In Salisbury we made easy reservations to fly to Rome, Italy, where we would find other reservations.

August 10—The South African Airways DC-7 was late. We left at 9PM. About 1AM we landed at Brazzaville (French Congo) across the river from Leopoldville. More refugees boarded the plane.

August 11—After a short stopover in Brazzaville, we flew on toward Kano, Nigeria, where we landed about 9AM. One propeller wasn't functioning properly and we faced the long flight over the Sahara Desert.

While the mechanics repaired the propeller, the SAA agent took us on a two-hour guided tour of Kano. It's an ancient mud and brick walled city, mostly Muslim, on the southern edge of the Sahara Desert. Camels were a common sight. The bus stopped quite frequently in order to allow us to take photographs. We couldn't enter the mosque but they allowed us to climb the tall minaret. This was the tallest structure in town and gave us an opportunity to take photos of the scenic areas around it.

With almost no rain in the area, the buildings were made of sun dried brick and mud plaster.

We left Kano at noon and landed at Rome about 4PM. This was one day before the 1960 summer Olympics were scheduled to open. We finally found a hotel room.

**August 12—No seats were available on any flights. We toured the Borghese Museum, Pantheon, St. Peter's Basilica at the Vatican, St Paul's Church, and in the evening ate at a sidewalk cafe on the Via Veneta.

The Via Veneta was "The" place to be and be seen in 1960. Late in the day we obtained tickets on Air France to Paris.

**August 13—In the early morning we visited the Sistine Chapel in the Vatican. In the afternoon, we flew on an Air France Caravelle jet to Paris. There we found a room in the Hotel Angleterre, where we'd stayed in 1952.

**Sunday August 14—We didn't feel well, but went to the American Church in Paris. This church has a splendid sanctuary draped with U.S.A. battle flags from the First World War.

As we thanked our God for a safe evacuation we felt sorrowful for the terrible situation unfolding in the Republic of Congo.

In the afternoon we went to the American Hospital to see an English doctor. He gave us medicine for anxiety and stress—we had both.

Our new friend, Miss Margaret Atkins, a Canadian, drove us around the city. We'd met her at the morning service in the American Church. With her as a guide, we saw a bit more than we'd seen when we walked everywhere in 1952.

**August 15—Visited several ticket offices, no luck. At the height of the tourist season, when everyone was going back to the USA, no seats were available. At TWA we finally obtained tickets for two seats that had cancelled reservations.

The Louvre Museum was closed on Mondays in August, which is the traditional month for nearly all French vacations. We visited other interesting locations on a three-hour bus tour. We rarely take bus tours, but we wanted one last look at Paris.

**August 16—Left Paris at 1PM local time on a TWA 707 and landed eight hours later at New York. Tired, but happy!!

**August 17,18,19—Visited the Board of Foreign Missions where we discussed the Congo situation and our scheduled furlough in the US. We turned in all expense reports and took our short physical exams. Very probably we could not have passed a psychological exam.

**Saturday, August 20—In the morning we visited a few places in Manhattan. Phyllis refused to fly anymore. We reserved a Pullman compartment on the *Southerner*, leaving Pennsylvania station in the early evening.

**SUNDAY August 21—We arrived in Atlanta. Mr. and Mrs. Lewis, Guy, May Belle and Mark Fish met us. From Musumba to Atlanta we had traveled 12,400 miles since July 12th, in cars, taxis, planes and trains. After a trip equivalent to halfway around the world we were exhausted.

BUT WE WERE HOME !!

SUMMATION OF OUR LIFE AS FOREIGN MISSIONARIES

When we arrived in 1952, daily life in a Lunda village appeared vastly different from daily life in any American or European location we'd experienced.

After serving two terms, these apparent differences almost disappeared. Granted, the villagers struggle for survival was more elemental. Each family had to hunt game, fish, gather wild natural foodstuffs and manually cultivate gardens or they didn't eat enough to survive. Without any kind of preservatives or refrigeration or grocery stores all edible items had to be obtained frequently, usually daily.

For their spiritual and psychological needs they believed in a Creator, Sakatang. They believed in supernatural spirits, witchcraft, bad luck and unseen powers that could be good or evil. In efforts to appease Sakatang and these spirits the people constructed tiny huts (Akish). In the vicinity of the huts, away from the village, the Lundas offered gifts of food, placed carved wooden human or animal figures and recited prayers. Designated mountains, hills, locations and trees were sacred. Hunters carried antelope horns filled with leaves, clay, insects and other things by the resident witch doctor. The hunter had been charged a great price for the magic horn that would render the hunter invincible against his quarry: the big, mean buffalo.

Lightning and violent storms were fearful phenomena. Good luck charms and actions were valued. Wrong words and actions could offend the spirit world. Misfortune, illness and death were always believed to be the result of misbehavior. Certain foods were taboo, could not be eaten. They would not eat predators.

We learned this on a hunting trip that we went on near the village of Chala.

Another time, when we carried away the antelope that had been killed by a pair of lions, our trackers left part of the entrails at the spot. They looked towards the lions and said "Brother lions, accept this food offering. Eat it and leave us alone."

With a certain lack of confidence in that prayer, they built nine fires around our camp tent that night.

Every Lunda village had a carved wooden statue called a Chipazu. A human face was carved on the front and the back. We were told that the Chipazu could see the past and look to the future.

Each village had a sacred tree. When the tree died, they moved the village. The Chipazu was left in place. At one abandoned village, the Lundas wouldn't touch the abandoned Chipazu. They generously said we could take the risk and pull it out of the ground. We did remove it, brought it to America and gave it to the Carnegie Museum in Pittsburgh. To the Lundas, it was potentially powerful and dangerous. They believed in its force.

How different is Lunda life and culture from American?

How many Americans will walk under a ladder leaning against a wall? How many tall buildings/hotels/motels have a 13th floor? Or a Room 13? There are very few commercial airplanes with row 13? What do we do when we break a mirror?

The struggle for survival is on a very different level, but real for most of us. Increased wealth brings the fear of scams, con artists and slick salesmen who want to relieve us of that burden. Lotteries, casinos and bingo parlors are filled with individuals who believe in good luck, or gain without work or strain. For gamblers any knowledge or skill seems to be irrelevant; chance and luck are paramount. Books and magazines are filled with information about miracle foods; diets, lifestyles an how to beat the lottery system. Crystals and pyramids are believed to have potent powers. Horoscopes are diligently observed. Some New Age disciples believe reincarnation can bring them a better life here on earth, IF they perform the proper rituals now. In the business world we are urged to power dress and power lunch in order to influence superiors or get an advantage over our opponents.

With expensive jewelry, clothing, automobiles and houses, we desperately try to prove we are important. Therefore, WE must associate with the right people and belong to the right organizations. How many Americans smoke, drink, eat junk food on the run and expect to live a healthy life forever? Illicit drug use is considered to be acceptable recreation. Violence with physical force is a valid solution to our problems. Inanimate weapons and explosives bring power to the possessors.

"Rights" have multiplied like rabbits. Responsibilities are rarely mentioned. Motivational writers and speakers exhort us to do whatever feels good while gaining all the wealth, prestige and fame we can acquire. Sin, Hell, judgment and conscience are old-fashioned and never, ever mentioned.

According to polls 85% of us believe in some sort of Supreme Being. WE want mercy, THEY should get justice. Does that Supreme Being govern our lives?

But the nagging question remains. How is life in a Lunda village really different from life in the USA?

Not very different! Many of our American and European friends would be shocked to realize the range of Lunda personalities, conduct, dreams and intelligence is identical to ours. Among the Lundas we encountered wise, stupid, intelligent, calm, violent, friendly, grumpy, cunning, skillful, irresponsible, responsible, thoughtful, honest, dishonest, and indescribable human beings.

In America and Europe we have encountered the same categories. There are strong Christians among the Lunda. There are strong Christians among us. We can all become God's children if we choose to do so.

As Wendell Willkie wrote fifty years ago, this is "One World". Twenty five years later the astronauts named it the "Blue Marble" because they could hide it behind a thumb.

BISHOPS WHO WERE OUR GUESTS IN CONGO

The following Bishops and their wives were guests for meals in our home in the Congo. All were talented and dedicated persons who enriched our lives.

Newell & Esma Booth..........Congo
M.W. & Ethel Clair.............Missouri
Richard & Lucille Raines......Indiana
Odd & Ruth Hagen..............Sweden
Edgar & Virginia Love.........Maryland
J. Waskom Pickett.............Massachusetts
John & Helen Springer.........Congo

VIII. FURLOUGH RESIGNATION EMPLOYMENT (1960-1961)

HOME

From our arrival in Atlanta on Sunday, August 21, until the following Sunday we made few entries in our diary. Our joy at being home was tinged with sadness as we read about the troubles in Congo, particularly in Katanga Province. Phyllis' Uncle Roy Warren helped us buy a 1960 Ford Station Wagon. His credit rating was excellent. As refugees from Congo our credit rating was non-existent.

Of course, we went to Rich's Department Store for clothes and accessories. Leaving Congo with a meager twenty pounds of luggage each, we'd chosen to bring irreplaceable slides, photos and movie film.

The clothes we wore were all we had with us when we got to Atlanta. During that first week we telephoned our family, friends and supporting churches with news of our safe arrival.

Sunday morning, August 28, we attended First Methodist Church in Decatur near Atlanta. Before I preached, the morning congregation was restless and not paying much attention. I began the sermon in Lunda, not English. Within a minute the people realized no one, except Phyllis, had the foggiest idea what I was saying. Soon they became quiet and attentive as they listened to the English words that were understandable. Nothing was wrong with their hearing aids! This church was one of our favorite places to visit. We enjoyed their friendliness as they faithfully supported our work.

For the evening service, we went to Saint Mark, but there we were simply introduced as one of the congregation. Many friends were happy to see us home safely. With Phyllis' parents, we left Atlanta Tuesday morning for the trip to St. Petersburg where her parents now lived.

GYPSIES

Missionaries must be part Gypsy in order to survive. From the time we arrived in Atlanta on August 21, 1960 until we moved into a garage apartment behind the Lewis home in St. Petersburg on February 21, 1961 we lived out of our luggage. Usually we were together, but not always. During the first two weeks we wrote letters, telephoned friends and churches, obtained Florida license plates and driver's licenses and took care of personal affairs.

After so many years overseas, it was taking us quite a while to get used to life in the USA. The speed with which we could share news by telephone across the country was amazing and pleasing to us. Shopping at supermarkets was a joy, not a 500-mile one-way trip.

On the 9th of September we celebrated our wedding anniversary:

Married in Atlanta, Georgia
1st anniversary in Brussels, Belgium
2nd anniversary in Bossey, Switzerland
3rd, 4th, 5th anniversaries, Kapanga, Belgian Congo
6th anniversary in Lovell, Wyoming
7th anniversary in St. Petersburg, Florida
8th and 9th anniversaries in Kapanga, Belgian Congo
10th anniversary in St Petersburg, Florida

The next day hurricane Donna blew straight into Tampa Bay with a high tide. Downtown Tampa became rather soggy because it's barely above sea level. Donna was a minimum category hurricane and did no serious damage other than flooding. As soon as the rains stopped, we drove across Florida to Titusville to be with Frank and Jessie (Phyllis' sister) Stodgell for a week. Frank was working as an electrician on US Air Force missiles being launched from Cape Canaveral. They'd recently adopted an infant boy, Claude, who was changing their life style.

When we returned to St. Petersburg, we went to Tampa to visit fellow Congo missionaries, Howard and Ruth Hardee. At dinner we enjoyed sharing news, and rumors, with fourteen Congo missionaries (Methodists and Presbyterians) on furlough.

For several weeks we showed our slides and shared news of Congo with friends but gave no formal talks. The news from Congo varied; usually it was bad or terrible.

We have not included much of it in this story because our knowledge was fragmented. Frequently the news reports were unreliable and biased. Our best information came from correspondence and conversations with fellow missionaries. It was so personal we kept it among ourselves. In the meantime we were enjoying life while slowly adjusting to life in the USA.

This pleasant life style came to a screeching halt on September 27th when we received a telegram from Bill Starnes at the Board of Foreign Missions in New York.

Working against much opposition, some of our missionaries in Congo arranged for the US State

Department to grant a seven-week tour of the USA to our Mwant Yav Ditend and a young escort, Jonathan Manung.

Mwant Yav Ditend didn't speak English and the State Department had no one who spoke Lunda. Could I be in New York to meet Mwant Yav Ditend on October 1st and act as their guide and interpreter across the US and Puerto Rico?

The State Department would make me a temporary employee, pay two-thirds of all expenses and arrange most of the appointments.

Bishop Richard Raines in Indiana and Bishop Gerald Kennedy in California would schedule one week in each state.

The Governor of Puerto Rico would schedule a week there.

Of course, my answer was yes. Afterall, I was fluent in Lunda, Mwant Yav Ditend knew me and trusted me to interpret all meetings fairly.

On the trip I kept a journal that filled forty-one typewritten pages. I felt obligated to send a trip report to the hundreds of people who'd helped make the tour a success. Simple arithmetic revealed thousands of pages would have to be printed and mailed. Six weeks of editing, deleting, condensing and rewriting resulted in the six-page informal report you will find in the ODDS & ENDS section. Almost 500 copies were printed and mailed.

SEPTEMBER 30 - NOVEMBER 19, 1960

While I toured the USA & Puerto Rico with Mwant Yav Ditend and Jonathan Manung, Phyllis lived with her parents on 13th Ave, NE, in downtown St. Petersburg. Her family had many friends in the area and so did we.

Our missionary friends, Howard and Ruth Hardee with their daughters, Dorothy (Dottie) and Ruth Ann (Ruthie), lived nearby in Tampa. Walter Rutland was the minister at Pasadena Community Church. We'd met and visited with Walter and Anne when Walter was in seminary at the Candler School of Theology in Georgia.

With no church membership for us yet, Phyllis attended First Presbyterian Church with her parents, who were active in a big Sunday School class.

Phyllis gave talks to various groups and explained our work in Africa with the slides from Congo and showing some of our souvenirs.

On one occasion she was interviewed by Dick Bothwell, a popular reporter with the *St Petersburg Times*.

Much of the time she kept track of me as I zig-zagged across the USA.

On November 4th I arrived at the Tampa airport with Mwant Yav and Jonathan. All of us were interviewed by the *Tampa Tribune* and television station WTVT (Channel 13).

I relinquished Mwant Yav and Jonathan to the Hardee's while Phyllis and I moved into the Barbara Ann Apartments for a few days of rest and recuperation.

Tuesday evening, the McCormicks, Dwight and Lynne, invited the four of us Mwant Yav, Jonathan, Phyllis and me to a formal dinner at their home. Dwight was an investment banker and had invited several influential friends to join us. The meal was delicious.

Before we started eating the meal our hosts, the McCormicks, asked Mwant Yav to bless the food. When he was asked to say the blessing Mwant Yav immediately knelt beside the table, as was his custom, and began to pray.

We are not sure how many of the bankers and guests had ever knelt to pray during the blessing. They did so that evening, although they didn't understand a word of the Lunda prayer. They did understand the sincerity of the chief as he knelt to pray.

On the 9th, I and company flew to Puerto Rico for a week's visit as guest of the Governor. Then they flew to Washington for a debriefing with the State Department concerning the entire trip.

One small item about the airport at San Juan, Puerto Rico. Large jet aircraft were rare. As my flight was still on the taxiway the captain set the brakes on the 707 and pushed the throttles all the way forward in preparing to roll onto the runway. He was new in jets and overlooked the fact jet engines do not need this procedure. Just taxi slowly onto the runway and take off. He rattled the wings on that jet and some of his passengers.

In Washington I put Mwant Yav and Jonathan on the train to New York where Bill Harvey would meet them and send them back to the Congo. I arrived at the Tampa Airport about 11:30PM, November 19, tired and weary. Phyllis was almost as glad to see me as I was to get home and be relieved of escorting two dear friends.

For details of that fascinating travel across America see the trip report in the ODDS & ODDS chapter of this story.

DEPUTATION

After I returned I was thrilled but exhausted. I rested for a few days but it was time to start visiting churches, friends and families. Long ago we'd made commitments to revisit Park Street Methodist and Saint Mark Methodist in Atlanta, First Church in Decatur, Powers Ferry in Marietta and First Church in Thomasville.

We had not yet visited any of my family and hoped to be with my parents for Christmas.

On Friday November 25th, we left St. Petersburg for Atlanta. Sunday morning we spoke at Park Street Methodist church. Sunday evening we spoke at Saint Mark Methodist. Monday and Tuesday included meals with the Grosecloses, J Tom Smiths, Huber Parsons and lunch with Dow Kirkpatrick at Saint Mark's parsonage.

Dr. Harry Richardson invited us to visit nearby Gammon Theological Seminary for talks with students. We enjoyed supper at a mid-week prayer service in First Church, Decatur. We showed our slides and gave an account of our service in Congo. There were other meals and visits with friends and family on Thursday, Friday and Saturday.

Sunday, December 4th, we spent all day at Powers Ferry Methodist church in Marietta.

On Monday we left for Fayetteville, North Carolina. Guy and May Belle Fish were stationed at Pope Air Force Base. They were an attentive group.

But our most memorable event was a "Thank You!" General Box, and his staff, had commanded the US Air Force rescue efforts for evacuating Americans from the Congo. We visited his office to tell him in person how glad we had been to see US flags on planes in Congo.

On the road again, we drove to Thomasville for a reunion with our dear friends, the James Reid family. Phyllis spoke to the Primary Department, I spoke to the combined adult classes, and then preached. We enjoyed dinner and informal talks with the adult classes while we trimmed their Christmas tree. At 6PM I showed slides and explained mission activities to the Methodist Youth Fellowship. We took turns talking as we showed slides for the evening service.

DEPUTATION AND RESIGNATION

While seeking employment, we continued our deputation visits to churches:

Sunday, Feb 12 ----Christ Methodist Church
Sunday, Feb19 ----Pasadena Community Church
Thursday, Feb23 ----United Methodist Men at First Methodist
Sunday, Feb26 ----Wesley Fellowship, Pasadena Community
Thursday, March 2 ---- Phyllis, Democratic Women, St. Petersburg
Saturday, March 4 ---Channel 13, Television show,

	"Great Decisions"
Sunday, March 5	---- Methodist Youth Fellowship, First Methodist
Sunday, March 12	---- Methodist Youth Fellowship, Christ Methodist
Wednesday, March 15	- Exchange Club, St Petersburg
Tuesday, April 4	---- United Liberal Church, St Petersburg
Sunday, April 16	---- Child's Park Methodist
Sunday, April 23	---- First Methodist, Leesburg

After I accepted employment with Florida Power Corporation on February 17, we mailed our resignation to the Methodist Board of Foreign Missions. After that resignation we ceased doing deputation as missionaries. But during the next five years or so, we would speak to hundreds of churches, schools, interested groups and civic clubs as "former" missionaries.

ADOPTION

For months we had been exploring the possibilities of adopting a baby. In Texas and Georgia the official agencies told us the waiting time for adoptions was two to five years. Our first appointment with the Florida Children's Home occurred on February 27, 1961, but it wasn't the last. They required many references, work records, educational background, medical history and a personal visit with both of us in the home we would provide the child. They approved us for adoption but warned us that we should not purchase any baby supplies until further notice. There was an indefinite waiting period with no guarantee that we would ever receive a child. On June 9th they called us into their office to advise a baby boy was available. We went that day and were pleased to accept him. Florida Children's Home required us to think about it over the week end and return Monday with our definite answer. That week end was hectic as we located a baby crib, cloth diapers, bottles, bottle sterilizer, baby formula, clothes and other items needed to care for an infant. The baby had been born on June 2nd.

We now had our first child. Our second, a baby girl joined us two years later.

The years flew by as I worked and we moved several times as engineering contracts changed and opportunities arose. We lived in Alabama, Florida, Pennsylvania, Georgia and Texas. We raised our children, Phyllis helped me with many of my jobs, and we continued our education. The children grew up and graduated college. Our son Melton got married and produced our grandson Miles. Our daughter Cathy is a school teacher and still single

In 1992, we headed to our first Congo/Zaire reunion.

IX. MISSIONARY REUNIONS

CONGO/ZAIRE MISSIONARY REUNION   1992

From June 11th to 18th, 1992, we went to the very first Congo/Zaire Missionary Reunion at Asbury College, Wilmore, Kentucky. Using our frequent flier miles for free tickets, we flew from Bradenton to Newark and on to Cincinnati. There we rented a Town Car and drove to Wilmore. About 135 missionaries were present for a great reunion.

Together, we represented more than a thousand years of service as missionaries. Ruth Piper Hardee was born in the Congo to missionary parents. Howard Brinton went to the Congo with his parents when he was six-months-old. Both Ruth and Howard returned to the Congo as commissioned missionaries. Others served up to forty years in Africa. We hadn't seen some of them in thirty years.

We participated in a beautiful memorial service for those who'd died. Some died in service in Congo; others died in their retirement years. From the younger generation, were little nieces and nephews who were responsible adults now. The month of June was a bad scheduling choice. Many former missionaries were active members of Annual Conferences that meet in June. They couldn't attend the reunion. We scheduled the next reunion for July 1995 at the Methodist Conference Center at Lake Junaluska, North Carolina.

CONGO/ZAIRE MISSIONARY REUNION—1995
BRADENTON to LAKE JUNALUSKA

Three years later, we were ready for the 1995 reunion. This one would be better than the first as it wasn't scheduled during the Annual Conference meeting dates.

We contacted Ruth Piper Hardee and invited her to ride with us.

After we left Bradenton on the 12th of July, we stopped in Tampa for Ruth, who'd had hip surgery and other medical problems. She doesn't travel easily. However, the back seat of our big station wagon offered reasonable comfort. None of us wanted to travel a long distance each day. A Holiday Inn in Thomasville, Georgia was our first stop. The second night we stayed in Franklin, North Carolina, about an hour's drive from our destination, Lake Junaluska.

LAKE JUNALUSKA

More than 200 active and former missionaries to Congo/Zaire assembled in the Methodist Conference Center at Lake Junaluska, North Carolina, on July 14th, 15th, and 16th, 1995.

Lake Junaluska is in the mountains of western North Carolina, near Waynesville, and has been used by Methodists for decades. It is large enough to have dozens of groups and hundreds of people use it at the same time.

Our reunion had exclusive use of the Lambuth Memorial Inn which has an excellent dining room and a large meeting room. This inn is a memorial to Bishop Walter Lambuth who went to Wembo Nyama, Congo, in 1912 with the Rev John Wesley Gilbert.

They started the work in an area later known as the Central Congo Conference. Bishop John Springer started our medical work in the Southern Congo Conference in 1914 with Dr. and Mrs. Arthur Piper. They were the parents of Ruth Piper Hardee, RN, who went to the reunion with us.

NIECES, NEPHEWS AND FRIENDS

Our reservations in Lambuth Inn were valid Friday, July 14, until Monday, July 17. As we waited for our room, we encountered old friends and made new ones.
We were delighted Immanuel and Valborg Bitsch-Larsen made the long trip from retirement in Denmark.
We hugged several missionary nieces and nephews who were now taller than us. Thirty-five years ago when we last saw Johnny Enright, Tommy Brinton and Ray Woodcock, they were mischievous boys.
Johnny now flies planes and builds projects as a missionary in Zaire. Tommy and Ray have responsible jobs.
Elaine Woodcock was a little red-haired girl who is now a wife and mother.
Harold and Elsie Amstutz became new friends. As a retired airline pilot, he now flies planes for mission work in Zaire, Kenya and Zambia. These flights are essential to mission activity.
Roads in Congo/Zaire are almost impassable because the dictator, Mobutu, wastes no money on road construction or maintenance.
For example:
1) total mileage of passable roads at independence in 1960 was 90,000,

2) total mileage of passable roads in 1995 is less than 5,000 miles, in an area as large as the United States east of the Mississippi River.

Mission airstrips have sprouted like mushrooms, since we built that first one at Kapanga in 1960. And everyone said it would never be used!

REUNION

The most formal reunion meeting was Communion Service on Sunday morning.

At other gatherings, we watched slide shows and shared stories about our time in Congo/Zaire. Several of our senior missionaries had converted old photographs from the early days (1915-1930) into slides that were fascinating.

Floodgates of memories were opened. Traveling across Africa, learning the local languages, hunting food, establishing livable homes, crossing old rickety ferries on rivers infested with crocodiles and hippos, dealing with government officials, enduring insects and infections, and just existing in Congo/Zaire has always been a challenge.

Some of the stories were hilarious now. Hearing each other's stories, we either laughed or cried, or both at the same time.

Learning of fellow missionary friends who died or were killed in Congo brought us to tears. One evening we had a memorial service for fellow missionaries who had either died since the 1992 reunion or had not been memorialized then. Sixty (60) candles were burning when the reader finished the list.

Now there are one hundred eleven of us among the saints. The next reunion of earthly missionaries is scheduled for July 1998 at Lake Junaluska.

One more statistic: As commissioned missionaries (preachers, doctors, nurses, teachers, builders, agronomists and engineers) we served 1,650 years.

The following paragraphs are samples of stories heard at the reunion:

Pat Rothrock: A church in Tennessee was threatening to give up their support of Doug Crowder because he'd left mission work to teach school. But in many a mission school, youths, both missionary and African, have come to know and love the Lord Jesus.

Holly Hammer Anderson: I went to the reunion 3 years ago at Wilmore and have told people since that the most wonderful thing was hearing the family stories—stories that we had grown up with and then meeting some of the people I'd never met: being able to see Ruth Piper after having stayed in the house her parents had built out at the falls. This was almost more family than my biological family.

H T MacLin: A lot of us were "aunts" and "uncles" or spoke of others that way. One strong impression of our meeting at Wilmore was that there were several there who shared things with us which they'd never shared in any other setting since leaving Africa. In this family it was understood.

Gran Godley: Ditto about what a family the missionaries really are. I was substituting for Faye Smith as a pilot. I landed at thirty-seven different airstrips, Kapanga five or six times, and learned what mission work was all about.

People have asked me "Aren't you afraid?" No. I believe the Lord provides angels 24 hours a day.

Howard Brinton: Some people think our religion was imposed over there, when really Methodism was invited to come and work with the people. An old chief, Mwant Yav, said to John Springer in 1910, "I want you to get two missionaries to come and work with my people, to cure my people of diseases that wipe out whole villages." That's when Dr. Piper went out and through his ministry, sleeping sickness and smallpox were brought under control

Virginia (Law) Shell: Talk about family...Bobbie Johnson told a story this afternoon that belongs to all of us at Wembo Nyama. When we were living there Ricky Deale and my little Paul went over to Elizabeth Ackerberg's house. One boy said to the other, "I know where the cookies are! I saw her get them out the last time". The other said, "But we shouldn't be getting cookies if she isn't here'. The first said, "But she's our aunt and she would want us to have cookies".

Hall Duncan: He talked about arriving in the Congo and being assigned to teach math in Mulungwishi. One day he had to teach a problem he couldn't solve. So he told his students they were going to be the leaders in the future and sent one of them to the chalkboard to solve the problem.. While the student was working the problem out, Hall was sitting in the back of the class praying the Lord would see him through this challenge. The student solved the problem.

Jim Decker: My daughter Sondra in St Paul has a friend who is from the Kasai. One Sunday at church, she met this man who had a lady with him who was also from Zaire and

who had a PhD in microbiology. He introduced the lady to Sondra. The lady said she was from Jadotville. Sondra said "So am I, I lived in Jadotville."
"What was your father's name?"
Sondra answered, "His name was Bwana Decker".
"I used to baby-sit you".
Sondra asked "Was I good?"
The lady said "No!".
This shows just how far the ripple goes when you drop a stone into a pool.
Dorothy Culp: Speaking of ripples. Our daughter had been demonstrating the use of machines in hospitals and in medical workshops. She was sent from Sacramento to Atlanta to a big medical convention. She was demonstrating microscan machines. You query the machine about what drug is effective with a certain bacteria. There was a line of people, and all were wearing name tags. One black man took quite a bit of time entering several queries. Three different cures for different bacteria came up.
She noticed the name Shungu on his name tag. Just then he saw her name tag and his mouth flew open.
"No! You weren't with a family by the name of Culp at Lodja were you?" he asked.
"Yes, and you're not Bishop Shungu's son are you?"
He was and had developed the cure for the three bacteria which came up on the screen in that demonstration.
Bill Starnes: Good to see Pete Hoepner here. One Sunday morning I took him with me to a service near Lubumbashi. I was preaching that morning. "If any man be in Christ he is a new creature."

New desires were part of it. Every time I used "new desires" Pete would scrunch up.

When we were leaving the village, Pete said, "Bill, before you ever preach that sermon again, you better look up the meaning of 'matako'."

I said I knew what it was, it was the plural for the word "desire". But I learned the people didn't use the plural as I had. Instead, matako is used by the natives as a word that means buttocks and I was preaching that they all needed new buttocks.

Don Shell: The Jesus film is transforming the population. We have shown it to about 150,000 people with about 15% responding positively to the invitation. We have difficulty with follow-up. It is shown in French now, and we use an interpreter, portable power, screen, etc. It is amazing how it is helping the people understand the life of Jesus, and that he actually hung on the cross. Even the Catholic people ask for it. Their people are telling their church leaders, "You're not telling the story right. We actually saw it happen!".

Rolla Swanson: I was a farm boy, but didn't know much about gardens in Zaire. I was in this garden and ants started coming up my trousers. It was unbelievable. I started to fight them and finally decided the only thing to do was to drop my trousers. But God has been so good and I just want to thank all of you.

Ray Watson: Some truck had broken the bac (ferry) at Lubefu, so I met Rolla (see previous paragraph) at the river as he came across in a dugout canoe, a nice young man in white shirt, straw hat, brief case in one hand and typewriter in the other. When he met those ants, I had my camera hanging around my neck and I was concerned about this nice guy who was a minister but interested in agriculture. I was there when he was examining this peanut plant and thought it was beautiful. All of a sudden he dropped his pants—

—I'm still sad and sorry I didn't take the picture.

Pat Johnson: More about that dancing. I learned that HT is a marvelous dancer, especially when he has motivation. One day, HT wanted to go monkey hunting. With Ngandjolo, we descended into the forest. Ngandjolo told HT to walk where he walked and not get off the path. HT looked up and saw a wonderful possibility for a shot high in the trees. Now he was watching for the heavens, but not watching for what the devil might do below. We heard some rustling among the leaves and then saw the most animated dancing in the world.

Virginia Shell: I remember the day when through misinformation the Africans were told that Burleigh (her husband) was going to move the hospital to Katako Kombe because he couldn't get the plans approved at Wembo Nyama. They marched together onto the station with their war drums, their terrible noise and yelling, and I was scared to death. I went out to the middle of the station and Isabel DeRuiter was standing there, one of those quiet saints of God. She turned to me and said, "Virginia, God has seen us through worse than this".

HT MacLin: Many here remember Ngandjolo. An insight I gained from him that I treasure was in 1958. Alice and I stopped in Brussels at the world's fair on our way back to Africa. The Belgian Government brought several thousand Congolese to that fair, perhaps to dazzle them with the glories of the "motherland" so they would remain content back home.

I met Ngandjolo at the airport and took him around Brussels. We went to Au Bon Marche. As we went up an escalator, the higher we went the whiter his knuckles became.

Later, when I took him to the airport for his return to the Congo, I asked Papa Moise, "What are you going to tell your people when you get back there? What's going to be your big memory about this?"

He replied "I will tell them that they sin here about like we do in Africa".

Lois Persons: As a new missionary, I didn't like being called "Mama" by people much older than me. Then one day a man came to our door and said, "Madam, will you buy these carrots?" My cook had a fit!! He said, "Don't you know she's no madam, she's a mama!" Thereafter I decided to be a mama was a good thing.

Woody Bartlett: A story that Mrs. Helen Springer told Woody. She said she was the originator of the mini-skirt. They were early missionaries in Rhodesia (about 1910 or after) and she wore the long woolen skirt down to the ground as they did years ago. They were traveling in the bush with a donkey and the rain just poured. The skirt got so wet that she could hardly move. She said to her husband, "John, come here". He came. "Do you have your knife?" He said yes. "Well, you cut the skirt off right there!"

Melvin Blake: One day at 475 Riverside Drive, Methodist Mission headquarters in New York City, I was going up the escalator and Julian Ray of Mozambique was going down.

He called out, "Mel, there is a bishop in your office." I didn't catch on.

Approaching my office, Ann said, "The bishop is in your office" and I still didn't catch on. On my desk was this box with the ashes of Bishop Springer. I put the box in a drawer until Omar Hartzler returned to Africa. The bishop was in my office for a long time.

Omar Hartzler: I was going out to be Bishop Booth's secretary. I hand carried that box onto the plane. When I got to Lubumbashi the customs official asked, "What do you have in that box?" I said, "I got a bishop!". The customs official didn't ask anything more.

Joe Davis {This paragraph was part of the memorial service}: Psalm 116 is full of thanksgiving to God, but in the midst of it, He said something unusual. "Precious in the sight of the Lord is the death of his faithful ones!". At first glance these words shock us a little bit. It's not the suffering of death that is lifted up here, it's the way God looks on us as we did when our children came home from school. What is said here is that God enjoys the presence of his children. God's priorities are on people not on things.

Nancy Woodcok: Nancy really appreciated then, and also now, all her missionary aunts and uncles. It's so neat to be here and visit with each one of you. Once, my best girlfriend back in Indiana just could not believe I had so many aunts and uncles.

Dorothy Ethridge: Traveling from Minga to Lubondai our family would usually stop in Lusambo. We loved tomatoes and Mom would pack a paring knife to cut tomatoes with. This time she forgot the knife. My dad volunteered his pocket knife. About half way through slicing a tomato, he stopped and with a twinkle in his eye, he shook the knife and said, "You know, I did an autopsy with this knife".

Tom Brinton: As a child growing up there, we had many fun times, whether on hippo hunts, or whatever. As I traveled with my dad, seeing him build schools and churches, I was thinking those buildings would last forever. In 1990 I had the good fortune to go out. It struck me that many of those buildings were gone, but what remained was in the spirit of the people planted by many of you missionaries. You put in so many years in that work. The work is still blossoming because of what you did.

Bill Starnes: I want to share something with you that Bishop Booth gave me 38 years ago and has blessed my life. I followed Maurice Persons as legal representative. I was also district missionary. One day I went in to see Bishop Booth and he asked how I was. I began to tell him that I was tired, felt overworked, etc.

He listened quietly and when I was through he said, "Bill, we're all tired. We're all overworked. We are all carrying heavy loads. It doesn't help if we talk too much about it".

HT MacLin: John Wesley Shungu was great with words. He came to our district when we had a bishop from the USA making his first visit over here. We had a great "mbulu" (revival) going in a village. Only Shungu and I both spoke English and Otetela. Bishop was asked to preach and Shungu translated for him. But soon the bishop used an illustration about a baseball game, which was never played in Congo.

Shungu whispered to him to tell the whole story. Then he would translate for him. Shungu said a few words and the crowd laughed.

The bishop was pleased that his message had gotten across so well. Afterwards he asked how Shungu could translate the illustration in so few words.

Without batting an eye, Shungu said, "Well, Bishop, I knew they wouldn't understand that story, so I just said that you had told a funny story. Please laugh now!"

Hall Duncan: As a cartoonist I got into trouble one time on the mission field. One missionary wanted to send me home from South Africa. The cartoon in question showed the bishop saying to a group of missionaries, "Now that we have been OFF the subject for four and one-half hours, I have a suggestion to make. "

John Enright: [John had returned from Zaire a few weeks before the reunion]. About three weeks ago, they just paid the school teachers for the years "93 and "94. It amounted to about 45 cents for two years work. Officials don't get paid. I have never experienced extortion, road blocks and beatings like I have this past year in Zaire. I had never seen the country so unhappy. Everyone is fixing for a fight. Katanga wants to secede from Zaire. "Tshombe" will rise again!

Where is the church? What of our fruit? I watched as thousands of Kasais were routed out of their homes and sent packing. The church didn't say a word against it. A pastor in one of our seminaries said, "Just as Joshua chased the Canaanites out of Israel, so we are going to roust the Kasais out of the Katanga. This is the will of God. This is what the Scriptures teach us to do." He is teaching in one of our seminaries.

Al Whelchel: Communion Service. The occasion of greatest importance was the one in the Upper Room. His

(Jesus') death was on the horizon. He sent Peter and John ahead to prepare for the feast of the Passover. There he made it a different kind of Passover than they'd ever had. Jesus didn't say remember our past, our deliverance from Egypt. Jesus brought it up to date. He'd asked that week, "Who do you say that I am?" Simon had said, "You are the Christ, the Son of God". Jesus said then, "I am He". He lifts the bread and cup, and bids them partake of it in remembrance of him. Not in remembering what he did, but in who he was, and is.

Three days is a short time for rekindling memories, but we did the best we could to revive as many as possible. Ruth enjoyed and savored this 1995 reunion because her ability to travel decreases each year. [However, we all plan to attend the next reunion at Lake Junaluska in 1998.]

LAKE JUNALUSKA TO BRADENTON

Leaving Lake Junaluska, we decided to take a different highway to Franklin and try to visit some friends.

That "different" highway is one we will never willingly travel again. It goes over and around the mountains in a narrow, twisting right of way. Seldom was a straight stretch of highway much longer than the wagon. Along the way we met several moving vans and huge soft drink trucks that occupied more than their half of the paved area. We never did find our friend's place. It is hidden somewhere along US 62 near Sapphire and Cashier. We asked for directions to the address we had written down. No one could help us.

On the road home we had many opportunities to talk with Ruth about life at Kapanga and mission activities in Congo in the years before we went to Kapanga. Ruth had talked with Howard Brinton and Omar Hartzler at Lake Junaluska. These two men had grown up in Congo. Howard went there in 1916 and Omar in the early 1920's.

Those conversations, and others, refreshed Ruth's memories. She shared them with us as we drove along the pleasant roads in Georgia and Florida. We had many questions she was able to answer.

X. EPILOGUE

You may understand why fictional adventure movies and/or television shows don't excite us. Our life story is being closed at the end of 1995.

Our Story may not be over, but the telling is. With our good health and genes from long lived parents we expect to have exciting years in the future. There are goals to seek, places to see and friends to visit. Watching Miles grow will be fascinating. Other active retirees have told us they don't know how they ever found time to work. We share that viewpoint. We have spent enough time on this story, other projects await our attention.

Our life story has taken many more pages than we anticipated. Daily routines and lots of trivia have been barely mentioned or left out. Perhaps there is still too much. Some events and impressions have been forgotten. Our diaries were incomplete and sometimes the entries were brief, almost cryptic. Others have written detailed journals, but we didn't do so. Unpleasant or painful incidents seemed to have disappeared. We didn't try to resurrect them. Our decision to stay in the USA and not return to Congo was selfish. If we had returned to Congo then Melton, Cathy, Rebecca and Miles wouldn't be in our lives today. We cannot imagine an existence without them.

I missed certain death in the North Atlantic, Louisiana and three times in Colombia. Was this chance or did the Lord plan for my missionary service in Congo? We both missed probable death at Luluabourg if that DC-4 landing gear had not fallen into place. I missed very probable death at the hands of the three angry cannibal witch doctors in Congo.

There were more incidents: the cobra, lions outside our tents, the violence in the Congo and the Middle East. Why? Why have the two of us lived this long when others have not done so?

By staying alive we have shared our witness with individuals, groups and churches. The hospital we helped build at Kapanga has eased much suffering and saved lives. In order of appearance: Melton, Catherine, Rebecca and Miles have entered our immediate family circle. At our wedding we were two, now we are six.

Several friends have now enriched our lives for more than 50 years. New friends are entering our lives as we close this story. Wherever we have found ourselves, we have tried to make that part of the world a better place when we left than when we arrived. Someday the Lord will tell us whether or not we succeeded.

We have tried to "VAYA CON DIOS" all our lives

XI. ODDS & ENDS

In this chapter we've included longer accounts about people and events that are mentioned briefly in the main story. We've been blessed with wonderful friends, unique experiences and close encounters with a cast of real characters.

Story One: Kayeka
Tshangand Kayeka was captured near Musumba/Kapanga by some Portuguese slave traders in the late 1800's. They took him westward into Portuguese Angola where they sold him. We've included a summary of his life story. He became a Christian who prayed effectively for a medical missionary. He died before we arrived at Kapanga.
[see XVII-24]

Story Two: Death Comes to a Missionary
We attended the Kennedy School of Missions with Max and Anita Ritter. I was having an emergency appendectomy in one wing of Edith Cavell Hospital, Brussels, when Anita was giving birth to their first born son, Halloween, 1951. We lived in the apartment beneath theirs in Brussels. Max was everything Anita writes in the included article.
[see XVII-17]

Story Three: Missionaries Fight a Crocodile to get their Hippopotamus

Originally this hunt for a hippopotamus was included in a letter to Phyllis's parents and it had no title. Mrs. Lewis submitted it to the *Atlanta Journal & Constitution Magazine* and they published it in October 1955. Credit, or blame, for the title goes to that magazine.

[see XVII-20]

Story Four Escape From the Congo—1960

This letter was written to Phyllis' parents, Claude and Thelma Lewis from Salisbury, Southern Rhodesia in July 1960.

Names of places have changed: today Salisbury is Harare and Southern Rhodesia is Zimbabwe. The letter was published in the *St. Petersburg Times Magazine*, July 31, 1960.

[see XIX-35]

Story Five Mwant Yav Ditend and Jonathan Manung, Diplomatic Tour in the USA—1960

This is my informal report on the Tour of the United States and Puerto Rico by Mwant Yav Ditend, Paramount Chief of the Lunda Tribe, and Jonathan Manung, School Principal in the city of Elisabethville, Katanga, Belgian Congo. The tour lasted from October 1, 1960 until November 23, 1960. It is a condensed report. My notes from the tour filled forty one (41) single spaced typewritten pages.

[see XX-2]

Story One) **THE STORY OF TSHANGAND KAYEKA**
INTRODUCTION

In the spring of 1986 while on a business trip for ARAMCO (Arabian American Oil Company) I went into a used book store in downtown Ottawa, Canada. Searching through a pile of books about Africa, I found and purchased *Currie of Chissamba* by John T Tucker, published by the United Church of Canada in 1945.

The foreword of the book is written by W W Barker, who compiled the first history of the Congregational Church mission work in Angola,Africa. Barker was a personal friend of Rev Walter Thomas Currie.

In Tucker's book we learned that Chissamba (which means peace) was the name of the Mission Station founded in Angola by Rev. Currie. While reading it we discovered the story of Kayeka, a young slave lad from the village of Musumba.

Musumba is the large capital village of the great Paramount Chief, Mwant Yav, of the Lunda tribe. Musumba is in the southwestern part of Zaire, known as the Belgian Congo until its independence from Belgium in 1960.

Among our other books about Africa we have *I Love the Trail*, written by Bishop John McKendree Springer in 1952. This book by Bishop Springer is a special tribute to his wife, Helen. It tells of their work together in Africa. On their second journey into the Belgian Congo in December of 1910 the Springers met Kayeka at Kalulua, a village in the Congo southeast of Dilolo.

Dilolo is the border town between Angola and Belgian Congo (Zaire) on the KDL (Katanga-Dilolo-Lobito) railroad. The KDL extended from the Angolan port of

Lobito on the Atlantic Ocean to the Katanga mining center of Lubumbashi (Elisabethville) in the southeast corner of Zaire. From there it connected to another railroad that went all the way south through Zambia (Northern Rhodesia) and Zimbabwe (Southern Rhodesia) to the port city of Cape Town on the Indian Ocean in South Africa. The KDL wasn't completed until the middle of the 1930 s.

In another of his books, *Christian Conquest in the Congo*, published in 1927, we found more references to Kayeka.

In addition to the information in these three books we have accounts of the life of Kayeka written by two United Methodist missionaries who knew Kayeka personally and worked with him and his family.

Ruth Piper Hardee was the first white child born at Kapanga Mission station, adjacent to Musumba. Her parents were Dr. and Mrs. Arthur Piper who began the medical work at Kapanga. Howard Brinton arrived there with his parents, Rev. and Mrs. Thomas Brinton, when he was 6 months of age. Howard and his wife, Elizabeth (Libby) would spend their lives in Congo and Zaire.

Our purpose in writing this account of Kayeka is to combine all the recorded events into one chronological order for a more complete story of his life.

TSHANGAND KAYEKA

In the late 1800's, on one of the last slave raids instigated by the Portuguese from the west coast of Angola, slave raiders entered the southwestern corner of the Belgian Congo and into the Lunda Kingdom.

Among the many African youths and adults they captured was a young lad named Kayeka, the little pledged one. Those captured were chained together in long lines and marched some 600 miles into Angola. Ill fed and harshly treated many died on the trek. (Slave Icon © 1990-94 CPTime lnternational)

Kayeka had the good fortune not to be sent on to the coast to go overseas. He was sold to an African chief who took a liking to this appealing teenager. Kayeka's African master lived across the Ukulongo River from a Canadian congregational Mission station named Chissamba, which means Peace in Umbundo, the language of the Bailundo tribe in that region.

The African chief sent Kayeka to work for Rev. Walter Currie at the mission station. When Kayeka was paid his week's wages, the money was taken straight to his master.

Kayeka learned a great deal from the tasks he performed and from his observations at the mission. He resolved to enter school himself—and learn to read like the missionary Rev. Currie.

Kayeka also watched as many people were healed from physical ills by medicine, care and rest. Only minor surgery was performed at this mission station. Rev. Currie wasn't a doctor but prayed for someone to come to Angola in order to give medical help to all who needed it.

His African master believed that Kayeka was intelligent and could probably earn more money in the future if he attended the mission school. Kayeka enrolled as a pupil. His books and studies were in Umbundo. He soon converted to Christianity and gave his whole heart to Christ.

Kayeka began to be "oppressed with an unbearable burden". He yearned for the conversion of his own people—the Aruund. He prayed daily for a way to return home to Musumba and teach his family about Jesus Christ. He also prayed God would send missionaries to Musumba. Unknown to Kayeka, but known to God, a great many other Christians were also praying for his people who lived in the heart of Africa.

Kayeka studied diligently and prayed often. He was close to the age of twenty. He had taken a wife, a former slave of Chief Kanundu. She was a member of the Baluba tribe, who were from northwest of the Aruund, partly in Angola and partly in the Belgian Congo.

His master converted to Christianity. After converting, he wanted to give Kayeka his freedom, saying since both were Christians, he could no longer keep Kayeka as a slave.

Kayeka wanted to seize this chance for freedom but realized his own freedom would cause a financial loss for his master. Therefore, he resolved to earn enough to pay for his freedom.

We read that Kayeka had "changed hands", meaning he'd worked for more than one master. After his freedom was achieved, Kayeka went on several trading missions on behalf of his former master. Time passed quickly.

It was almost 1900. News came that the Portuguese Republic, recently established, decreed the release of all slaves: "by whomsoever owned," and anyone who wished, could return to their home lands carrying permission issued by the local European authorities.

Kayeka, however, continued his trading trips. He bought salt, needles, thread, beads and food as he went into the interior. He continued to pray throughout the years that missionaries would come to his homeland.

It was on one of these trading excursions in 1910 that Kayeka met Rev. John and Helen Springer. Bishop Springer wrote in a letter dated December 9, 1910, "that day proved to be a surprising, a revealing, and an historic occasion. They came to our veranda on that day, an African nearing 30 years of age. He regarded us with quiet but intense interest."

"Sir, is it true that you have come to open a mission among the Aruund, the people of Mwant Yav? I have heard that this is your purpose". He spoke hesitatingly, in the limited English he'd acquired.

"Yes, that is our appointment," I replied. "And why do you ask?"

He was visibly much affected. Gradually his story came out.

Kayeka said for years whenever he heard of the arrival of any white men of God in the interior, he traveled to meet them and find out if they would come to Musumba. He told Reverend and Mrs. Springer he had prayed for their arrival for years.

Reverend Springer said, "And here we are, just at the border of your tribe, with a definite appointment to your people."

Here was the concrete answer to Kayaka's prayer that had continued for more than twelve years".

No wonder that we, that day and long afterward, found our hearts stirred to their depths in wonder and praise to God.

The Springers and Kayeka met on December 9, 1910, at Kalulua, on the border of the Belgian Congo.

Earlier that same year, in October, a Belgian government official had met the Springers at Kansanshi and asked where they were going. John Springer told him they were appointed to the Aruund tribe.

"Oh", he replied, "we just abandoned a temporary government post at Kalulua right on the border. If you find the buildings still standing, you are welcome to use the camp in the rainy season".

The Springers found the post in good repair with several buildings and some furniture left behind. "Surely, God planned to bring us to this very place," they said to each other.

Kalulua was only 10 miles from the Fisher's British mission station at Kalenge Hill. It was good to have such fine neighbors near. Kayeka must have visited with the Springers for several days.

In the conversations, they learned Kayeka's father was the chief at Kazembe on the Lukoshi River, some eighty miles north of Kalulua.

Chief Kazembe was a brother of the Mwant Yav.

Therefore, Kayeka was a nephew of the Paramount Chief (King) of the Aruund. Kayeka may have had other relatives and friends in this area of the Belgian Congo. Surviving records are sketchy.

He explored this territory on his many trading trips. Again, he asked the Springers to travel to the court of the Mwant Yav at Musumba.

John and Helen Springer already knew something of the geography and territory of the southern Belgian Congo. They'd walked hundreds of miles in Africa as they searched for the right places to start mission stations.

For example, in May of 1907, on their way home to the USA from their mission work in Southern Rhodesia, they felt the need to explore the possibilities of opening new mission stations in the very heart of Africa. They traveled north by railroad to Broken Hill in Northern Rhodesia—end of the line at that time. From there they continued northward on foot. Their caravan consisted of fifty native carriers. They took food, supplies, clothes and trading goods in order to bargain for food in the villages along their route. They needed local food for their carriers and for themselves.

The first 200 miles took them past a few mission stations and government outposts on their way to the Belgian Congo.

Geologists had recently discovered huge deposits of copper ore and other minerals in the Katanga region of the Congo. The Springers realized Europeans from many nations would flock to work in these new mines and smelters.

Natives from central Africa would also be needed as workers. Northern Rhodesia was already mining in many areas and British missionaries were there. The Springers knew the mining areas in Congo would be a strategic center for any evangelistic work for God.

The Springers spent a Sabbath day at Kambove, in the Congo, where six years later they would build a mission station. The next Sabbath was spent at Ruwi, where gold had been found. Later copper would be found also. Mr. Harrison, manager of the mine, became a good friend of the Springers. The railroad to Broken Hill was being extended northward into the mining area of the Congo. Plans were made to connect it with a railroad (Katanga-Dilolo-Lobito) coming from Lobito, Angola.

In July of 1907, they traveled south across the Zambezi River to visit a new British mission station named Kalene Hill. There they first met Dr. Walter Fisher and his wife, a nurse.

From Kalene Hill they traveled to the Garanganza Mission Station at Kavungu.

Leaving that station, they followed Dr. David Livingstone's trail of 1853-1854 to the Atlantic coast near Luanda, Angola.

On their way they visited the Methodist Mission Station at Malange, Angola, on August 16, 1907. This station was the most interior Methodist Mission Station in Angola.

After three weeks of rest, they sailed from Luanda on the Portuguese steamer, *Africa*, to Lisbon, Portugal. [Kavungu to Luanda is about one thousand miles, on foot.]

On October 16, 1907, the Springers arrived in New York City. John and Helen Springer took all the new information they'd learned on their 1,500 mile trek across Africa to challenge the churches of America.

John wrote a book *The Heart of Central Africa*," subtitled "Mineral Wealth and Missionary Opportunity."

Helen put her story articles together with many photos taken in Africa. Her book *Snapshots From Sunny Africa* was published. They were both tired and Helen was ill, so they stayed in the United States for some years. When they returned to Africa in 1910, it was with a new appointment to move into Central Africa—the Belgian Congo—and open mission work there.

After his meeting with the Springers, Kayeka returned to Chissamba, Angola, to take his family and move to Musumba. He took with him the Good News of Jesus Christ and also the good news that missionaries would soon arrive to work among the Aruund. He longed to tell his people about what Jesus had done for him.

Kayeka gathered together his wife and children, their family possessions, bundles of clothes, blankets and food for their long journey. There were a few other Lundas who wanted to return to Musumba under Kayeka's leadership—some were unattached men, boys and girls.

It took them eighty days to travel inland on foot all the way to Musumba. Kayeka was inspired not so much at the prospect of physical freedom as by the hope and confidence that his people in remote Congo would respond to his preaching about Jesus. He sought their release from sin and death in order to find the New Life in Christ. He prayed as he traveled towards home.

Kayeka traveled straight to the Mwant Yav at Musumba with all the good news! Slavery in Angola was over and many Lundas were now free to return to their homeland. He told the court about his own life in Angola—working and learning at the Chissamba Mission Station.

He told them about God and his son, Jesus. He told them all he had learned from Rev. Currie—and more importantly—that missionaries would soon be coming to Musumba.

When Rev. John Springer and his wife, Helen, arrived at Musumba in the dry season of 1912, they were greeted with an enthusiastic celebration. Because of Kayeka's testimony and influence, the Mwant Yav asked the Springers to meet with him.

The Paramount Chief had heard about "Totolo", Dr. Fisher, of Kalenge Hill station and his work. The Mwant Yav asked Rev. Springer to send two missionaries: first, send a doctor to help his people and second, send a man of the Book, the words of God.

This Paramount Chief, Mwant Yav Muteba, went with John and Helen Springer to choose the physical site for the Mission station. They chose a large piece of land adjacent to Musumba—a good place with a deep spring of cool, clear water. Leaving Musumba, the Springers traveled south to Dilolo and back to Elisabethville.

In 1914, Dr. and Mrs. Arthur Piper arrived via Kambove. The Springers traveled part of the way to Musumba with them. Mrs. Piper (Maude Garrette) confessed years later she and her husband felt, at that moment, like "children left alone in the woods."

On June 22, 1914, news reached Kayeka of the impending arrival of the young white doctor and his wife from America. Kayeka gathered between three and four hundred natives and headed out to meet the missionaries. This crowd was excited and happy; they had no better way to express their emotions than by singing. As they walked out from Musumba and down the trail, their voices could be heard a great distance away. They traveled nearer towards each other until they could see one another. The new missionaries were overcome with emotion when they saw all the people who had walked out to greet them--singing "Jesus Loves Me" in Lunda. The Africans lined the path for miles as the doctor and his wife passed. Many held palm branches arched over their heads.

When the Pipers reached Musumba the crowd gathered around them. Kayeka offered a most heartfelt prayer to Almighty God for His Goodness to them. After the prayer there followed a stirring message of welcome from the Mwant Yav. Their missionaries had at last arrived.

The work became established and the new Mission Station was named Kapanga. During those first months and years, no person worked as faithfully and patiently at the missionary's side as did Kayeka. The joy of Kayeka's experience found expression in several hymns he composed. Those hymns were included in the first Lunda hymnal printed years later. Mrs. Piper, in writing to a friend, described Kayeka as the most Christ-like person she'd ever met anywhere.

The first hospital was small with a grass roof. It was used for surgery, with light from a Coleman lantern at night. There was a medicine closet and dispensary for outpatients. This hospital clinic was set on the main road through mission property—west to Musumba and east to the modest Belgian government post on the Lulua River.

Dr. and Mrs. Piper served faithfully for more than thirty-eight years on this mission station and retired in 1952. (Non-medical missionary personnel were often moved around to various stations.)

A 200-bed fairly modern hospital was built over the course of many years. Construction was completed in 1954 and it was dedicated that year. The Pipers returned to Musumba in 1959 for a great celebration; they hadn't been able to attend the dedication.

During the intervening years, the original little building was given a permanent metal roof and used as an out-patient clinic.

In October 1916, Rev. and Mrs. Thomas Brinton arrived at Kapanga with their six-month old son, Howard.

The "Man of the Book," as requested by Mwant Yav, had arrived. His work of teaching God's word began.

Miss Marie Jensen, a Danish nurse, came with the Brintons. Miss Jensen came to the USA from the Methodist Church in Denmark in order to study midwifery in Chicago. She'd applied to the Board of Foreign Missions.

Mrs. Brinton was a school teacher and knew nothing about medicine. The Brintons had asked the Board if they could find a trained nurse to go to Congo with them. The Board accepted Miss Jensen's application for service and sent her to the Congo with the Brintons. She was with them on the voyage and during the final thirty-one day trek (walk) from Kambove to Kapanga in the rainy season of 1916.

Unless you have experienced a rainy season in Congo, it is impossible to appreciate the difficulties in walking thirty-one days while caring for a six-month old baby.

Rev. John Brastrup, from Denmark, arrived in 1920 to help with the many mission duties at Kapanga. Miss Jensen would spend her career at Kapanga hospital and return to Kapanga in 1959 with the Pipers.

Rev. Brastrup moved on to the Sandoa Methodist Mission years later to join the Brintons and spend the rest of his career there. He died in retirement in Denmark.

The Mwant Yav of 1912 died in 1921 and a new Paramount Chief was chosen to guide the Aruund tribe. The position of Paramount Chief is not hereditary.

It was this same year Rev. Thomas Brinton was asked to open a new mission station at Mwajinga (Sandoa). This station was south of Kapanga on the edge of the Lunda territory that bordered the fierce Bachokwe tribe.

Rev. Brinton was conducting a Bible Training School at Kapanga he'd begun in 1917 with the help of Kayeka and many other faithful African Christians. By 1922 Rev. Brinton had translated and published the four Gospels and Acts in the Lunda language.

Rev John Brastrup took over the work of the Bible Training School and the circuit of village churches at Kapanga.

Kayeka and a group of his friends were asked to move to Sandoa to help start the new mission. With his family, his wife and children (Sala, Rachel, Esther and Moses) and several relatives, Kayeka moved south. Many of Kayeka's friends, some from his years in Angola, decided to go with him. Together they established the village of Kayeka near Sandoa Station.

Kayeka's ability to lead and manage people, his great patience and good judgement were of enormous value to Rev. and Mrs. Brinton. He helped bring goodwill and understanding between these two tribes (Lunda and Chokwe) that "in olden times" had been so hostile to one another. Politically, the Chokwe were subject to the authority of the Mwant Yav at Musumba.

Rev. John Springer returned as Mission Superintendent of the Congo Mission Conference in 1922. On a trip to Sandoa he found that Rev. Brinton and the men helping him had cleared a large site for the mission station. They'd planted gardens and fields, opened roads, and built four major buildings. Rev. Brinton was again teaching Bible classes and leading a new training school. The school term lasted forty weeks each year. Rev. Thomas Brinton was working to complete the translation of the New Testament. He was also doing some translation work into the Bachokwe language.

When Kayeka and his family originally returned to Musumba from Angola, they brought with them seeds from orange, lemon and grapefruit trees. He planted some citrus trees at Kapanga. He planted more and more trees at Sandoa. Fruit trees were important to him. He had been so hungry as a young man, he wanted to help his people with improved agriculture and gardening.

Although Kayeka loved sharing God's word with his people, he and his friends from Angola also wanted to teach them the building skills they'd learned from Rev. Walter Currie at Chissamba. They knew how to make bricks and lay them properly. They knew carpentry as they built lintels, doors, window frames and strong rafters.

But Kayeka's great love was agriculture—At Sandoa, he centered his life around agriculture and cattle raising.

Kayeka chose to be a Christian layman in the church, telling his people agriculture wasn't dependent upon the pleasure or displeasure of the spirit world with all its witchcraft and evil superstition. It was dependent upon hard work and knowledge of the proper care of the land that God had created.

"More than twenty years after his return to his homeland, Kayeka revisited Currie's village at Chissamba. He recounted to a generation which knew not Joseph, how he, Kayeka, had been taken as a slave into a foreign country." He told about his blistered feet and a deep hunger in his stomach as he plodded along, yoked to the one in front and to the other one behind him. He told how he had finally reached Chissamba.

There he heard the Gospel of Jesus Christ which brought relief for his soul. It was a moving recital. "Men meant it for evil, but God meant it for good". Just as it had happened to Joseph in the Old Testament.

Kayeka shared with the Rev Currie and people at Chissamba how God sent missionaries to open new stations: one at Musumba which was named Kapanga and another at Mwajinga (Sandoa). He told of the ways he and his fellow "workmen" from Angola had helped with building these new mission stations. Rev. Currie knew that God indeed had sent his word through Kayeka into the heart of Africa.

Tshangand Kayeka lived to a ripe old age, loved and respected by everyone. He died in the early 1950's and is buried in the family burial plot at the Mwajinga (Sandoa) Mission Station on the edge of Kayeka's village.

"In 1990, Rev. Howard Brinton was invited back to Zaire by Bishop Katembo Kayinda, Southern Zaire Conference, to be the conference preacher. One afternoon the whole conference gathered around Kayeka's grave for a moving memorial service".

We have created a Chronological Timeline below:

DATE	LOCATION	AGE
1884	born in southwest Belgian Congo	birth
1898	captured by slave raiders, In Angola worked at Chissamba Mission, attended classes, converted to Christianity, Prayed for his tribe, the Lundas (Aruund) Portugal decreed "release all slaves	14
1910	Met Rev & Mrs. Springer at Kalulua in southwest Belgian Congo	26
1914	Dr. & Mrs. Arthur Piper arrived at Kapanga and started medical work	30
1916	Rev. & Mrs. Thoms Brinton & son, Howard arrived at Musumba, Miss Marie Jensen, Danish nurse and Rev. John Brastrup, Denmark, arrived	
1922	Kayeka moved to Mwajinga (Sandoa)	38
1930	Kayeka returned to Chissamba Mission after 20 years in Belgian Congo	46
1950	Kayeka died and is buried at Sandoa	66
1960	Belgian Congo granted independence from Belgium and became the Republic of Congo, later renamed ZAIRE	

BIBLIOGRPHY
1. SPRINGER, John Mckendree: *Pioneering in the Congo*, published in 1907.
2. SPRINGER, John Mckendree: *Christian Conquests in the Congo*, published in 1927.
3. TUCKER, John T.: *Currie of Chissamba*, published in 1945.
4. SPRINGER, John Mckendree: *I Love the Trail* published in 1952.
5. PIPER, Ruth B. (Ruth Piper Hardee), *Kayeka, The Faithful* written in 1949. A report prepared for a class at the Kennedy School of Missions, Hartford, Connecticut.
6. BRINTON, Howard
   A personal letter to us in 1996.

Story Two) DEATH COMES TO A MISSIONARY.. by Anita Ritter
Published in the *Christian Advocate*, September 30, 1954]

Thoughtfully, I reread the words of the letter at the front of the memorial book I was organizing for the children:

Max darling,
In our four years of marriage, we have created together with God, among many other beautiful things, our two children. Mark, whom you have loved and guided and known; and our unborn child, whom you loved yet unseen.
One of the things which hurts most deeply in your sudden passing is your absence from our children. We both talked so often of the importance of both parents-- the tremendous influence a father should have on his children. Darling, the hurt is lessened somewhat when I realize the precious heritage you are leaving to our children, absent though you may be physically.
                                        Anita

Yes, our children's heritage from Max will be great. So often since his death I have thought of the times friends have said to me, "It's a tragedy, yes! Such a fine man, so capable, only 27 years old, it's true. But, Anita, think of what he has done! Think of the lives he has touched, think of the witness he has been to so many during those 27 years. Many of us shall never accomplish one-half as much, even though we live many times as long."

Shortly after my return to the States, still ill and lonely, I had a letter from one of our professors at college. "Often I have spoken of you and Max to my classes", he said. "You went into the Belgian Congo because there were some things in which you really believed. I was and am proud of you both. Little did I know that you were to sacrifice so supremely and so much. Yet if I know Max as well as I have led myself to believe, if the decision were to be made over again, it would be the same."

That's true! As our beloved professor went on to explain, it is quality rather than length of life that counts. Surely Max contributed much in the things he did for the time he was here. During his high school days, he was leader in the Epworth League, YMCA work, and elected to a national honor society. Three of his four high school years he was elected class president.

After graduation from high school, he joined the navy. For two years he served in the South Pacific, participating in the Okinawa and Iwo Jima campaigns. He was honorably discharged as a pharmacist mate with hopes of becoming a doctor.

As time went by, Max felt his call was in the teaching field and transferred to Ball State Teachers' College from Los Angeles City College. Majoring in social sciences and geography, he was a serious student. It isn't surprising, then, that he was elected to three honorary societies. He was very active in college "Y" work among other things, and it was in the Office of the. Director of Religious Activities that we first met.

During our first year of marriage and Max's first of teaching, something was missing. Max talked about it often. "This just isn't it!", he would say. "It has to be more".

Shortly afterwards we began to discuss educational mission work, and soon Max's correspondence with the Board of Missions was renewed where it had been left off when he decided to become a teacher. We discussed different fields. We decided we would go anywhere but to a tropical country. But then came the word that the greatest need for educational missionaries was in the Central Congo. Max and I prayed about it and I remember his saying, "Honey, if we're going to do it, let's go all the way! Let's go where we're needed most and contribute all we can!" The decision reached, inspired by those great pioneers who had gone before us, we tackled the long battery of questionnaires, references and physical exams.

All the time, we prayed. Our chief aim was to discover God's will for our lives and fulfill it.

After one semester of study at the Kennedy School of Missions, we sailed in August, 1951, for Brussels, Belgium, where we were both to study French and Max was to take the Belgian government's colonial course. Neither of us knew French.

Our first child, Mark Owen, was born on November 1, 1951. The 15 months (in Belgium) were difficult but Max passed the government French and colonial examinations successfully.

At Lodja, Belgian Congo, we continued our years of preparation by studying Otetela, the language of our African tribe, for six months.

Finally, on April 1, 1953, we arrived at Wembo Nyama, the central station of Methodist work in Central Congo. After nearly six years of study, we began actually to work in Christian education. Max was a principal teacher in the teacher training school, supervisor of student teachers and in charge of the boys who boarded at our mission school.

I worked with the mission women in the Women's Society and, after Annual Conference in June, taught four hours of pedagogy in the training school. Max and I jointly headed work in the Christian home.

Soon after our arrival in Congo, Max had his first attack of malaria and was bothered regularly afterwards. We hoped he would develop a normal amount of resistance to the disease. But in July 1953 he had an attack that didn't respond to medicine. He developed violent headaches, ached all over and suffered waves of nausea. Both of us were feeling ill, apparently experiencing the same symptoms. We had blood tests. They showed we were both carrying a lot of malaria in our systems, but by late afternoon Max's symptoms were beginning to differ.

By 11 o'clock that night, he was having difficulty breathing. By three he was unconscious and artificial respiration was begun. The doctor, nurse and pharmacist at Wembo Nyama worked desperately to keep him alive. Teams of African students came and went all day the next day, applying artificial respiration. Another doctor arrived at noon, and members of the Presbyterian mission worked unrelentingly to overcome the terrible vastness of Congo space to get an iron lung in time. {Congo is as large as the USA east of the Mississippi}

That afternoon he was gone. It was bulbar polio.

I heard Mark's cry. He had been sleeping in another room and seemed to awaken at the same time Max left us—very much as if he knew his daddy had said goodbye. About an hour afterwards the sky grew dark and a violent rain came up. The wind felled a huge palm tree in our mission village and the storm was unusual even for Congo. That storm was a consolation to me. As a close missionary friend said, "It seems God is grieving, even as we, over our loss"

The next day, as we prepared for the service, again the sky began to cloud up. After the simple yet beautiful service, we hurried to the graveside as it seemed the clouds did too. As we stood there beside the grave, again a strong, sudden wind came up. My heart was strengthened and uplifted as the wind forcefully caressed my shoulders and face, for it seemed Max's presence with me was vivid and real.

At a time when it would have seemed I was surrendering my husband to the grave, I had a vivid, reassuring awareness of his spirit with me. As the wind blew with a strength so like Max's, I knew he was there--that no grave could hold his wonderful stubbornness, his admirable fighting always for the principle of the thing, his strength of character.

As a palm branch fell above the heads of some of the Africans watching and sudden fear of the wind's power whipped through the crowd, my heart was calmed, for I knew Max was with me as never before. There was such a powerful, glorious, mystical quality about the strength that came to me, that I humbly and gratefully received it, aware in my heart that there was much I didn't and wouldn't understand until I was free as Max is now.

Knowing and loving Max as I do, I shall always associate him with a great search for truth. In history and sociology he sought the truth, the facts of the situation. In life he sought the true meaning and believed it lay in complete acceptance of Christ and his way of life and in discovering God's will for his life,

Many times he reminded me that the only permanent factor in this physical life is "change". The only "changeless" things in our lives are spiritual. In the world in which we live, he felt the realistic application of Christ's truths the only solution--the key to a peace with the real brotherhood of man supreme.

One life is all we each possess. We must do all we can to further Christ's kingdom on earth with that only life wherever we are most capable. The words of John 14--16 are thoroughly marked up by Max in our Bible. And he loved the verse: "Jesus said to him, I am the way, and the truth and the life, no one comes to the Father, but by me".

Max's quiet, calm, forceful faith was evident always in his life but especially so the last few hours that he was conscious. When the doctor had left his side earlier in the evening, he turned to me and said "Honey, if I don't breathe easier soon, I think I'm going to die". There was no fear, no hysteria. Later when he was sinking fast, he calmly offered suggestions to the doctor.

Later that afternoon, after our doctors, nurses and African students had exhausted themselves from applying artificial respiration to no avail, I went in to see Max. The Africans were standing around him, sobbing quietly. My grief was inconceivable.

Then I saw his face. Max wore a smile that was truly of another world. No one can ever know the way in which that peaceful, heavenly smile comforted my heart. I was so thankful that the Africans with us were seeing it, too. It must have been a dynamic sermon on immortality for all who were there.

As one of our dear professors from college wrote, "To understand why the heavenly Father called Max home now would tax our finite minds beyond their power to comprehend. To love his memory and cherish his ideas does lie within our power".

While I was yet in Congo, so stunned, heart-sore and lonely for Max as I prepared for our trip home without him, I turned to the Bible which we had shared so often with each other. To my surprise I found brief notes in Max's beautiful hand of the last worship hour he had had for us missionaries.

I had stayed with Mark at the time and hadn't heard his talk. As I read his notes now, each word seemed a comforting message direct from him to me. He was discussing the power of faith and the Holy Spirit.

Stephen full of faith and the Holy Spirit. The presence of the Holy spirit in our lives—a beautiful story. Stephen full of grace and power. "His face was like that of an angel." His (Stephen's) defense in which he speaks of Abraham, Joseph, Moses…but he, being full of the Holy Spirit, gazed into heaven and saw the glory of God. "Receive my spirit…do not hold this against them"…he fell asleep…And Saul was consenting to his death…laid waste the church. The amazing transformation in Paul's life through the revelation, presence and power of the Holy Spirit…Spirit of Truth, Counselor, Comforter.

In the precious memory I have of Max, especially that of his heavenly smile after he died, I shall always remember his notes of Stephen's death. "Stephen full of grace and power. His face like that of an angel...But he, being full of the Holy Spirit, gazed into heaven and saw the glory of God".

Story Three. MISSIONARIES FIGHT CROCODILE TO GET A HIPPOPOTAMUS.
[October 1955]

In the Congo we found that it was a whole lot easier to kill a hippopotamus than to get him home.

Our adventure started when the leper colony here at Kapanga, Belgian Congo, Africa, received a free permit to kill two hippos for meat because we have been going through a rather severe meat shortage. So three of us, Dr Bitsch-Larsen, Everett Woodcock and I, all missionaries, went hunting in the jungle. There probably are dozens of the animals within 15 or 20 miles of the mission, so it was no great feat to find the area where they ranged. We left home about 5:30 AM and picked up a number of Africans as guides.

About 7 AM we arrived at the Lulua River and started upstream in two dugout canoes. For the next two hours we saw nothing of interest and no fresh signs of hippos. Then we sighted one floating along in the middle of the stream but he disappeared in a hurry. A short time later we saw more hippos. We pulled ashore and walked along the bank, trying to sneak up on the game. But the big animals had stopped playing and gone underwater. We split up. Doc went upstream, Everett downstream and I stayed put.

Everett had a small-bore rifle and naturally he was the one to sight game first. He ran back for me.

The hippo we saw playing around was small, so we waited for bigger game. In a few minutes, up came a real giant, who snorted and bellowed in fine fashion. Just as the hippo reached the top of its leap, I let it have a .375 Magnum bullet from my Winchester.

Later we discovered it was a perfect shot—directly through the hippo's left eye. {This established me as the Great White Hunter in Kapanga)

When you kill a hippo it sinks. All you can do is wait until it bobs back to the surface, which may take several hours. As rigor mortis begins after death, the stomach and intestines gradually fill with gas. The hippo becomes lighter than water and begins to float. Everett went back to get the carriers and the truck while Doc and I walked down the river bank a ways and took up their vigil, expecting the hippo to come floating along.

After an hour I could stand the suspense no longer and went back upstream looking for our prize.

It rose to the surface, just about where it was shot, about the time I stumbled out of the underbrush. It wasn't moving.

Then it DID begin to move, but in an up-and-down motion instead of downstream with the current.

A moment later I observed two big eyes on a long snout. A crocodile was holding the hippo. The crocodile quickly submerged. I went after the doctor. Doc has a telescopic sight on his rifle, so he crept back ahead of us. The croc was still there. Doc's heavy soft-nosed bullet made the croc jump high out of the water. As he disappeared, he thrashed the river into foam.

Our hippo was then free to drift downstream. We walked along the bank as an escort to make sure another crocodile didn't try to steal it. We hoped to let the carcass drift to a ferry some distance down the river. There we could lead the two tons of meat directly into trucks, without having to pack it out through the undergrowth on the river banks. We would have to pass a long series of tricky shoals about a mile above the ferry.

The canoes arrived about noon, bringing helpers, lunch, ropes and knives. Our hippo drifted to the head of the shoals around 2PM and we three missionaries went into the water with it. We weren't expecting much help, since most Africans are afraid of water. Few of them ever learn to swim, for nearly all the water in their country is infested with crocodiles.

The shoal water ranged from a few inches to four feet deep—too shallow for crocodiles, we hoped! We shoved and pulled, with the natives hauling on ropes when it was possible. Meanwhile, the sun dropped lower and lower in the west, and we hadn't even reached the worst part. We determined to get through that stretch of rough water before quitting, and we did. About 5:30PM or a little later we pushed into deep water and left the carcass floating near the bank. A rainstorm came up, but we'd been in the water all afternoon, so it couldn't make us any wetter.

Next morning we found crocs had nibbled at the underside of our hippo but hadn't done much damage.

A hippo is so large and round shaped, crocodiles can't open their jaws wide enough to bite into the carcass.

Again we went into the water and pushed and shoved the carcass downstream. We made fine progress for about fifty yards, then we hit deeper, swifter water, which ran over and through two barriers of sharp rocks. This stretch of river kept us busy until noon. By then we were so tired and discouraged we gave up the idea of floating our kill down to the ferry. Fortunately, we were near a sloping bank, so we heaved our hippo in that direction. With about fifty men pulling on a one inch rope, we got the animal completely out of the water onto a mud flat.

The picture was taken as the hippo floated in the river near the bank that was our target.

A few minutes after we began the butchering job, a crocodile came drifting along, drawn by the scent of the dead hippo. All three of us fired at the same time and this croc jumped out of the water as he thrashed around, too.

In a few minutes, he surfaced again, we fired several more times. About half-an-hour later, he came up a third time. We went after him in dugout canoes. Those .375 slugs are enormous chunks of lead and brass. We shot thirteen times. The croc's struggles grew weaker every time we hit him, until the thirteenth bullet took off the top of his head. He settled in the water. Our boatman brought the canoe alongside and Doc grabbed one of the critter's legs while I slipped a noose around the toothy snout of the dying croc.

We towed our quarry thirty yards to the bank. The beast measured four meters and seventy centimeters-- 15 ft/6 in. We removed the skin and cut the head off with the skin. It took eight men to carry the skin & head. Lundas will NOT eat crocodiles!

[Incidentally, the Basala Mpasu tribe to the north of Kapanga will eat crocodiles, but the Basala, also ate people. The Lundas wouldn't eat people and wouldn't eat any animal that ate people: such as crocodiles, leopards, lions or cheetahs.]

Wives and children came walking up the trail just after we got the crocodile out of the water. While the hippo was recognizable, the work of butchering stopped while Kodaks clicked and a 16mm movie camera recorded the scene. We had scales with us and weighed each piece of hippo as the meat was cut up. We were able to estimate the beast's original weight. Four thousand pounds, or two tons, was our guess. All of it had to be carried about a mile over rough country to the truck. The last piece was loaded at 9PM.

By this time the hippo had a fairly strong odor-and so did we—but after being together for the last two days, we didn't notice it very much. By 10PM we'd divided part of the meat among the carriers, given a portion to the boatmen, and were back at the mission station with the rest of the hippo. Most of us just plopped down to rest, but Doc went with Bill Davis to take the meat out to the leper colony for distribution on Sunday morning.

During our two terms of service we went on ten or twelve hippo hunts. Not one hunt was uneventful.

Once our canoe almost swamped and sank in a rock-filled rapid.

Another time we were charged by an extremely unhappy Mama hippo. Our canoe was between her and her baby who was in the grass on the bank of the river. She looked like the Battleship Maryland headed towards us!

Once we killed two hippos, but only had a license to kill one. How do you hide a two-ton hippo? We simply ignored the second one; the Lundas promptly disposed of that evidence.

Story Four) ESCAPE FROM THE CONG0—1960.
(JULY -- 1960)

Dear Folks,
Salisbury, Southern Rhodesia

This is to let you know that we are well and safe at the mission near Salisbury. What we both feared—but never dared predict—has happened. The Congo we have known these past eight years is in a troubled state—for the present, at least.

As you probably know from the news stories coming from here, the trouble began soon after Independence was proclaimed. A number of army units mutinied and the military uprising spread. We're sure that you understand that it wasn't the people who caused this uprising. They have been wonderful.

At any rate, some bad things have happened, according to stories we've heard from people who were at other missions. Some were badly mistreated. Others were involved in heavy fighting. Everyone we've talked to was forced to leave their home and most of their belongings. Many will never see them again.

Our first word of serious trouble came at 1PM, Saturday, July 9, when the American Consul at Elisabethville broadcast an appeal for all Americans to leave the Congo without delay. Our staff discussed evacuation plans, but Kapanga is over 100 miles from the nearest border crossing.

On our mission radio network, we heard that Southern Presbyterian missionaries south of Luluabourg were fleeing towards our mission station. The fighting there was serious and getting worse. It was reported moving in our direction. There was no panic at our station. Our Congolese friends begged us to stay; they said no harm would come to us. But we'd been asked to leave by our government, and we knew we had to leave before long.

That afternoon, two families arrived, tired and hungry. More came during the night. There were twenty-seven in all. Most of them had little more than the clothing they wore. We fed them and bedded them down and tried to make them as comfortable as we could.

Sunday we heard our escape road to the south was blocked. We asked for evacuation by air. Thank God for our new airstrip! (The Kapanga airstrip was completed just three months prior under my direction.)

That afternoon a U.S. Air Force C-47 was to have come for us, but it was diverted to a more urgent flight. There still had been no violence at our station, though reports had it coming closer all the time. Tuesday the C-47 came for us, making two trips. We sent the Presbyterians out on the first flight, then took the second ourselves.

It broke our heart to leave Kapanga. We carried only one small suitcase of clothes, a briefcase containing our slides, our camera bag full of movie film and a travel case with some toilet articles in it. We had to leave behind our home, most of our possessions and our little Volkswagen. Most of us felt bad about deserting our possessions, but we were really heartsick at leaving those people and the work we feel is so important. None of us know yet when we can return--if ever. We feel fortunate that we left our church with good leadership.

The C-47 took us to the Belgian Kamina Air Force Base, where we slept on blankets on the floor of the officer's club ballroom for two nights—about 150 of us in one room. The food was quite good. There were about 250 American missionaries and hundreds of Belgian and other nationals at Kamina. A huge US Air Force GlobeMaster came in Wednesday and took out 202 people, mostly elderly, sick or families with small children. The GlobeMaster came again Thursday and took 193 more of us.

We took off at 9:30PM and landed at Salisbury about 12:30AM, Friday. Customs and registration were held to a minimum. The people were hospitable, offering us soup, coffee, sandwiches and warm clothing—It was winter this far south of the Equator. We got to bed about 5AM for a few hours of sleep.

Early in the morning, our Methodist friends came for us and took us to various stations in Rhodesia. We were fortunate to be assigned to our friends at Nyadiri station, the Hunter Griffins. We knew them in Atlanta.

Our next move was uncertain. News from the Congo was not encouraging.

During the weeks preceding the Independence, we told the Lunda people "not to fear." Several months ago we went through a period of "fear" of things to come. But that soon passed. Before we left, we were all working very hard for "our Congo." Now we pray that we may try to help her and her people again.

   Harry & Phyllis

Story Five) MWANT YAV DITEND and JONATHAN MANUNG

An Informal Report on their Tour of the United States and Puerto Rico from October 1 to November 23, 1960

Mwant Yav's visit was officially approved by the United States Department of State. Contacts and reservations with non-Methodist groups were made by the Committee on Leaders and Specialists of the American Council on Education, Mr. Frederick Mangold, Director.

The success of Mwant Yav's trip was due to the excellent cooperation and hard work done by government officials, council members, airlines, universities, schools, churches, bishops, company officials and many friends. All of these people gave generously of their time. Please accept a grateful "Thank You" to all of you who helped us.

This informal report was written by Harry Little, who acted as a state Department escort-interpreter during the trip. Therefore, I accept sole responsibility for any errors or misinterpretations.

JANUARY, 1961   Harry Little

~ ~ ~

This informal report was condensed from forty-one pages to seven pages. A huge number of people had been involved in the trip. We mailed 500 copies of the report to Puerto Rico, Europe, Congo and across the USA. Not one copy came back.

The report is in two sections. The first section contains some of the impressions I gathered from the two Africans. As you read this section carefully, you will see America with a fresh vision. The second section is a chronological account of when and where they traveled.

~ ~ ~

King Mwanta Yava, Chief of the Lunda Tribe in the Congo with his son and Harry & Phyllis Little while touring the United States

"ALL THE STARS OF HEAVEN HAVE COME TO EARTH!"

"Here are some of the impressions I gathered from Mwant Yav and Jonathan Manung during the 50 days we traveled together".

"All the stars of heaven have come to earth!", said the chief, when he first saw the lights of metropolitan New York City.

Their first ride on the subway was exciting but too far underground. They preferred ground or air transportation, they were not afraid to fly.

We were in New York during Kruschev's visit. Mwant Yav didn't think it very necessary for a real leader to pound on the table with his shoe. It seemed to him most undignified.

The young school principal was highly pleased to be in the United Nations building. In the past he has taught about the UN from books, now he will be able to teach from his experience. {We got into the UN sessions because we were temporarily a part of the US delegation to the UN. All tourists and visitors were banned from the chamber while Nikita Kruschev was in New York}.

In New Jersey we saw some roadside displays of pumpkins, cider and scarecrows for Halloween. Have you tried to explain Halloween to a visitor? (from Africa?) Their visit to the Museum of Natural History encouraged them to try harder to preserve the things of the past that are slipping away so quickly. The elephant group truly fascinated them and they spent a long time trying to name the many antelope in the Africa exhibits.

During the train ride from New York to Washington, they noticed the cities, towns and factories. But their most excited comments were about the great size and productiveness of the farms. This is a reflection of the wide-spread African concern with inadequate farm resources and machinery.

The many trees and parks of Washington encouraged Mwant Yav's desire to have such park areas in his capital village, Musumba. After viewing a small portion of the Library of Congress and its 35,000,000 items, they said to me, "You white people really do not have as many books in your homes in Congo, as we thought you did. This library has millions." At the Bureau of Engraving, they made the inevitable request for samples of the $5 and $10 dollar bills we saw being printed. Their request wasn't granted. They were most respectful and silent at the changing of the guard at the Tomb of the Unknowns in Arlington Cemetery. They watched very carefully two funerals being conducted nearby, a sailor and a soldier.

While talking with men from the African American Institute, International Cooperation Administration, State Department and the American Council on Education they said repeatedly they were looking for educational opportunities, scholarships, knowledge, for know-how, and for educators to eventually come to Africa.

The quality and quantity of research being done at the Agricultural Research Center in Beltsville overwhelmed them. Now they began to understand a little bit why American farms are so extremely productive and food so abundant.

One evening they were invited to a private home. Here they got their first look at a washing machine, modern kitchen, home workshop, etc. Later, Jonathan asked if it really was a government employee, and not a high official.

In Indiana, during the drive from Indianapolis to Ft. Wayne, we saw the marvelous farmland of the Middle West. The large storage bins of corn astonished them. [Corn is a part of their diet]

After a few minutes of conversation the Governor of Indiana, Mark Handley, gave up his chair to. Mwant Yav. The governor told the chief to take care of the state while he went to make a speech!

Later in the day, the Mayor of Indianapolis made a real friend when he gave Mwant Yav the key to the city.

At Purdue University we visited the Agricultural Extension Office, where the assistant director gave us a long explanation of the extension work. They felt the idea of county agents, home demonstrations, and field exhibits would be applicable to spreading agricultural knowledge in Congo, and other parts of Africa. Literacy is not a prime prerequisite for doing the demonstrations.

The fabulously complicated machinery used in making capsules by the millions at the Eli Lilly plant amazed them.

In Indianapolis, the Foundation for Fundamental Education helped groups of people build better homes for themselves, sort of a large scale do-it-yourself project. This is similar to the houses now being built in the chief's home village, so he was interested.

King Mwanta Yava, his son & Harry Little

The fabulously complicated machinery used in making capsules by the millions at the Eli Lilly plant amazed them. In Indianapolis, the Foundation for Fundamental Education helped groups of people build better homes for themselves, sort of a large scale do-it-yourself project. This is similar to the houses now being built in the chief's home village, so he was interested.

The Allison Company has an exhibition known as the Powerama. They saw a full-size cut-away jet engine used on various aircraft. The commanding general of the Army Finance Center had arranged an informative tour of the center's operations. Two fascinating gadgets were the automatic sorting machine, and automatic electric typewriter, which was tape controlled through a portion of its cycle. {The two Africans could see the typewriter in action, but the young woman had moved on to another job.}

At the Indiana University stadium they all had seats in the governor's box near the sidelines. Their opinion of football is "It is not sport, it is war!" The Indiana U. team must have thought so, they lost 35 to 0.

One highlight of their trip to California was the day at Disneyland. The voyage on the Congo River is almost too realistic, especially if you have actually been on a river filled with hippos', crocodiles and huge pythons draped over tree branches along the banks of the river.

If my notes are correct, we were told that 400,000 chickens were in cages at the poultry farm in Orange County. That is more chickens than they'd seen in a lifetime. In Katanga, someone with a few chickens is considered fortunate. The men at the dairy farm performed an artificial insemination while we were watching. Mwant Yav and Jonathan expressed great disbelief and dismay at such a method. It is messy to watch.

Bishop Gerald Kennedy was well known in California. Through his Hollywood connections he got us on a one-hour television show at the CBS studios. The host was interviewing Zza Zza Gabor, Danny Thomas and Jack Benny. The three of us were added to the show and Mwant Yav became the "star" of the show. He was a man with great natural intelligence and smile. All three of our stars treated him with great respect. Zza Zza was a charming woman.

At Tuskegee Institute [Alabama], they were most interested in the George Washington Carver Museum. Both had read about him and knew something of his life work. They were pleased to see his equipment and souvenirs of his endeavors.

Another interesting trip was a visit to the Russell Nursery School. Here the Congolese made their first acquaintance with one-way glass. The kind used for observing the behavior of little children without distracting the children by the presence of the observers.

During the visit to the zoo at Tampa [Florida], Mwant Yav was pleased to give names to some young lions. He and Jonathan were flabbergasted to see lions so close. In Congo, some village children never see a lion, or an elephant, or a monkey.

In St Petersburg, we visited a polling place on election day. The orderly, calm and efficient voting by machine made a deep impression on them. They want machines in Katanga. The elections there in June 1960 were not orderly or calm.

In Puerto Rico, they were interested in three things. One of their biggest interest was in the InterAmerican University at San Germain. At this university, international students and international professors are gathered from North, Central and South America; from Europe and from Africa. They enjoyed their visit. It was one of the few places they expressed a desire to return to someday.

Second, they were interested in the cooperative projects that are so numerous on the island. They felt this idea could grow in the Congo.

Third, they were eager to see the self-help building and educational projects for the rural areas of Puerto Rico. These, too, are definitely possible now for the Katanga.

In Washington, they thanked the Committee on Leaders and Specialists for planning the trip so well and for their sympathetic understanding. This expression came at the Annual Meeting of the committee, which we were privileged to attend in November.

THANKS TO ALL OF YOU WHO HELPED US. It is impossible to name individuals because truly your numbers are legion.

Twajikitish nakash Kamu!
(WE THANK YOU ALL VERY MUCH!)

AFTERWORD:

This book was condensed from a significantly larger volume which was an autobiography written jointly and separately by my parents, Harry and Phyllis Little. We have attempted to focus on the portion of the book that specifically related to their African experiences and accomplishments which they celebrated and remained proud of throughout their lives.

At the writing of this forward, Harry has gone to the Lord, passing away on September 11, 2015.

Cathy Little married Douglas Strate and became Cathy Strate on November 17, 2007.

On November 25th, 2002, a second grandchild, Aiden John Harry Little was born. Miles Little, now a man of 25, presently resides in Honolulu, Hawaii, after obtaining a degree in Applied Economics from Florida State University. Aiden Little is entering his freshman year at the International Baccalaureate Program at Southeast High School, where Cathy was a teacher for 27 years.

Phyllis (my mother) was instrumental in the editing and printing of this book, as was my sister, Cathy. Phyllis is a resident of the Woodlands in Bradenton, Florida, where she has many friends among the residents and staff. I continue to practice law, as I have for the past 30 years, in Bradenton, FL. Should any reader be interested in more information regarding all portions of this story, they may contact me.

Respectfully,

Melton H. Little

I WATCHED

I watched as the wisps and curls of the cigar smoke
raced towards the heavens
Come with us they whispered
The sound of the wheels slowly returning to the bed
From which he would never rise again.

I watched as he lay motionless
The breaths becoming ever shorter
Stay with me, I whispered "live to 100."
The sound of the fan whirring
to take away the stale air of death

I watched as I held his hand
Strong, they had always been.
"Can you hear me?" my love shouted,
A small nod
The sound of my tears
as they dropped from my face

I watched as the parade
of those who could do nothing came and went
"Leave him be," my mind screamed,
But silent I stayed
The sound of shuffled feet in and out

I watched as the face of the phone lit up
"He has gone,"
The voice in my head wailed
The sound of the wheels against the road
Taking me closer to what I did not want to see

I watched as the bed rolled through the halls
"I love you," I said to him
Though I knew he could not hear
The sound of the bed
Rolling into the back of the black truck

I watched as the truck drove into the dark
"I miss you," I said to no one.
The sound of my shoes against carpet
Returning to an emptier world

I watched as the memories ran through my mind
like a movie
"I am with you in those,"
I heard in his voice
The sound of a funeral dirge off in the distance.

I watched as he set on the bed
Just as he always had looked
"Don't worry and don't be afraid."
The sound of my sweat dropping
onto the pillow

I watched as the sun came up on another day
"I can make it,"
I heard my thoughts say
The sound of life swirled about
As it went forward around me.

Melton—December 9, 2015

Made in the USA
Middletown, DE
24 November 2025